# GODFATHER
# OF NIGHT

# GODFATHER OF NIGHT

*A Greek Mafia Father,*
*a Drug Runner Son, and an*
*Unexpected Shot at Redemption*

## KEVIN PAPPAS

BALLANTINE BOOKS

NEW YORK

Published in the United States by Ballantine Books,
an imprint of The Random House Publishing Group,
a division of Random House, Inc., New York.

BALLANTINE and colophon are registered
trademarks of Random House, Inc.

LIBRARY OF CONGRESS CATALOGING-IN-PUBLICATION DATA
Pappas, Kevin.
    Godfather of night : a Greek mafia father, a drug runner son,
and an unexpected shot at redemption / Kevin Pappas.
        p.   cm.
        ISBN 978-0-345-51223-9 (hardcover : alk. paper)
    1. Mafia—United States.        2. Organized crime—United States.
    3. Criminals—United States—Biography.        I. Title.
HV6446.P37 2009
364.1092—dc22
[B]          2009018744

Printed in the United States of America on acid-free paper

www.ballantinebooks.com

9  8  7  6  5  4  3  2  1

FIRST EDITION

Book design by Mary A. Wirth

*To my wife, Cathie, for never giving up and always giving me the strength to continue on*

*To my daughter Jourdan, whose loving smile carried me through*

*To my only son, Mikal, who carries the name without blemish*

*To my younger daughter, Paris, who is the light of all of our lives*

*To my mother, for giving me life*

*To Lukie Pappas, who has given my mother the joy of love*

*To Rhaz, for helping me to put my thoughts down on paper*

*To Mickey, for keeping me in check during this entire process*

*To the Band of Five, may they rest in peace, for putting their lives before mine*

*Daytona*

I hate to be alone. It's one of my personal superstitions. I avoid it any way I can. Even today I have two cell phones to be in constant touch with people even if physically I'm by myself. Nothing good can happen to you when you're alone.

But that July day in 1988, I had left my crew, or what was left of it, behind. I had driven down to Daytona Beach in my slant-nose Porsche 944 to relax and get some sun. I felt I deserved it. We had been making a killing in Atlanta. We'd climbed to the top of the cocaine game in the Southeast. I was bringing in so many kilos from Medellín that I was stuffing them in the ceilings of unsuspecting tenants in the buildings I had bought with my profits. But they were selling just as fast as I could get them.

I was laid out on my towel, I remember, looking up at the sky through my sunglasses. They have those airplanes at Daytona that fly back and forth advertising wet T-shirt contests at local bars. I followed them, listening to the surf. Then I noticed a helicopter out of the corner of my eye.

I prided myself on the fact that I was hypervigilant. I had an escape route out of every situation I walked into. I never did meets in hotel rooms or apartments. It was always in the open—alleyways are good, but any open space will do. I even had a Browning 9mm strapped to the inside of my Mercedes trunk door in case anyone ever threw me in there during a kidnapping. This is why I led the best co-caine crew in Atlanta: I always had an exit strategy.

But nothing ever happened to you in Daytona. It was one of the places we went to get away from the twenty-four-hour insanity of our lives. I'd gotten one phone call from Texas that morning that had wor-ried me—about a renegade deal I hadn't known about—but I thought things were under control.

And besides, what can go wrong on a beach?

So I just watched this helicopter buzzing past the airplanes. It came closer and closer to me. It was black, unmarked. It came right to where I was sitting, hovering over the waterline.

And then I noticed the ropes falling out of it. Looked like an ad for the Navy SEALs. And sure enough, right after the ropes came guys dressed in black, rappelling down the ropes to the sand. On the back of their jackets it said U.S. MARSHALS. And that's when I started to get nervous.

They touched the sand and immediately turned and started pounding up the beach toward me, six agents with their M16s and Glocks drawn and pointing straight at my forehead. They came right up to my spot.

Finally, they were standing over me and the lead agent said, "Are you Kevin Pappas?"

I gave it a minute. "Well," I said. "I'm not Santa Claus."

The Marshals jerked me up off my towel, handcuffed me, and marched me off in my flip-flops to a van waiting on the beach road. And here's the thing about the Marshals. They won't tell you any-thing. The Georgia State Police or the DEA will laugh in your face like they just scored a touchdown on your ass in the Super Bowl. They scream at you: "How does thirty years sound, Pappas?" or "We got your ass this time, motherfucker!"

That way you get a sense of how bad it is. And you can shoot the shit with the cops because they're on a natural high from arresting Kevin Pappas, international drug trafficker.

"Is this about my tab at the hotel bar?" I said to the guy who was pulling me along.

But the Marshals were silent as a tomb.

That made me nervous. And that black helicopter made me nervous. I knew that I was going down for something big. But really, I had no idea.

As I sat in the federal detention center that night, I thought of my father. I felt that he was the reason that I was alone and that I was in the cocaine game in the first place.

I felt the bitterness just surge up inside of me. Years of frustration, of loneliness and anger.

The Greeks believe every person has two sets of parents: God is the spiritual parent, and your real father and mother are the physical parents. The two are almost equals. You have to ask for your parents' blessing for any important step in life, like marriage, just as you would pray to God for success in those things. So to turn away from your parents is to turn away from God, and to be cursed by your father is to be cursed by God. The Greeks literally believe that when a father or mother curses you, those words fall on the ears of the Lord and he withdraws his protection from you. This is called *parahorisi*.

Sitting in the federal holding center, I felt like my father had cursed me. I didn't know it, but I would soon get the chance to pay him back, in full.

# GODFATHER
# OF NIGHT

I grew up in Tarpon Springs, Florida, during the 1970s. Twenty miles from Tampa, the town looks like a quaint tourist spot from the outside, but in reality it's controlled, from the docks to the courthouses, by Greek immigrants and their descendants. My name was Kevin Cunningham—an outsider in the heart of Greektown.

If you walked out of my house, turned right, and went down two city blocks over the cobblestone streets, you came to the church. Every Sunday morning starting at about seven you heard this chant that started "*Na na na na . . .*" coming over the loudspeakers, the sound bouncing off the waterways so the whole town heard it. It was the old priest singing the church hymns. It's like when you go to Egypt or Morocco and they have the Islamic call to prayer. But this was the Greek version.

The next block over from my house was the Smyrlis Bakery, and the smell of bread would come through our open windows and into my room. This scent would always wake me along with the sound of the chimes and the bells and the singing of the hymns. And every afternoon I would head to the main strip, right by the water, on my bike.

As you approach the wharf, the street signs start appearing in Greek and English, and you see the old ladies dressed in black dresses even in hundred-degree weather, just like they would be back in Sparta. In front of the coffee shops on Dodecanese Street there are men flipping worry beads, very ripe old rough guys who look like they've been in the sun forever. These are lower-echelon gangsters in the mob. Inside, the captains and the soldiers are gambling for high stakes—forty, fifty thousand dollars on one throw of the dice. Women are not allowed in the coffee shops. They don't even walk down that side of the street. Instead they cross over.

Really, it was like growing up in a small town in Greece. Everywhere you went, you saw the blue of the Greek flag—on signs, on roofs, on house trim. It was like a painted border that circled the town, and it said everything inside this line belonged to us.

Pedaling my bike, I would make a right on the harbor street off Dodecanese and see the little wharf, where octopus hung on string lines to dry out and the masts of the shrimp and sponge boats spiked into the air like mini oil derricks. The names on the boats weren't average American ones—there was sure to be a sponger named the *St. Michael* or the *St. Nicholas,* very important saints in the old country. And all along the harbor road you heard music playing, you smelled the food from the diners, and you heard the chatter of the people speaking in Greek.

Today at the end of the harbor road, you come to the Pappas restaurant. Out front, there's a sculpture of a man in a deep-sea diver suit, with the round metal helmet and the grille, straight out of *20,000 Leagues Under the Sea.* It's a statue of Louis Pappas, the man who brought the clan to America, and it honors him and the other divers who made the town the sponging capital of the world, the place where the natural sponges from the bottom of the sea are harvested and sold. Louis died under the water in a mysterious accident years back—some people say it was a hit, but the town likes to think he died doing what he loved.

Under the statue, there is a plaque that tells how Louis brought "honor and fame" to Tarpon Springs. If he had been another nationality it might have said "riches" or "commerce" or something like that. But the Greeks want above all to be respected by their countrymen, and that is what that plaque is about. The Greeks feel that their nation invented the modern world, that they are unlike any other culture out there, and that they will survive when all others are gone.

I would park my bike outside the old restaurant and then walk in and start working. My job was as a delivery boy and busboy or whatever the owner, Lukie Pappas, Louis's grandson, wanted me to do that day. Lukie was a big man in Tarpon Springs. He owned racehorses in the Tampa Bay Downs and he had Arabian studs and trainers and a 120-foot yacht. It seemed like he owned half the town. Later, I would learn that wasn't quite right. In reality, he owned only the most important parts.

Lukie was a quiet person, but commanding—very Greek, very compassionate. He made me feel accepted and wanted. When he was going out to do something, he would come over and say, "You want to come with me?" That meant a lot to me. I just found him to be a very compelling man, and I spent more time with him than I did at home.

And when I had done a good job, worked extra hard busing tables or mopping the floors, he would take me to the bar, lift me up onto a stool, and order me a drink. God, I loved those moments. I felt like I was a big man like him, having a cocktail at the end of a hard day. "Give the kid anything he wants," he'd tell one of the old Greek bartenders. The guy would think, turn and look at all the bottles of gin and whiskey and rum behind him on the wall, then make me a Shirley Temple. And he'd always make *my* drink first, then give Lukie his Tanqueray and tonic or his Crown Royal with a splash of ginger. Then Lukie and I would sit at the bar looking out at the tourists and the boats coming in and out of the harbor. I was king for a day, or for an hour.

By the time I was ten or so, I knew Lukie did more than run the restaurant—he was the head of the biggest Greek crime family in the Southeast, a prince of a great mob syndicate.

Lukie wasn't a pushover. I had to work hard, and I did. There's no quicker way to lose a Greek's respect than to be a lazy bum. I started working in the kitchen in high school, sweeping floors and making salads. Then Lukie graduated me to short-order cook. I went right after school and stayed there and worked and ate my dinner. I'd drop into bed in my family's miserable little shack at the end of the day, exhausted but happy.

# CHAPTER 2

My mother was the bookkeeper at the restaurant, and I would see her there—slim, 110 pounds, seventeen-inch waist, black hair, hazel eyes, her body as taut as a ballroom dancer's, which she was. She's a mix of Cherokee Indian, Italian, and Sicilian blood. You would notice my mother, believe me. The Greek men sure did.

She was born in Flat River, Missouri, and raised in Detroit, Michigan, off Telegraph Road. She's the female version of me: loving but extremely aggressive in her attitude. To her, "no" was just another way of saying "yes." Eventually she was going to hear "yes"—the only question was how much charm or abuse it was going to take to get there.

She met Jim Cunningham in Detroit at a dance hall during the mid-fifties. He was 6′1″, thin face, salt-and-pepper hair—a good-looking man. He was from Scotland originally, and I guess he had his good qualities: He loved animals, especially dogs. And he was a sharp-looking guy. He liked his shoes buffed to a shine, a sharp crease in his pants. All good dancers are like that, and Jim Cunningham was a fabulous dancer.

But he had a fucking mean streak a mile wide, especially when he drank hard liquor. Today he'd probably be diagnosed as bipolar, but back then I just thought he was a mean bastard. And the thing he hated more than anything in the world was me.

It must have been fun for my mother and Jim in the beginning, dancing in the Detroit ballrooms to Benny Goodman and all the big bands during the fifties. Of course one thing led to another, she got pregnant with her first son, Charles, and they had to get married. Then it wasn't so much fun anymore.

My mother had a bad case of asthma and the marriage was hanging by a thread in Detroit, so they decided to move to Florida for her lungs' sake and hopefully for a fresh start to the marriage. The miraculous salt air healed her asthma in no time. The marriage was a different story.

In Tarpon Springs, Jim Cunningham got a bread route and my mom took a job as Lukie Pappas's bookkeeper. We lived in an 800-square-foot shack on the wrong side of the tracks—literally. The train ran by a few blocks from my house. The place was an oven in the summer and too small for our family all year long.

Behind the house was a small garage. Jim Cunningham was a motorcycle nut, and he had Triumphs and BMWs all through my boyhood years. Sometimes I would go out to the garage on a summer night, hoping to help him with an engine or something, and he would see me and his face would just twist up. "Get the fuck away from me," he'd say in his Scottish accent. "Go to your mother; she's the one that loves you."

I just couldn't understand why he hated me so much. He was fine with my brothers and sister. So I needed my mother to stick up for me and, man, did she.

One night when I was about thirteen, my friends and I threw some park benches into the bayou. We ran when the police showed up, but this one cop, Officer Crane, started chasing us. We knew the neighborhood so well that we knew when to duck under clotheslines in the dark and when not to, and there was this little wall that we all hid behind. But the cop didn't see the small obstacle in the darkness, and he hit it. He went catapulting over our heads and ended up breaking his femur bone.

Everyone else ran, but I stood over him and watched him screaming and clutching that leg. So the next day, whose house did they knock on? My mother answered the door and I was standing out of sight just to the side of her.

"Mrs. Cunningham?" the cop said.

"Yes?"

"Is your son Kevin here?"

"Yes."

"Well, we have an issue. Could you please step outside?"

So she stepped onto the porch. I was terrified.

The cop proceeded to tell my mother what had happened. And I was ready for her to come tearing into the house after me and give me up to the cop. But then I heard her.

"I'm sorry, my son was here with me last night. We were at the Kingdom Hall for Bible school."

The cop got hot on her, but she stuck to the story. Finally he left in disgust and she came back into the house and closed the door. I looked at my mom and we locked eyes. She didn't say a word. I felt so close to her then, like we could share anything in the world.

I was very sheltered by my mother. I could do no wrong in her eyes. She gave me compassion that she showed no one else. And they all resented it. My sister, Kathy, and my brothers, Charles and David, Jim Cunningham, the extended family—everybody resented it. If you feel my shin even today, you can feel the bone is serrated like a fish knife—that's from all the kicks I got from Kathy, who got blamed for everything bad I did. I have more scars from Kathy than I do from my drug trafficking rivals. Because she wanted that love that I was getting.

My mother was my best friend, and I lived and breathed to make her happy. She was the only individual who I could turn to on every aspect of life, from girls, to spiritual things, to anything. We were inseparable.

But I was living a double life, even as a kid. I was getting more and more fascinated with Greektown and the culture there. But at the same time, my whole family on my mom's side are very high up in the Jehovah's Witnesses: elders and ministerial servants who travel regularly to Bethel, which is like their Vatican. They were the powers that be in the church, just as the Pappases were the kings of Greektown.

By day I was in school or in Kingdom Hall. I was your average poor, white, mullet-wearing Jehovah's Witness living in poverty and waiting for the end of the world. I would knock on people's doors and talk about God's Kingdom. Those dreaded visits from the Jehovah's Witnesses you get on Saturday morning? That was me. But very few doors closed when I was doing the talking.

When someone answered the door, I would launch into my speech about how the Witnesses would rule the earth with Christ and ask people if I could leave *The Watchtower* with them. The worst part was going to my friends' homes. Their parents would answer the door, and I'd go right into the spiel: "Hello, my name is Kevin and I'm here in your neighborhood today to talk about God's Kingdom." And my friends would be in the background, laughing, because they knew I was playing both sides.

But I'd have to do it. It's a Witness's duty to bring the good news to nonbelievers. I'd knock on the door and the people would answer, "Yes, can I help you?" And I'd say, "Could I please just give you a message?" And, since I was a little kid, they'd give me a minute or two. And I'd say, "Do you know the Lord's Prayer?"

"Thy kingdom come, thy will be done, on earth as it is in heaven."

I'd interrupt right there. "Great point. So the scriptures say there will be a kingdom on earth."

And they'd think about it and say, "Yes."

"Well if you would turn to Psalm 37, verses 10 and 11"—I'd open my Bible and show them the verses—"it says that only the what will inherit the earth?"

"Only the meek."

"Right. So the scriptures tell us that there is going to be a heavenly and an earthly kingdom. Isn't that great to know that we're going to be able to be resurrected and to live on earth with the people who we love and not float around in heaven and not know who's up there?"

And they'd go, "Wow."

I had them interested. "Let's see who we're talking about here. What's the name of God?"

"Well, Lord."

"Oh, that's interesting. There are many lords and many gods. What is the name of God?"

And they'd say, "I don't know."

"And how long have you been going to church?"

"Thirty years."

"And in thirty years, the man up in the pulpit *never told you the name of the guy you're worshipping?*"

Silence.

So I'd say, "Turn to Psalm 83 verse 18. 'The name of the father our lord is Jehovah God.' "

I'd say, "Oh look, he's got a name." Like we had just discovered this together. "So when you're praying to God, wouldn't it be nice to pray to Jehovah God, as that's his name?" And that would all make sense.

And from there I would bring them into the knowledge of the Jehovah's Witnesses.

I was a great salesman. But I believed in what I was selling. At least for a while.

Every Thursday in the Kingdom Hall they had the Theocratic Ministry School. It's a training session that teaches you different concepts of ministry. So I'd go up there and give a twenty-minute talk, and one of the elders would study and evaluate me. He'd say, "Kevin, you did a great job. Your voice was good. You escalated and you punctuated well. The only thing you need to work on for next week is your gesturing—it needs to be a little more accentuated. I think you need to be a touch more animated."

And I'd say, "OK."

I was a perfectionist. I was always looking for approval, trying to excel in things that would get me noticed. And I also began to understand that I was always being judged no matter what. It wasn't, "Oh he's so cute, God bless him. He's such a natural." He was like, "You did a good job but you damn well could do better next time."

But most of all, it taught me to control the room and how to persuade and motivate people. I would use that later in Atlanta in the drug game. What the Witnesses didn't know was that they were preparing me not for the Kingdom of God in the afterlife, but for survival here on earth.

**E**ven though I had my mother in my corner, I still got depressed. When my father, Jim, told me I was a piece of garbage, I believed him. When I was down, I would go for a ride on my bike with my dog Hambone, my closest friend in the world at that time. Hambone would follow me to school and then he would wait for me at the school door when I got out. I loved that dog more than anything in the world.

When I felt upset I would go riding around town on my bike and try and calm down. And then I would make my way to the docks. Something about the wharf would soothe my mind. And that's where Black Spot was.

One time, I had just gotten bullied at school by a kid, and had also been in a bad fight with Jim. He always seemed mad at me, and this day things got real ugly so I just took off running, and scooted down the alley next to our house, past the railroad tracks to the little corner grocery store. I was hungry, but I didn't have any money in my pocket. So I kept on walking, past the Greek Orthodox Church, and headed down to the wharf. I could always count on three things happening: The sun setting. The tide going out. And seeing Black Spot.

I ran up to where he was sitting on his driftwood stump. His face was dark, all tanned and leathery. He was clipping away at his sponges. Black Spot was a pretty big guy. Black hair with a lot of gray.

He looked like a man on an old Greek coin. He talked like he came from the old country, and as long as I had known Black Spot, he'd been my friend. I watched him as he clipped a wool sponge and picked the barnacle bits out. At his feet were more sea sponges and a raw loofah soaking in a large bucket of salt water, softening.

Black Spot was always dressed the same: baggy blue work shirt that matched the sky; long, loose brown pants (never shorts); and dirty worn-out leather sandals that creaked whenever he walked. His hands were huge and callused, his fingers big and chewed up. Most of the kids thought he was weird. Some thought he was some kind of devil or ghost. He had a big old black mole on his right cheek that gave him his name.

Whenever Black Spot wasn't clipping sponges, he flipped his worry beads and muttered a prayer or two under his breath. Or else he'd take a break and drink coffee at one of the cafés on the boardwalk. After dark, it was poker and shots of ouzo. He'd spent most of his life sponging on the island of Kalymnos. Then he came to America to teach the locals how to do it.

Black Spot loved the salty wind and the sound of the waves. After he stopped going out to sea, the local shopkeepers set him up on the wharf to clip sponges for the tourists. I guess having Black Spot around was good for business; he was a living embodiment of the old country. I don't think he had any kids. His wife had died many years before.

"The ocean is my family," he said. "I know nothing about you kids."

Black Spot told me a lot of stuff about the people in town, and this place, Tarpon Springs, and how practically everybody who lived here was a *padaya* (a part of the brotherhood) like him. Everything he said began with "I remember . . . I remember . . ."

I snuck up behind Black Spot and tapped him on the shoulder. He pretended like I startled him. Usually I was happy when I saw him, bragging about my day and all the money I made selling sharks' teeth jewelry to the tourists. This time I had a shiner and red eyes from crying. He spoke to me in Greek.

"*Ti'ka'nas*, Kevin. *Yassou* (hey buddy), what's up? You okay? Rough day?" Black Spot asked me. He helped me with my Greek and corrected the words I used.

With Black Spot there was no such thing as a dumb question. He didn't yell at me when I asked him stupid stuff: Why is the sea so salty? Why don't those big fishing boats sink? He told me stories: how the red tide killed the sea life, and how there wasn't as much sponging as there used to be when he first came over from Greece.

"*Te'egg'a'nay*," he asked me. "What happened to your eye, sport?"

"Some big kid called my mom names." They had called her a whore, and it wasn't the first time.

"Everybody calls everybody names. You don't think I got a name? They call me Black Spot."

"Yeah, but that's because you got a big black spot on your face."

"And you've got a black spot around your eye," he says, snapping his finger near my bruised face.

I told Black Spot what happened, and how I got two ass-whoopings in one day, and a written warning from Mr. Gambos, the principal. It was a bad day, but fairly typical.

"Nicky is bigger than me," I said. "And he punched me out at the bike racks."

Black Spot shook his head. "*Ray malaka* (fool)!" he spat out, "I remember his poppa was a no-good bully back when he was little like you. And he never learned his lesson. Thought he knew everything about everything. That's why one day he went out to sea and never came back."

It was cruel, but that made me feel better.

"You know, school really sucks. I can't win. It ain't fair," I said in Greek.

"Life ain't meant to be fair." Black Spot picked up another sponge from the pile. "Life is to be lived. You wait. Tomorrow will be better. Live each day brand-new. Let things happen. Stand up for yourself. But don't go looking for trouble, or it'll find you first."

Black Spot let me cry on his shoulder, which helped.

"The kids call my mom bad names. They're all liars."

"*Ketasay* (look)! The walls have ears and the *mati* (the all-protecting eye) lies within you," he said to me in Greek.

"So what'll I do about Nicky? Maybe I should just run away."

Black Spot barely looked up from clipping his sponge. His face grew serious, and he put his crusty hand on my head.

"Kevin, you're different," he told me. "You're blessed to be around strong people."

And then he would get on to his favorite subject: the Greeks. How they had been the first real civilization and they would be the last on earth. He told me about Alexander the Great, his battles with the Persians, his invasion of India, and the greatness he embodied. Man, he could go on for hours about that shit.

"The Spartans and Athenians," he said in Greek, "whenever they needed answers, like when to go to war, they'd go to the oracle at Delphi. The old woman at the oracle would tell the Greeks what advice Apollo offered. You need to listen closely to what your heart and your blood tells you."

I didn't really understand why Black Spot was telling me these things. After all, my parents weren't Greek. But he knew I loved the culture and the stories of Alexander. Black Spot planted a love of the Greek world deep within me and it never faded. I'll always be grateful to him for that.

# CHAPTER 4

Even though I was American, I always hung out with the Greek boys. I loved being part of their culture. I took Greek lessons, I learned how to dance the traditional dances, and I soaked up every bit of history and culture I could from Black Spot and the other old-timers.

But you couldn't escape it in Tarpon Springs. At noon on Greek Easter, the Archbishop would come from Greece and parade through the town. They would tape off the entrance of the town so he could walk through the streets undisturbed. And the Archbishop would say in Greek, "Christ has risen." Then he would lead a procession down to the water carrying a cross, and there would be forty or fifty Greek men in the water in white robes, and he would throw it above their heads and the water would churn as they fought to get it. There's even a statue of a guy catching the cross in front of St. Michael's. The guy who grabbed it would have a year of good luck.

The Bible says that the earth shook when Christ rose, so the Greek boys and I would run around the town all night setting off homemade firecrackers, which were called "Greek bombs." We'd go from house to house where the old grandmothers were cooking lamb and rice, and it would be so much fun. And I was right in the middle of it.

That was the beautiful part of Greektown. As I got older I saw the other side, too. The part that no one really wanted to talk about.

People have seen so many Italian mob movies that they think the only way organized crime works is the Italian way. But the Greeks have their own style and traditions. Take punishment, for example. The Italian Mafia will exact their vengeance on you as the wrongdoer, but the Greeks, they go for the family and leave you standing. If you've disgraced the group, you can count on the fact that someone close to you is going to pay. This isn't mercy—if anything, it's more tortured, more suspenseful, and therefore more Greek. They want you to think about it. "God, who's it going to be? When's it going to happen?" The *drama* of that appeals to the Greek soul.

I remember when I was in ninth grade, we started hearing that something had happened with a lieutenant in one of the Greek families. It was all very vague. *Something didn't go the way it was supposed to go.* And that was real fucking bad.

The guy knew what was coming. He had to. Our school was across the street from a very stereotypical Greek neighborhood. We were outside at lunchtime and we heard this old lady screaming in Greek, "Please don't do it. Please, I'll talk to them. Please no." She was terrified. And the lieutenant said back to her, "If it's not me, Mom, it's going to be you. You know how this is." And as soon as he said that, we heard this enormous *PPPOOOOOOOOOWWWWW.*

He had taken it. He had rigged a double-barrel shotgun to the door. It was aimed straight at his own face so when anyone opened up the door, it would blow his brains out.

I had seen things in Tarpon Springs before. But this was the first marker that told me this Greek thing was a serious business, and Tarpon Springs wasn't like other towns. Maybe it should have scared me off. But I didn't see it as a dark side. I saw it as another side of something I wanted to be a part of, desperately.

The Greeks have a word, *phsadaua.* I heard it all the time. The old ladies would come when I was a little kid and they would pinch my cheek and they would spit "*phsadaua*" in these loud voices. I never really knew what that meant. As I got older, I learned. It means, "The devil is within you," or "Get the devil out of you." It was a kind of blessing, but a warning, too.

And I would go to the cafés on Dodecanese and Greek-dance for the old mobsters. They loved me. They'd throw money at my feet and clap their hands. And they'd talk to me, tell me what to do and what not to do. And every so often they would tell me things like "This is the real one." That made me feel like I was destined for great things. They were tough old bastards, and they didn't give out praise lightly.

I was trying to live in both worlds, but you couldn't. The Greeks hated the Witnesses and vice versa. One time I was going door-to-door with my mother, and I don't know what we were thinking but we went to the house of the Orthodox priest. His wife came out and she says to my mother, "Get away, you devil, get away." But my mother is very stubborn, like me, and wouldn't back down. I told her, "Ma, let's go, this lady's no good." But she wouldn't. So the priest's wife stepped closer and slapped my mother hard, bursting her eardrum. To this day, my mother's deaf in that ear.

Later the Witnesses disassociated me from the church. They put me on restriction because I was getting too close to the Greeks. They said I couldn't have any interaction with members because I was bringing reproach to the church.

It was like nothing ever gelled in my life: not religion, not my family, nothing. My soul was sort of dangling for someone to grab it.

I gravitated to Greektown more and more, and to the Pappas restaurant. After class I would hustle over and get to work, sweeping up, cleaning. But most of all I watched Lukie. How he dealt with people. How he carried his power. By high school I knew what he did at night. The Greeks say, "He's a businessman by day but a *nounos* by night." *Nounos* means godfather.

The different levels of that power were revealed to me one by one. One time when I was in high school I made a trip to Greece with a dance group called Levindia. We performed for the prime minister, Papandreou, at this very formal ceremony at his official residence. We came out in our traditional costumes and I was so proud to be doing it, smiling and concentrating hard on my steps. I looked up at the prime minister and his group and all of a sudden I started recognizing people from Tarpon Springs. From the Pappas family. And I was like, "Jesus Christ, I can't believe what I'm seeing. *The prime minister is hanging out with a bunch of mobsters.*" From my American point of view, it was as if John Gotti was at the Inauguration Ball with President Bush. It made no sense.

But in Greek life, everything is connected. On the feast of the Epiphany, which is held every January 6, the Pappases would fly in the Orthodox Archbishop—the equivalent of the Pope in the Catholic Church—and they would parade through the streets hand in hand with the man. Lukie and his brothers would lead the procession and everyone else would follow behind. I didn't get the symbolism of it when I was younger, but it was the Archbishop blessing Lukie. Just as Lukie had the chief of police, or a judge, or a congressman, he had the Orthodox Church there with him, by his side. It went so much deeper than money. The leaders of the local syndicates actually had to be approved by the head of the local Orthodox Church. People would go to the Archbishop and kiss his ring, but if they wanted something, if they really needed something, they would go to Lukie and say, "*Nounos, nounos,* please."

So I came to believe there was no separating out criminals and civilians in the Greek world. It was all part of this incredibly rich culture that spread over the water to all the corners of the earth. And yet it remained hidden, mysterious, complex. When I went to prison, there were almost no Greeks in the place. I still marvel at that. But they're hidden beneath layers, so deep in the Greek-American society that you hardly know they're there.


I spent all of my growing-up years watching men like Lukie and his brother Yani operate, and I was just enamored of it. I saw that people brought them gifts, I saw that they could give an order and it was carried out, and they never left the house. It was so pompous, so *brazen*.

The Italian mobsters would come to Tarpon Springs and gamble and relax, and Lukie took them out on his yacht and showed them a great time. I cleaned up on his yacht and I saw them there, saw the respect they paid the Pappases. But deep down Lukie considered the Italians to be his operatives, the guys who wanted the headlines. They like the attention. They love the violence. They want the fancy suits, the notoriety. They like to be the muscle.

But the Greek? He's happy being the power behind the muscle. The Cubans were the "do-boys" for the Colombians. And the Italians were the "do-boys" for the Greeks.

People might say it was the money that I fell in love with, the gold Rolex Submariners that every Greek mobster wore, or the Stamas yachts, or the mansions on the water. But it wasn't. It was the respect and the power. The Witnesses told me to wait until Christ arrived and I would be among the chosen of the earth. But the Greeks held the world in their hand.

Which one would you choose? I felt like I belonged with the Greeks. I chose them.

# CHAPTER 5

In 1980, when I was sixteen, my mother picked us up and moved us out of Tarpon Springs to the small town of Zebulon, Georgia. My mom sold the house in Tarpon Springs for $38,000 and bought ten acres in Zebulon, and we lived in a small trailer on a dirt road, sleeping on the floor, woods and ticks all around us.

I was dumbstruck. Why would you move me away from everyone I knew and loved to this shithole filled with rednecks and bugs?

"I did it for you," she told me. "The schools here are better."

Which was complete bullshit. Our household was not one that gave merit to education. We were always told growing up that you don't need to go to college because the end of the world is coming. Why get educated when Jesus is coming to judge you? You need to get saved before you learn calculus.

And just a few months before we left Tarpon Springs, something had happened that changed me and made leaving that much more bitter for me.

There were maybe a hundred blond girls and guys in my high school. Everyone else was typically Greek: dark eyes, dark hair. They matured quicker. Ninth graders looked like they were twelfth graders. They were big Greek boys with broad shoulders and deep voices. And they had the culture. They weren't typical American high schoolers, rejecting everything their parents and grandparents believed in. The values had come down to them, especially the code of loyalty and the respect for family.

It's different with the Italians. They run around trying to be notorious. They'll say things like, "My last name is Gotti" or "My father is with the Gambinos," or they'll trade on their name. In the Greek community, that's disrespect. Number one, it brings shame to your family, and number two, this is the family's business, so why are you talking about it to strangers? Greeks are so tight-lipped. In Tarpon Springs, they didn't need to talk. Everyone knew who your uncle was and who your dad was. If you had to talk about it, your family had no power.

And I was becoming part of it. There was one hallway where only the Greek kids could walk down. If you were an American and you tried to go that way, a Greek linebacker from the football team would smack your face for you. But I could walk down there every day. Somehow I had become an honorary Greek. I was even becoming fluent in the language.

One night before we moved to Zebulon I was hanging out with the American kids at a keg party. There was a girl called Jennifer Page who was the high school slut. Every guy made out with her and played with her boobs. So Jennifer got drunk and somehow my name came up. She started saying, "Oh, Kevin did this and that," and the American boys came to defend her honor, which was ridiculous because most of them had already slept with her. But they had decided to whup on me.

A guy named Brian Stewart came up to me while I was sitting on my Yamaha 400 motorcycle. Brian was a senior, probably 6'3", 235 pounds, a popular guy who actually went on to play pro football for a while. And he started breaking bad on me pretty hard and saying all kinds of nasty things. I was about 165 pounds soaking wet at the time.

Brian grabbed the keys from the Yamaha and threw them in the pool, and the other American boys started gathering around me. I had no extra key and I was stranded there out in the middle of nowhere. I told Brian, "If you touch me, I'm going to bust you in the mouth." And of course he touched me, and I took my helmet and I shoved it in his face and I popped his two front teeth out, literally knocked them out.

I knew I was fucked at that point. The American boys wanted to beat on someone and I was it that night. They told me we would have it out at this place called the Sahara, a deserted field on the wrong side of the tracks. Of course I knew I was going to get my ass whipped but I had to go. I was a big-hearted kid and I'd rather get beaten into a coma than be known as a pussy.

I had a buddy who lived up on the hill named Leon Malcromontes, which in Greek means "the black eye." He saw what was going on and he went into Greektown across the railroad tracks and told all the Greek boys, "Oh my God, Kevin's going to get killed." I had no idea this was going on. I was walking to my doom at the Sahara.

When I got there, it was dark as hell, and I saw Brian coming toward me with a crowd of the American boys behind him. But all of a sudden I hear this rumbling of four-wheelers and four-wheel drives. I looked across the field and there were fifteen Greek boys charging across the Sahara. I couldn't believe what I was seeing. They piled out of their cars and went up to Brian and said, "Listen, he's one of us. Put your fucking hands on him, and we'll kill you."

The Greek boys stood up for me. It was a small moment but for me that was the most monumental thing. It was the beginning of my quest to really become one of them. I had two American brothers and a sister who I didn't really even know. I had a Scottish father who hated my guts. But these Greek boys stood up for me, and from that point on I was accepted.

And then my mother had taken me away from it, everything I believed in.


In Georgia, our lives were boring. There was nothing to do and I had nothing in common with the rednecks we lived near.

My father went to work as a psychiatric nurse at this rehab center called Anclote Manor. It was a top-flight place; the heir to the Campbell Soup fortune went there. If you went insane in Georgia, that was the place to end up. They called my father JC there, and this sounds totally fucked up, but the crazy people revered him, they loved him. They put him on a pedestal like he was Jesus Christ. I'm not kidding. He was their fucking savior. And he would do anything for them.

But then he would come home and see me and he'd say, "Go fuck yourself, you little shit" in that brogue of his. I freeze up when I hear people talk like that now.

People say to me, "Well, he must have been nice to you once in a while," but I honestly can't bring up a single good memory of him. There's *nothing*.

And I had no idea what caused him to hate me. I would rack my brain looking for things that I'd done to Jim Cunningham that might make him despise me that way. I felt tormented by this. It was a mystery I couldn't solve, and it just got more painful every year. I would rather have been beat with a fucking pole than be emotionally abused like that. But the treatment also stoked an anger inside of me, a feeling that I was being mistreated. And it had to erupt eventually.

A year after we moved to Georgia, Jim Cunningham went into the ICU ward at Clayton General Hospital in Atlanta. He'd been bitten by a tick and gotten some weird disease and it had slowly destroyed his kidneys. I watched him get sicker and sicker, and I have to admit that sometimes I was glad that he was suffering. Let him have some of what he was dishing out to me.

My mother was torn up over it. They had problems, and he could be cold and bitter toward her, too. But they'd been together for more than twenty years and she had some good memories of him in the early days.

So we kept a vigil at the hospital, going back and forth to our house and to work and then going to see Jim at night. We knew he was dying, but we didn't talk about it. Finally we were waiting outside his room one day and the doctor came out, closed the door, and said Jim was probably not going to make it through the night.

I didn't feel anything when he said that. I was at the hospital just to console my mother—I had no intention of seeing Jim. He could go on his way without ever talking to me again for all I cared.

But later the nurse came into the waiting room.

"Are you Kevin?" she said.

"Yes, I am."

"Well, he wants to see you."

I was confused. The guy ignores me his whole life and on his deathbed he wants to see me? I just wanted to get out of there, but for my mother I kept my mouth shut. She gave me this strange look as I walked away like she wanted to stop me.

As we came to Jim's door, I could hear him moaning in pain. They had shot him up with morphine to give him a few minutes with his family, but when I walked in there he was suffering. He would arch his back as if an electric current had shot through him and then sink back down onto the bed. He was in so much pain that his eyes were glazed over and his face was a deathly white.

If I had loved him, it would have been painful. But I didn't. And I didn't fear him anymore. He had shrunk into his body and he had tubes coming out of his nose and his wrist. He looked like he'd aged twenty years in the last two weeks.

So he was in and out of these convulsions, but then his eyes cleared for a minute and he saw me. And he grabbed my hand.

"I have something I want to share with you," he said. "I made a promise. Please don't be upset with your mother. I made a promise when I found out something about your mother and I made her swear that she would never tell the secret to anyone."

I said, "Well, what's the secret?" I had no idea what the hell he was talking about.

He couldn't get it out, though. "I've tried to be the best I could be for you," he told me. "I know I've not been a good father to you but I tried to do all I could."

And I said, "And?"

He looked at me. "I'm not your father."

I didn't get it. "Well, you've never been very good to me, but . . ."

"No," he says. "I'm . . . not . . . your father. Your mother had an affair with another man and you're not my son."

I couldn't really process what I was hearing. I said, "What do you mean?" a couple of times. And then—and by this time, I was shouting—I asked him whose son I was.

He looked up at me.

"You're Lukie Pappas's son."

My mind went blank and I felt like throwing up. I let go of his hand, big tears running down my face.

I wasn't in shock. It was more anger that I'd been deceived. And that this man who I felt nothing for had been the one to finally tell me, instead of my mother, the one who I loved and always supported me, the person who was my best friend and last refuge in life. That made it worse, somehow.

"So you wanted to clear your conscience before you went to hell?" I yelled at Jim. And then I asked him what I'd always wanted to. "Why did you ruin my life?"

No answer. I don't know if it was the morphine or he didn't have anything to say, but it was just silence.

I turned and I stormed out of the room.

Jim Cunningham died that night. I didn't even go to the funeral.

# CHAPTER 6

I was so angry that I could barely talk. I wanted answers. I went home and waited for my mother. I sat in the swing on our front porch, and when she walked in, I hit her with it right away.

"What reason did you have to do that to me? Why didn't you just tell me?"

She played innocent. "Tell you what?"

When I blurted it out, she tried to blame the story on the fact that Jim Cunningham was delusional—his mind messed up on the painkillers. She couldn't bring herself to tell the truth.

I said, "Mother, come on. Tell me." I was begging her and the tears were burning my eyes. But she kept lying and that just made me angrier.

I had a glass of wine in my hand. Being dramatic by nature and filled with rage, and with seventeen years of total confusion built up inside me, I broke the glass of wine and started to cut myself. "Is this what you want? Is this what you want to see? You want to see me suffer? You need to see it?"

I'd never done anything like that before, and I haven't since. But I felt if I didn't let the pain come out of me some way, I'd do something far more drastic. Like cut my own throat.

My mother broke down. "I didn't mean to lie," she said finally. "I had to. I swore I would never tell." And she started justifying herself.

And the truth finally came out, how she had been lonely and had the affair with Lukie and finally told Jim when I was six or seven, and he had made her swear never to tell anyone.

Now that I'm a father I understand Jim Cunningham better. I was someone else's fucking kid. Every time he saw me it was a reminder that his wife had fucked around on him. I mean, I love my children and I love my family, but I don't know how I could deal with that if it happened to me.

But if they had just sat me down and told me, I could have dealt with it. My whole life is the product of a couple of conversations that never took place. If my mother and Jim Cunningham had dealt with it back then, I would have been fine.

People are careless with other people's lives. That's what I learned.

I thought my mother spilling the beans would help, but it really didn't. I hated her, I hated the man who raised me, I hated Georgia, I hated myself, I hated the bugs, and I hated the trees. I was a resentful kid. I stayed in Zebulon briefly, and then I told my mother, "I've got to go."

"Where are you going?"

"Back to Florida."

"No explanation?"

"You didn't give me one when you brought me here. I'm not going to give you one now." I was a mean bastard to her, but she had earned it.

I flew back to Florida, got my own little apartment. I found myself a beautiful girl with violet eyes. She looked like a young Elizabeth Taylor. She was one of my girlfriends down there.

All the time, I was thinking of what to say to Lukie. I wasn't ready to confront him yet about the secret, but I wanted to see him.

As I was getting up the courage to go, I went to a party at Boot Branch, a beachfront area in Tarpon Springs. I hooked up with a local girl named Alisa Aposstolis who I'd known forever. We'd had this secret crush on each other for years, but we were always paired up with someone else. That night, though, I was feeling the effects of my stepfather's confession, and I'd had too much Jack Daniel's, and one thing led to another. Years of pent-up passion just came pouring out and we started making out on the sand. I was kissing her and felt happy for the first time in months.

Things were getting really steamy and we were practically ripping each other's clothes off, but then I felt this weird sensation. Something was wrong. Something had changed. It's like when you try to push two magnets together—there was this electric sensation that we shouldn't go any further. I pulled away and she looked at me.

"What's wrong?" she said.

"This feels really strange."

"I know," she said. "I was feeling it too."

I knew her dad was the lawyer for the Pappases, but what I had forgotten was that he was Lukie's nephew. I told Alisa what happened in Georgia and she started crying.

"God, I can't believe it," she said. "Does that mean we're related?"

"I think so," I said.

We went to her mom to get the full story. She was shocked and told us, "Listen, I'm sworn to secrecy." We begged her to tell us what she knew, and I'll never forget, she said, "You have to swear to me that this stays between us." And then she told me, "Yes, Kevin, you're Lukie Pappas's son. But we never thought the secret would get out."

I felt like the world was mocking me. I'd finally hooked up with my dream girl and she turned out to be my first cousin.

I was a Pappas but I wasn't. It was like this secret life had been forced on me. And the only one who could make it right was Lukie.

I started to put the pieces together. There were still things no one would tell me, but I got hints. I was convinced, for example, that Jim Cunningham must have caught my mother in the act. Maybe the talk in the town reached his ears and he tailed her. Or maybe he just caught a look he shouldn't have. There was no other way she would have told him voluntarily.

Memories from my childhood changed. I remembered the times Lukie Pappas would drive his silver Mercedes 560 SEC—the most beautiful car I'd ever seen—out to a place he had called Pappas Ranch, and my mother would meet him there, supposedly for business. Sometimes she would bring me along, and I would go and swim in the pool. I felt like I had gone to another world, and I was so grateful to Lukie for having me over. Now I know they were inside fucking, and the pool time was just to keep me distracted.

Lukie's home life, including his marriage, was a disaster. His wife would come into the restaurant raving about this or that, just totally melting down. But the Greeks, when they have kids, they don't divorce. Lukie had mistresses forever and my mother was his main mistress for a decade and a half.

He would do little things for our family around Christmas. He would come the day before and bring my mother an enormous amount of toys and clothes. My father would scowl, but I got a warm feeling every time I saw Lukie. Even before I knew, I was drawn to him.

# CHAPTER 7

I was truly alone for the first time in my life. Jim Cunningham was dead, and once I found out the truth, the cat was out of the bag. It was no longer a secret and I was dead set on letting everyone know it. I thought I would gain sympathy. But instead, I was ostracized and disowned by my very own brothers and sister. They wouldn't even talk to me. They were mad at our mother and felt they had been deceived their whole lives and now more than ever they resented the favoritism she had shown me. The Jehovah's Witnesses had a meeting to decide my fate because I had been raging against them, and they disassociated me. My mother had tried to protect her own soul because she could be disfellowshipped if they discovered she had an affair.

It didn't matter. My faith had died that day when Jim Cunningham told me that my whole life was a lie. I would still keep the Scriptures close to my heart, but I was no longer a practicing Witness. I couldn't believe any God would put a boy through what I was going through.

I replaced religion with anger. And a burning desire to know who I *really* was.

While I was in Georgia, I had made my mother write a letter about my pain and unhappiness and send it to Lukie. I finally went down to see him. It was a beautiful day and I walked into the restaurant bar where he was sitting, drinking a Tanqueray and tonic—his summer drink. In the winter, he drank Crown Royal with a splash of ginger.

He looked at me. I still remember the scene. He was immaculately dressed. Crisp white shirt, black slacks, gold Submariner on his wrist, slicked-back hair—the classic Greek mobster summer uniform. Lukie was always calm, elegant, unemotional. Everything I wanted to be but wasn't.

"I read that letter," he said. "What do you want me to do?"

I was nervous but I got to the point. "I want to carry the Pappas name."

That shocked him. "What are you talking about? Your mom worked for me and she's a good lady, but you know I can't run around and say that you're my son."

I said, "My mother knows who the father is. She's sure of it."

"Well, she also could have been screwing around with other people."

I kept my cool. "Listen, Lukie," I said, "my mother isn't a slut. She fell in love with you."

Then he looked at me real serious. "Let me explain this to you," he said. "When you become a man you'll realize you just don't spread your business all over the streets."

"Yeah, and when I become a man and I have a son out of wedlock I'll also know to stand up for my blood."

It was his first denial of me.

I told him I wanted to see Greece, the place that I had come from. He gave me four thousand dollars in cash in an envelope to go make the trip. I would have rather had his recognition, but I felt it was a start.

This was the first time I was able to experience the culture and people firsthand for myself. I spent two months in the old country, looking into the Pappas family history. The moment I got off the boat in Kalymnos, someone approached me and recognized me as one of the Pappas boys. It blew my mind. Kalymnos is an island near the southern tip of the Greek Isles known for fishing and sponging. It was also known as a haven for ex-pats and fugitives from the United States. This island reminded me of what Tarpon Springs was built from, and it stirred up deep feelings in my heart for my heritage. Everywhere I turned, the Pappas name would appear. The main drag is called Pappas Avenue. There was the Pappas Restaurant and Pappas diners. No matter where you looked there was a street, a business, or a monument with that name. And these were my Pappases, my father's family.

I found my friend Mikie Conomanos from Tarpon Springs, one of the Greek boys that I was raised with. I told him the story of Lukie and my mother, and he walked me around the island and introduced me to everybody. Then I started hitting all the islands. I went to Sparta and I got to see where the Pappases originated from, where my grandfather lived, and I just drank it in. I felt that sense of being home that I had always missed as an American boy in Greektown. I knew who I was. This was what I had yearned to be a part of my whole life.

Only one bad thing did happen that freaked me out. It had to do with the *mati*.

The *mati* is a Greek symbol, the evil eye. I wear a marble *mati* around my neck at all times. It wards off evil directed at you by your enemies. I was in a store and as I walked out my necklace broke and the *mati* fell to the pavement and shattered. And this Greek lady who was walking into the store stopped dead in her tracks and looked at the pieces of the *mati* and then at me. And she whispered the old phrase—*Get the devil away from you.*

I had been feeling so good, but that scared me.


I thought that the trip would cure me of my hunger to know who I was, but it didn't. If anything, I wanted Lukie's acceptance even more. When I got back, I changed my name to Kevin Lucas Pappas.

But every time I went back to Lukie, I got the same answer: *You're not my blood. I can't recognize you.* The same old-world Greek shit about hiding your mistakes and keeping your public face clean.

It was the same thing that had happened with Jim Cunningham. If Lukie had sat down and spent one hour with me and told me I was his son, treated me like his son, I would never have needed to see him again. But he shrugged me off.

Still, word had gotten out in Tarpon Springs. The old Greek ladies would see me on the streets, and now they could be open. "Look at you now; you're beautiful. You look like Lukie." When you're thirty, forty, fifty, you keep quiet. When you're seventy, they can't do anything to you. They'd tell Lukie Pappas he was a prick to his face. What are you gonna do?

I was really on my own now, and I needed to get money for food and rent. I began to hustle. There was no one else who was going to take care of me, so I decided I had to do it for myself.

To make ends meet, I created a jewelry business in Tarpon Springs. I had five 200-gallon fish tanks that I transported around town on this wheeled frame that was shaped like an octagon. I built the whole thing myself, and I would tow it to wherever the tourists were—the sponge exchange, which my grandfather Louis Pappas had created decades before, was one of my favorite spots.

In the tanks were oysters that had cultured pearls in them. I bought them wholesale, $175 per crate. In my little mobile shop, I had an enormous amount of settings behind me; tourists would come by and pick out their oyster and their setting. Then I would take the black pearl or pink pearl or the white pearl and I would set them in a ring or necklace for twenty or twenty-five dollars. I would sell sometimes up to two hundred oysters a day. I was making a killing.

But I wanted a legitimate store. I've always loved gold and diamonds, and when I was growing up in Florida, I would take shark teeth to make bracelets and necklaces and sell them to the tourists. A jewelry business was so natural for me.

Most of all I was trying to do the right thing, to show Lukie I could do business just like him. Things were working well. I was making money. But it didn't make an impression on him. He looked at me like I was just a punk. I thought the store might change that.

I had a friend named Jack Edwards whose father was the president of the United Bank in this small town in Georgia, population 810. It's the only bank I've ever seen that operated out of a trailer on the side of the road. So I went in to see Mr. Edwards.

"I want to start a jewelry store."

He started to chuckle.

I said, "No, I'm telling you, I need a loan to buy jewelry."

He said, "How you going to pay it back? You don't have any credit."

I said, "My mom will sign for me."

"I could ask her?"

"Sure." She owed me that much.

"How much you need?"

I told him $10,000.

"That's a lot of money."

"I know."

It was in June or July. "Christmas is coming and I'll pay you back by the time it gets here."

I found a location in this little town, Griffin, Georgia, that cost me $800 a month. I had a cabinetmaker make me some custom cabinets, named the store "The Gold Mine," bought a sign, and I started hustling. I was very, very driven.

I paid the loan off before Christmas. Soon I had a line of credit with Mr. Edwards: $20,000, then $50,000, then $100,000.

I used to have airplanes with signs trailing behind them saying, THE GOLD MINE. I was dating a *Penthouse* centerfold and she would come in and do signings. And I got to know the Atlanta Falcons because I was selling them custom pieces and I would have them come in and do autographs. People would be lined up outside the jewelry store, thirty to forty deep. Every month I had a different promotion: "Come see the Falcons." "Come meet the *Penthouse* Pet." "Come get a free Falcons hat." And I was selling a shitload of jewelry, driving a slant-nose Porsche 944, and just hustling like crazy.

It was amazing. I was the youngest entrepreneur in the country to own two jewelery stores at age seventeen.

In the back of my mind, I thought I would pull up to the Pappas Restaurant in my flashy car, with diamonds dripping from my wrists, a hotshot businessman, and my father would come out the door and embrace me.

It didn't happen that way. He gave me no recognition, no respect at all. But I knew what he was, I knew what he stood for, I knew what kind of secrets he held, and I knew what kind of business he did at night.

I was looking to get his attention. That's when I started dealing a little coke.

# CHAPTER 8

I t was the eighties. I had cut myself off from my past. My fake past, you could say. And my real one didn't want any part of me.

I had even cut my mother out of my life. She had betrayed me, chosen Jim Cunningham over me. I really lost two fathers and one mother in that deal.

I was depressed, but finding out the truth also opened life up. Nobody had any claims on me. Within three years, I would go from a 165-pound hick from the backwoods of Georgia to a bodybuilder, entrepreneur, Chippendales dancer, drug trafficker, friend to the rich and famous, and ex-con. It was like I was going through a new life every three years.

And it seemed like Atlanta and I came up at the same time. In the eighties, the city started to heat up. And I was right there; I knew everyone who was worth knowing. If you walked into a club or a party where the Atlanta Falcons were hanging out or the music business was out in force and there were famous pro wrestlers doing lines of coke on the countertops and the finest women in the city were represented, you better believe you would see me there.

I was a jeweler by day and a dancer by night. I had always loved to dance; it was something I got from my mother. And when I was in high school, I had gone to the Arthur Murray School and become one of the top guys there. I even signed up for a *Dance Fever* competition: If you won you got a chance to be on the show with Deney Terrio. I wanted to get on that show so bad I would do anything, practice any amount of hours, to make it.

I made it to the finals and won the contest; I was so happy I thought I would burst. I was supposed to fly out to L.A. to tape the show, but then the producers found out I was just sixteen—I had used a fake ID at my audition—and cancelled the trip.

I was crushed. It took me weeks to get over that disappointment.

By the time I was eighteen, I was dancing for Chippendales and the Male Encounter, a bunch of big, cut boys who went up and down the Atlantic Coast doing shows for women.

That's where I first saw the drug scene up close. The girls out for their bachelorette parties or whatever would want something to bump the night up. And so I started dealing a little crystal, coke, speed— whatever they wanted. My friends were doing the same thing. We'd make a few grand a week, take two weeks off, and go down to Miami to windsurf and hang out.

It wasn't a business then. It was just a way to finance chilling out. You've heard of recreational drug users. Well, I was a recreational drug dealer. I didn't really see the potential. But I've always been a fast learner.

We'd be in the Atlanta clubs like the Cheetah and the Tattletales and the Lemon Peel, and we'd have what we called spotters out there in the crowd. They would basically take orders for whatever kind of powder or pill you wanted, and they'd come back to me and I'd give them the product. The bouncers and the bartenders would direct people to me, too. So there I was in a Speedo like a dumb piece of meat, but really I was watching over the merchandise and the buyers. Within a couple of years, I had five or six clubs that I was dealing out of.

In the beginning, it wasn't just the money. I was making peanuts compared to what I would soon be bringing in. But drugs draw people to you. They draw death closer, too, but first they bring you attention. Doors open. You're invited to mansions you would never have seen the inside of. You meet people who would have never wanted to shake your hand. And at that point in my life I wanted attention. I wanted people coming to me.

I was getting my dope from Cubans and some Lebanese guys I'd run into. Mid-level guys, nothing too heavy. But then I decided to start buying kilos, and I nearly got my ass shot right off the bat.

I cooked up my first major deal with my friend Jose Diaz. I built my organization through friendships. The guys in what became the Band of Five—I guess you'd call it my drug-trafficking gang—I either met through dancing or the prison system. The Band wouldn't all come together until a few years later, but Jose I met in 1982 at Packets, dancing on Ladies' Night.

Jose came to America on the Marielito boat drop. His dad was a painter back in Cuba who had very little time for him, and his mother was out partying for most of his childhood. He grew up as pretty much an abandoned child—and one who was under suspicion because his family had been a supporter of Batista. By the time he was a teenager, the pressure was too intense. He had to get out. He came to this country with a pair of high-water pants, a T-shirt, and not a whole lot of fucking else.

I'm not ashamed to say that Jose was absolutely and unequivocally the most beautiful man I'd ever met. He looked like a sculpture. He was a former Mr. Georgia, a bodybuilder with green eyes and that typical woman-killer Cuban look. But above all, Jose was loyal. I knew that he would die for me. He was my first partner and I trusted him with my life. Jose was also very methodical, a guy who thought before he moved, and I needed a person like that in my life because I'm so headstrong; too many times in those days, I made a move before I thought things through.

We had a Cuban connection down in Miami, and like a couple of hicks we thought we'd go down there Wild Bill Hickok–style, buy the merchandise, head back up to Atlanta, cut it up, and make a fortune. But there is no beginner's luck in drug trafficking—a lot of the times, it's the amateurs who end up getting shot.

The deal went down in an alleyway behind a hair salon in a light industrial section of Miami. A lot of deals went down in that area. It was like a drug bazaar. But it was half-deserted in the early evening. That's one of the things that Hollywood gets wrong, at least for my clique. We never did business in hotel rooms or motel rooms or anywhere enclosed if we could get away with it. I like four directions of escape, not just a single door. Do your business out in the open. If they have surveillance on you, you're nailed anyway. But always give yourself a chance at getting away.

So we rolled up to this block on Flagler Street to meet the two Cubans. It was a two-kilo deal. I had the money in a brown paper sack.

We showed up first. We'd been driving around Miami all day, killing time, and we were real anxious to get the deal done. The Cubans showed up fifteen minutes later. One was very thin, about 5′10″, with what I can only describe as white features but very dark skin. His eyes were dead, no emotion or even interest when he looked at you. The dude looked like someone who could kill you and then use your body as a chair while he counted your money. He was dressed in a guayabera shirt, buttoned all the way to the top, untucked. The other guy was the talker and the planner. He was shorter, a little fat, light-skinned, and wearing an Adidas shirt. The tall dude kept flicking his eyes between Jose and me as his partner did the talking.

I tried to see if I could spot a gun in either of their waistbands. If you have a gun there, you move differently. I knew how to spot that, but these guys were acting completely natural.

Jose spoke to them in rapid-fire Spanish. I kept looking to him for a sign of how the deal was going, and he kept nodding at me. I knew Jose sometimes got a bad feeling from the way someone was talking— if they were changing their story, trying to delay us, or some other sketchy behavior. But this time he kept nodding and smiling.

"They say that this time is COD, but if we do good, next time we can get five kilos on credit," he said.

We didn't want to hang around. They brought out the coke in plastic sacks and we handed over the money. The fat guy kept nodding and smiling. He looked me right in the eye. That gave me a good feeling.

Jose handed the coke to me and I started walking away. Jose was a few feet behind me, still talking to the fat dude. All of a sudden I saw movement in an alleyway to our right and a guy jumped out. What I remember were the dreadlocks. He must have been Haitian or Cuban. And he had a pump shotgun in his hands.

Thugs don't yell "Freeze!" As soon as I saw him, I turned and started to run. The shotgun went off. I felt fire along my backside and in my hand. I yelled to Jose and I saw our two contacts had also pulled handguns. They obviously thought we were suckers and they were going to take our money and the coke and let us bleed to death in that alley.

But Jose was not going to let that happen. He pulled out his Desert Eagle—Jose liked big guns, and the Desert Eagle is the biggest—and started blasting. We both turned and started running as the guns were popping off, and I got a load of buckshot in my backside. I also got a piece of lead in my hand that's still there between the index finger and the middle finger; it's too close to the nerve to remove. Jose was wounded, too—he took buckshot in the side and in the back of the leg.

If you've ever heard a Desert Eagle fire, it's like a cannon. It freaked the Cubans out. They left the money bags where they were and we went back and grabbed them. We drove back to Atlanta with the money *and* the merchandise.

We couldn't go to the hospitals because they would call the cops. We called up a contact I had in Miami called Birdman and he gave us the address of a Colombian doctor. We drove to his house, went around back, and rang the bell. His assistant, this plain-looking girl dressed in blue hospital smocks, let us in. He'd rigged up a little mini emergency room in the back of his home, with a bed to lie on and supplies in jars. He wasn't set up to do heart surgery, but that's not what his patients needed.

The assistant cleaned us up, washed out the wounds, and ten minutes later the doctor came in. He was all business. He hooked up Jose to a saline IV and pumped him full of antibiotics. I had six pellets in my ass, one in my hand, and three in my left calf. They weren't deep. The doctor dug them out and cleaned me up quick. He had to spend more time on Jose, who'd been closer and whose pellets were deeper.

We drove back to Miami that night. We were feeling good. We kept telling the story over and over again, laughing at how dumb the Cubans must have thought we were.

We came very close to dying that day. But we'd stood up to a couple of thugs and started our little business.

There was another time during the Gold Mine days, when I didn't know what I was doing, that I had the brilliant idea of bringing the dope in underwater. Jose and I went to a meet off Key Biscayne, where we were supposed to hook up with other Cubans with some product to sell. There were five of us in a Zodiac: Jose, myself, and three other guys who were there mostly for protection.

It was two in the morning, pitch-black. You could just barely make out the lights on shore. We were dressed in wet suits and our air tanks were topped up and ready to be strapped on.

I must have seen too many Navy SEAL commercials. We were going to get into our full scuba gear, trail the dope (which was in waterproof bags) behind us, and just head for shore. I figured the DEA was looking for boats, not frogmen.

We saw the lights from our connection coming toward us from the south. The supplier's boat pulled up to us, and we took their ropes and tied us together. Then we started transferring the cash and the coke over the sides of the boats, using flashlights to make sure everything was right. Finally, the transfer was made and we'd put on our fins and were getting ready to go over the side into the water.

Then we heard another outboard—a big outboard—coming at us, and then saw lights flash on. What we didn't know was that the dope didn't belong to our connection: They had jacked it from some other Cubans, and somehow the owners had gotten wind of our deal. And they were here to get their dope back.

They opened up on us with rifles from about 150 yards. We started screaming, "What the fuck is going on?" But for obvious reasons our connections weren't giving us any information. We started blasting back at the white-orange bursts that we saw in the darkness, but all we had were handguns.

It was chaos. We were sliding around the boat in our flippers. I'm like, "Jose, if the tanks take a bullet, do you think they'll blow up?"

He shouted back. "How the fuck should *I* know?"

So we were firing our guns and struggling to get the tanks off, but it was impossible in the chaos. Finally, I screamed to Jose, "Fuck this! Just head for shore." We left the coke there and dove into the water, and our buddies turned the Zodiac around and got the hell out of there.

The underwater thing was actually a great idea. But our execution wasn't the best. I hadn't researched our suppliers enough, and it came back to bite me in the ass.

Again, we got out with our lives, but every fuck-up like this showed me how *not* to run a drug-trafficking business. It's not as easy as it looks.

# CHAPTER 9

My first real connection to the drug business came through the Gold Mine. These young black guys started coming in and buying enormous amounts of jewelry. They'd pull up in their Mercedeses and their Lexuses and go on these shopping sprees. One day I remember this guy came in and picked up probably a hundred grand worth of merchandise. He walked out to the car and brought out two eelskin satchels shaped like boots. He unzipped the bags and they were packed full of money, new hundreds wrapped in bank wrappers.

I was like, "Oh, my God." I knew they weren't ballplayers or musicians, so let's face it, there was only one other major possibility at that time: They were gangsters. Tyrone Meeks was the first one that I got friendly with. He pretty much ran the cocaine trade in black Atlanta. I started at the top of the food chain, which became a habit of mine. I always wanted to deal with the top guy.

Tyrone was a local guy who lived in Griffin and made good in the cocaine trade. He was in his early fifties by the time I met him, and he had the black neighborhoods locked down. He wasn't hustling and scheming anymore; those days were gone. Tyrone was the cocaine establishment. He was the go-to person in the black community if you were in trouble, especially if your family was involved. And he took his profits and put them into three things: women, gambling, and jewelry. That's where I came in.

I learned a lot from Tyrone. He was a very keen, very intuitive street hustler. He'd never really held a job, but instead had been a dope slinger his whole life. He worked with the young boys on the corner like on Nickel Street growing up. So he'd seen every aspect of the business. You don't do that by being stupid. Tyrone was very smart and, by the time I met him, very wealthy.

He was more than a drug distributor. He could walk the neighborhoods and talk to the people about their kids, about the prison system, about the cops. Everybody went to Tyrone to either handle a situation or make peace. He was the caretaker of his neighborhood. And he turned that into a side business. If someone needed a loan, he'd give him or her $5,000 with fifteen points on the dollar.

You'd never know Tyrone was a drug dealer. He dressed beautifully and had perfect manners. Plus he had a beautiful wife who lived with their two kids in a mansion in Griffin.

But all along he was probably the highest-volume sack dealer on the south side. Sacks were clear baggies of base cocaine. Ten years later it would have been crack, but that hadn't been popularized yet. They didn't puff it up and process it; they just took a kilo of coke and broke it down into twenty-dollar pieces and put it on the street.

Tyrone owned that business. He was the big time. I wanted what he had.


After he bought a bunch of pieces from me, Tyrone and I became friends. He thought I was a cool white guy, the new kid in town, and he introduced me to everybody in his world. Tyrone saw I was hungry and hooked in to social circles that he didn't travel in—which meant new customers for him. So I became Tyrone's protégé. And with that came money and opportunity.

I got to know his guys and soon a personal relationship became a business relationship. Meaning money laundering. Tyrone and his guys had so much cash that they were looking for ways to wash it. So I thought that was an easy way to make money. It wasn't like I was selling drugs. I would bring them to my suppliers and they would pick out merchandise—emeralds, diamonds, and Rolexes were the main items. They'd pay an inflated price on paper and it would be a legitimate transaction.

I kind of eased into the business. It's a small step from being legit to laundering a little money. It's another small step to selling a quarter kilo here or a half ki there to people you know. From then on, it just snowballed. Pretty soon you're flying to Colombia to arrange the deals yourself.

# CHAPTER 10

W hat made my business in the beginning was my Rolodex. I knew everyone in Atlanta, beginning with the Falcons. I got to know the players and the staff so well that even the Falcons' coach walked me into the locker room one day. It was like being introduced around by the Pope.

My first real sales were to football players. There were a few guys who grew up in Griffin, Georgia, who would come into the Gold Mine and buy diamond stud earrings or custom necklaces. I started hanging out and partying with them. Pretty soon I was going to bashes at mansions and meeting the Atlanta Hawks. Through them I met musicians: Atlanta was just beginning to be a powerhouse in the industry. I moved into a penthouse apartment next to this R&B star who had a string of big hits during the eighties, and soon I was hanging at his place, too. My circle of customers and friends just kept getting wider and wider.

Maybe my Tarpon Springs days paid off in Atlanta. I knew how to be the outsider who made friends in a community he didn't belong to. I was the white guy at every black party, just like those years when I was trying to fit in with the Greeks. I could dance, I could talk shit with the best of them, and I was a comedian. Plus I had powder for sale. You just couldn't have a party in Atlanta without me.

During the Falcons games, I would hang out with the wives and girl-friends in their section, talking them up. The only difference between me and a regular fan was that I had a .38 strapped to my ankle in a leather holster. I had started wearing it after I started dealing. I had guns everywhere: my glove compartment, under my seat, a shotgun behind the counter at the Gold Mine.

One time I was hanging with the Falcon families at a game when cops started running down the aisles toward our seats. They had their guns drawn and they came right to my row. Someone had seen my holster and called 911. Luckily, it was empty—I'd left my gun at home.

But the incident didn't help my PR. The Falcons' coach found out who I really was and banned his players from contact with Kevin Pappas. He said I was a bad influence. Never mind that his guys were coming to *me*.

I felt it was safe because I knew who they were; I knew their families, their girlfriends, their wives. They weren't informants for the government. They had enough money to pay for the merchandise and they had enough smarts not to fuck up their contracts and their business because they were professionals. So I kept telling myself this wasn't real drug trafficking.

I was spending money like water. The jewelry business was doing well, but I was living over my head. I needed another source of income. So I started letting people know that if they needed a ki or a half a ki, I was the guy.

Word got out fast. We'd get calls from the rich people in Buckhead. We had politicians. We had cops. We had street people. We had a lot of weightlifters, a lot of bodybuilders, a whole bunch of strippers. We had corporate America. We even delivered to some of the best office buildings in Midtown Atlanta—lawyers needing their morning refresher or mortgage brokers celebrating a big sale. Car dealers, for some reason, were big clients of ours. There was one guy who owned a string of exotic car dealerships. He was good for half a ki a week. And that was just for him, his buddies, and his clients. In the eighties, coke was what a good cigar is now—the capper at the end of a deal.

And just like the Vegas casinos, drug dealers have whales. High rollers. And you had to service them like they were special. Anytime of the night they called, you got out there and took them the dope. Big sales meant lower risk. You had to take care of your premium clients.

The junkies were different. They got no respect. They were barely hanging on to life anyway. We had a way of testing the purity of the stuff when we wanted to confirm it; we'd take it to a street guy and give him a hit. People laugh when I tell them, but there's actually nothing better than taking it to a junkie. Sometimes they would come close to OD'ing and then we knew it was pure, 97 or 98 percent. And the funny thing was that was the shit that the junkies wanted. They didn't resent us for almost killing them, not at all. They'd be like, "Hey, can I get some more of that?"

It was like a medical trial for addicts. We had people lining up to be test subjects.

We also had test kits. We cut a triangle in the ki and we put the kit in and if it turned a royal blue it was 98 percent pure. Later, when we were buying directly from the Colombians and the Ochoa clan, everything we got from Colombia was guaranteed at 96 to 98 percent. Everything. It came with a money-back guarantee. If the purity was anything less, they'd make it up to you on the next load.

Tyrone had a friend he introduced me to during this time. He was a good ole boy with a mullet haircut, looked like Billy Ray Cyrus with a really bad complexion. Pure country. He always wore jeans and a T-shirt and big belt buckle. Everyone called him Lee.

Lee didn't draw much attention to himself, but he was always around. I thought he was just a local boy who was living large. He was a car wholesaler, which meant he was always driving around Atlanta looking for new merchandise and had plenty of time to hang out at the Gold Mine. And he had a wicked bad coke habit.

I never thought much about Lee. He was an OK kind of guy. A casual acquaintance. I should have been paying more attention.

The scene wasn't like it is today. This was before crack, before Miami became the murder capital of America because the Colombians were killing everything that moved. Before the war on drugs. It was socially acceptable to bust out a bullet casing—that was the carrier of choice for the club crowd—and tap out a few lines of coke.

I didn't feel like a criminal. I knew what I was doing was against the law, but being a cocaine dealer was different. It had cachet. It was cool to be a coke dealer. Everyone wanted to be my friend. I'd walk into a club and there would be an "Oh, wow, look who's here" look in people's eyes. They knew the party was on.

At this point, I was doing odd jobs. Whatever you needed me to do in the drug trade, I was available. I was still learning my way and so I couldn't pick and choose my assignments. A lot of the times I was asked to go down to Miami and take a package up to Atlanta. Sounds simple, but it wasn't.

Using the highways during the eighties was dangerous. There were so many profile checks being done on A1A coming out of Miami that you had to basically be in disguise just to have a hope of getting through. The guys they had working those checkpoints were phenomenal. If you were driving a Chevy Malibu looking like a surfer, but you had a Rolex on your wrist, they'd pull you over. So you had to make sure that you profiled your own guys before they went out onto the road. You couldn't put Kevin Pappas in a Malibu. You'd have to put him in a Porsche—with my jewelry, my tan, and all that, I just looked like a Porsche guy.

The roadblocks could make your hair turn gray while you waited to go through them. They had these big ladders with high-powered lights that would shine down on the car, and they had two dogs. We got to know the setup so well that we even knew the dogs' names: Champ and Bear. I'll never forget: They even had the Highway Patrol vests on with their names on them. Champ and Bear held my life in their hands and you would actually have to spend hours thinking how to outsmart them if you wanted to survive. Forget the cops—you had to think like a drug-sniffing dog to beat the game.

You'd see the red taillights ahead of you and then the lights thirty feet up in the air, and you'd say to yourself, "Oh my God, is the stuff packaged right?" You'd have five or ten ki's in the trunk, and there'd be forty cars ahead of you, so you'd have time to go over every step of the wrapping and storing of the dope to see if there was a shot at getting caught. Some idiots would see the roadblock ahead and they'd pull a U-turn to get away from it. But of course the GHP has chase cars waiting for you to do that, and they'll get you before you've gone two miles.

So you just don't turn around. Not when you're loaded. You bite the bullet. I remember coming up to Champ and Bear with ten ki's in my trunk in a black Porsche 944 and my heart was practically coming through my chest. The handler brought the dogs up and they walked around and sniffed, walked and sniffed. I was sitting there, trying to act bored, flashing my diamond bracelet, trying to seem like some hot-shot lawyer who has a hot date waiting up the coast. I tried to look annoyed but I was terrified.

There were no hits. I sailed through. But if you don't think a drug trafficker earns his money, you try sitting on a baking-hot piece of asphalt with enough dope to put you away for the rest of your life sitting six feet behind your ass.


A lot of these runs were for a guy named Billy Solomon. Tyrone introduced me to him, and he was like Tyrone on an international level—a step up. Billy was Bahamian, and back then the Bahamas was the transshipment point between Colombia and the United States Billy was heavy into the heroin business, the cocaine business, and money laundering. He was a big dude—6′2″, 285 pounds, with a goatee, black as the ace of spades.

So when Billy gave me the job of delivering five kilos to his contact in D.C., I said yes right off.

I called Jose and he agreed to come along with me on this other job. We took along two other hard-asses who did runs with us. We drove the shit up 95, hoping we wouldn't get spotted. Everything went fine, and we breathed a sigh of relief when we finally pulled into D.C. But then we realized we had another problem: We didn't know where the fuck we were going.

The directions were off, because pretty soon we were wandering the city craning our heads out of the car window looking for street names. It doesn't take long in D.C. before you end up in the wrong part of town. We started on Pennsylvania Avenue and passed the White House—with five ki's in the trunk and guns all over the car. I'd never seen the White House before, and I just couldn't believe I was seeing it on a drug run.

"Jose, this cannot be happening."

"Yeah, it's happening," he said. "Where the fuck is this house? I'm going to kill Billy when we get back."

We drove around and finally pulled up to what we thought was the house. But we were in shorts and T-shirts and it's like forty degrees out. We looked like hicks on steroids. And we quickly became a target.

We were sitting in the car talking about what to do next when we saw four or five black guys, neighborhood guys, walking toward us, all dressed in Timberlands and down jackets and jeans. They didn't look like they were coming to offer us directions. One of them pulled up his jacket and I saw a flash of silver.

"Get the fuck out of here!" I yelled.

Jose hit the gas and we nearly ran over one of the guys as we peeled off. I could see his face as we went by. He wasn't scared. He was angry. We were fat targets who were getting away.

We finally found our way to the entrance to US 95 by sheer luck. The whole ride back, I was thinking, *There has to be a better way.* I needed to figure this game out or I was going to die a very stupid death.


I liked to put forward the image of invulnerability. If you don't care about living, you can appear to be indestructible. You'll take any job, no matter how dangerous. But a year after the D.C. job, I had a load on my back hauling ass through Alligator Alley coming out of Miami. I was in a truck with 150 kilos packed in a red convertible Chevy, kind of a surfer ride. And all of a sudden, I just felt exposed. I looked at my situation from a profiler's point of view.

I pulled over. I called the guy I had just done the pickup from and said, "I can't do it. I'm a dead giveaway." Truth was, my nerves were shot. I was done. I knew that part of my business was finished. So when you start thinking about the repercussions, it's time for you to get up, get out, or change up.

At the time, I felt it was a strike against me that I couldn't go through with the drop. But now I see that I was just getting smarter. There's no profit in risking your ass as a mule. I wanted to be the guy making the deals.

# CHAPTER 11

There were three types of merchandise. You had a yellow-based petroleum cut, which was what we called the wash cocaine, the bottom of the barrel, the sludge. It was popular for some reason with our black customers. They liked it because they were remelting it and stepping on it and because it's got a real strong flavor to it. It's pasty, it's sticky—a nasty cut in my opinion, but some people loved it.

The second wash is acetone. It smells like nail-polish remover. That cut is what you called a high-level norm. It was the industry standard. It melted very quickly, so it was good for freebasing. And it held up well when you stepped on it, so the traffickers could make money on acetone wash and they loved that.

Then you take a pure cocaine that's 98 percent and it has ether-based wash. That ether base is so potent that it can break blood vessels and make your nose bleed. So if you're snorting cocaine and you're leaning down to do a line, that ether-based shit was so strong that often your nose would be squirting blood.

You could take this tablet and you could hold it up and thumb your finger on it, and it would actually flake and cascade down. If you know anything about cocaine, that's good. It was like the finest caviar; the quality was amazing. Cesar Uribe cut the coke for the Ochoa clan and his nickname was the Mad Cook. He knew how to take the coca leaves, process them into a paste, wash that, and purify it in such a way that the stuff was like candy. It was really a connoisseur's cocaine. We took a lot of pride in that. Later when I hooked up with the Ochoas, people knew that we had good merchandise and they would pay five grand more for it because that'd mean that they could take it to the streets and put more weight on top of it.

The price of the product depended on how much you were buying. You'd sell ki's and half ki's at one price and you'd sell small weight at another price. Then you'd gram it down and eight-ball it and quarter-ounce it down to another price.

This is how the math worked: Each kilo had two tablets, or bricks; each one was 500 grams per. At that time, kilos went for $18,500. You'd take that kilo and you put another half a ki on it—cutting it with baby laxative or whatever. Now you've got 1,500 grams. You break that into eight-balls at three grams per. By the time you're done you can piece out that ki and make $100,000 on it.

But when you break a ki down into 1,000 grams and try to sell those one at a time, that's a thousand chances to go to jail. You make a better profit but you increase your vulnerability. I'd rather flip ten ki's and make ten grand a ki than have four ki's and break it down and make a million. Because I'd rather be more secure.


South Florida was glorified because of *Miami Vice,* but everyone understood that Miami was hot as a pistol. If you lived the high life in Miami, your life was very short.

There were rabid gun-shooting crazy jackasses on every block. And while Atlanta was controlled by American-born gangsters, black and white, Miami was filled with cultures you might think you understood but you didn't: Jamaicans, Haitians, Cubans, and Colombians.

The murders there were terrible for business. Life expectancy for a drug trafficker was low. Rule of thumb was you wouldn't last more than five to seven years. Not only does the violence make the local news every night, but you get the feds interested. Once it becomes a headline, prosecutors and the DEA and the ATF want to come to your town and make their reps.

And another thing people don't realize is that all that killing messes with your personnel. The turnover of people within the hierarchy of the trafficking gangs was so rapid you didn't really know who to trust and who not to trust. You'd go down there and make a deal with X and come back two months later and X had been found dead in a mail sack by the side of the road. So who do you deal with? You open yourself up to danger every time you make a new connection. You couldn't really put your stake in the ground in Miami because the players there were so big and so ruthless. For me, it was a fun place to go and visit but not a place to do business.

Atlanta, on the other hand, was the hidden jewel. Big city, glamorous, southern women, a sun town. And you didn't take your life in your hands stepping outside your door. It was still a major cocaine hub, but it didn't make the headlines. I got into the cocaine game at the exact right time, and in the right place, too.

Cocaine was innocent back then.

# CHAPTER 12

I wanted to become a player in Atlanta. But I couldn't spend a lifetime doing it like Tyrone had. I wanted to impress Lukie. I was in too much of a rush.

At that time I needed cash up front to get the merchandise. It wasn't like that later on in my profession when I could get $10 million of coke fronted to me on a handshake. You needed to show the money.

I called up Tyrone. "Listen," I told him. "I've got a deal. You want to get in on it, I'll partner with you."

Basically, I was offering to do all the work and take all the risk if he put up the cash. It was a good deal for him and he knew it.

Tyrone said, "What do you need?"

"About a quarter of a million dollars."

He didn't hesitate. He said, "Call me back in an hour."

So I called him back. "All right, I talked to Douglas. Go to his house on Hill Street and he'll take care of you." Douglas Barker was a relative of his. He was also Tyrone's enforcer. He was the kind of guy who said three words and it carried the weight of a hundred.

So I pulled up to this typical southern wood-frame home. Douglas met me at the door and took me back into one of the bedrooms. He was a tall dude, looked like an Olympic sprinter, with a thin pencil beard. He was dressed in a tight T-shirt, jeans, and sneakers, and his BMW was parked out front—he was a fanatic for them. He was a nice guy, but the word was, if Douglas was called in, Tyrone had stopped negotiating. If he wanted you roughed up or your jaw broken, he had thugs to do that. Douglas was the last resort. He'd kill you without saying a word.

The little stash was low-tech for sure. There were no safes or sliding doors or vaults under the carpet. Douglas just pulled back a piece of the paneling and there were stacks of cash between the wall studs.

I was like, "Good lord, I can't believe what I'm seeing." There must have been $3 million in there. Douglas wasn't even trying to impress me. That was just an average stack for them.

He took out a quarter of a million dollars, put it in a Ziploc bag, and said, "All right, let us know when it comes in."


As I started making more connections and dealing more coke, I started to plan out how to organize a drug-trafficking gang. I think I gave more thought to my management style than most CEOs of *Fortune* 500 companies. After all, I had a lot more to lose if my people failed me. If a CEO has a bad quarter or a bad year, he gets fired or retires to the Bahamas with a fat golden parachute. If I made the wrong move, I'd be dead or in the pen.

Seventy-five percent of multi-kilo dealers and traffickers are brought down not by what they do, but by what one of their lieutenants or captains do. You not only have to keep yourself out of trouble, you have to keep your people out of trouble—because if they're facing the rest of their lives in jail, they're going to give you up. I loved my guys, but I'm not sentimental. The drug game has the least loyalty of any aspect of organized crime. There's too much money and the turnover is so great that you're constantly having to watch out for a new set of people.

And so I thought a lot about how to motivate and—let's face it—control people. I have to say I got very good at it.

I was a horrible student growing up. I'm dyslexic. In school, I got around it by being a clown and trying to compensate for it. But I do have two assets: I can read people like I was flipping through a magazine and I have a near-photographic memory. Very good skills in the drug game.

And I must be the only trafficker who learned his techniques from the Greek Mafia and the Jehovah's Witnesses. Those were the two organizations that taught me the most.

The Jehovah's Witnesses had told me how to bring a message to people. As a child orator, I would be on stage with six to seven thousand people in the District and Circuit conventions at the Macon Coliseum and it didn't frighten me. But they also told me how to get inside people's minds. To be a good preacher, you have to know what people want, what they really want deep in their souls. And then you tailor your message to that.

What I did was to replace the message of religion that I had learned—that desire for salvation—with what my men really wanted. Some of them wanted money and power. OK, I can lead you there, I can teach you how to get that. Some of them wanted women, to be loved. Some thought that they wanted gold and women, but what they really wanted was to belong to something larger than themselves.

The lower echelon of the drug trade is full of castoffs, misfits, people who have no family or who've been rejected by the family they have. I can't tell you how many times I took my posse to the Bahamas or Miami Beach for Thanksgiving or Christmas just to get their minds off the family dinners they weren't part of. You had to watch your people around the holidays. They'd get crazy without even realizing why. None of them had real strong connections to their parents. And if you gave them something to replace that, they would die for you.

That was my specialty. I showed people how to believe in themselves and to go after what they dreamed of becoming. I was the father they never had.

Which brings us to my other teacher, my biological father, Lukie. But my dad's management style was very antiquated—he did things the same way they did them in Greece. It was strictly about rewards and punishments and loyalty to the family.

It worked for him because he was embedded in a deeply Greek community. The families wouldn't put up with disrespect toward Lukie. They wouldn't let their sons or daughters blab about crime business. Plus, he was recruiting his own family members for his soldiers and his captains. The Greek culture did the work for him, in a way. He was building on a thousand-year-old tradition and all he had to do was not fuck it up.

I was beginning from scratch. I had no family and I was managing Colombians, Americans, black dudes, Cubans, Vietnamese. There was nothing to build on but what I instilled in them.

So I managed my guys based on emotional needs. And I confided in my group, but never gave them enough information so they could turn and flip and hurt me.

I made them feel part of something important and exciting. I let them know that hurting me would be hurting themselves. And I was sure to find out what their Achilles' heels were. I held that hole card close to the vest and used it only when I had to.

I'll give you a couple of examples. One of my boys, Carlos Ramirez—a cousin of Jose's—actually crossed the line by getting behind in his bills and running his mouth. And what mattered to Ramirez was his image as a tough bastard. He was 5'11" and 260 pounds, a street brawler. So I took him out to a public park at one in the morning and handcuffed him to the monkey bars and beat him with a two by four. I told him as I was doing it, I said, "Listen, this is going to hurt." I brought my whole crew with me, and some of his family members, too, and I told Ramirez, "I'm disciplining you because you made a mistake. You did not do it maliciously, but if I let these mistakes go on we're going to have issues. Now, you're probably not going to like what I'm going to do but I've got to make an example." So I smacked him across the face with the plank and broke a couple of ribs. I worked him over pretty good, and I let him know that if he didn't use his head, he was going to lose what was important to him.

I was respectful because I didn't want to turn him against me, but I took away something he valued. His rep.

There was another guy named Tommy Madden who was one of my guys in the clubs. He was from Louisiana, had a thick Cajun accent—a big fat good ole boy. Tommy owed me money, half a million, and after giving him a few reminders without any response I went over to his condo with a U-Haul truck. We kicked open the door and he was sitting on the couch with this sloppy blonde and a bunch of coke on the table.

"Hi, Tommy," I said.

"Uh, hey there, Kevin, how you . . ."

I stopped him right there.

"You know, Tommy, you're giving the Cajun people a bad name. Not paying back your debts, not returning phone calls. If it wasn't for that catfish you guys make, I'd be prejudiced against people from Louisiana."

"Kevin, I was . . ."

"Shut up."

He was freaking out. He had a little Chihuahua named Guido and it was barking its head off. I walked over to Tommy. His date shot her ass to the other side of the couch.

"You owe me close to half a million, Tommy. Where the fuck is it?"

He was stuttering some bullshit. I knew the money had gone up his nose and so did he.

So we took everything he owned: all his furniture, his TV, his pots and pans, his jewelry, his clothes—everything. And we loaded it right up on the U-Haul as he watched.

We left him with the couch, a bowl of popcorn, and his date.

Tommy couldn't believe it. "But I have no clothes, man!" he shouted as we were leaving.

"Go steal them like you stole my coke," I said.

Tommy knew that because he had nothing left the next time we had to come back we'd be taking the debt out on his fat ass. So he paid up. And he got his furniture back.

But I did it calmly. I didn't go in there waving a machete like a lunatic or bashing people's heads in with a baseball bat like Al Capone. I didn't yell and scream and make the whole thing into a personal vendetta. That's what I got from watching Lukie all those years back—control.

If I made it personal, the anger I felt would have come back at me a hundred times stronger. I was businesslike. Lukie would have been proud.

# CHAPTER 13

As all this was going on, I was still looking into my family's past. I wanted to know who they were. Being lied to for so long had given me this need to know the truth.

The deeper I investigated, the more information was offered to me by friends of the family and the streets. We can call them concerned citizens. The façade that I once thought was innocent was now unraveling to expose a behind-the-scenes business of huge scope. It was common knowledge that my father had dealings with well-connected families in all the leading industries in the Sunshine State: citrus, tourism, you name it.

What houses were put where and who could put a hotel on what beachfront was often decided by the family. Without a payoff or a piece of the action, you'd be guaranteed to get nothing. They had strong connections with congressmen and judges, and they could get real estate projects blocked with a single phone call.

Members of the family simply called it good business. But if you asked the feds, they actually have a different term for it, and depending on which agent writes it up in their field notes, you'd learn your fate from a higher power.

What I learned was that the Pappases were in charge of a lot of stuff from waterfront properties to the Gulf Coast cities. They would involve themselves in only what interested them. The older generation was able to keep the dealings within the immediate family. But it is my understanding that when the younger generations started to come into play, their decisions were not always the best for the family. That was the eighties generation. We all lived fast and furious. We didn't have Xboxes or PlayStations. We had orgies, Ecstasy, and cocaine. We settled our differences not by the courts, but by the butt of a gun. It's when the American dollar meant something and actually went a long way.

In my day we had to pay people for information. There was no such thing as Google. Times certainly have changed but some things haven't.

For example, like my future posse, my father had a team of guys around him. His brother Yani was the oldest son, and he was the patriarch, the face of the family. His brother George was the loudmouth; I don't think he had much power whatsoever. Lukie was the politician; he made the deals. And his right-hand man—they called him Nickie V— was the muscle. If you reneged on a deal with my father, Nickie V was going to take it up with you.

Another close associate of my father, my uncle Theo, is also an interesting guy. I don't think he was a true uncle, but we grew up calling anyone close to the family "uncle." He owned an island in South America and he was a scientist with a specialty in exotic animals. He wrestled snakes as a pastime. One time, he wrestled the largest anaconda in the Amazon. And he also discovered the pink dolphin in the Amazon.

But from what I heard he was also a very, very large worldwide distributor of cocaine. At one point, he was caught with several tons, more than a billion dollars worth of drugs. It was one of the largest busts in Florida, ever. His guys would hollow out exotic woods from the Amazon and they would stuff them with drugs and then ship them into Florida via family-controlled ships. Eventually everybody was doing this, but "uncle" Theo was ahead of his time.

Supposedly, Theo played on both sides of the law. He supplied both regular buyers and every so often black ops needing to launder funds. Theo was active even when I was a kid. There's a famous bridge in Tarpon Springs, called the Humpback Bridge, near the inlet where I used to go cast-fishing when I was in high school. It's just a normal concrete bridge that you wouldn't look at twice, but it's where my "uncle" Theo almost died. In the late eighties, when I was already gone, someone planted a remote-controlled bomb under the middle of it and detonated it when he was driving across one night. His car was blown to shit but Theo lived.

They never found out who did it, officially. It must have been a competitor looking to get him out of the way. I'm sure whoever planted the thing eventually got a visit from Nickie V.

Theo was smart. Lukie's real problem was the next generation. His son, my half brother, is named Louis and he's the heir to the throne. But he's an impulsive guy. I've had plenty of confrontations with Louis myself.

One time I went down to see my father, and my brother came charging out of the restaurant yelling at me that my mother was a whore and that he would never accept me as a brother. He was bigger than me at the time and clearly had an advantage. Louis came at me, and we fought it out right there in the parking lot. He caught me with a couple of shots and hit me to the ground. I was bleeding and I got up and wiped my thumb across my face and then took my blood and swiped it across his cheek.

"You see that?" I yelled. "That's your blood, too, Louie, and there's nothing you can ever do to change that."

I felt like I was the true heir. I had Lukie's smarts; I had *improved* on his leadership style. But with the Greeks, the legitimate son is given the family business no matter who else is in the picture. It's been this way for a thousand generations. Louis was the heir and that was that.

My being so successful and good at what I did didn't make me a true threat to Louis. Every time I pulled off a ten-million-dollar deal, I would have liked to think it made Louis look bad. But actually, it didn't matter. I had the wrong mother.

This was the first time I had been back to Tarpon Springs to see Lukie since he had given me the money to visit Greece. During this time, I had grown a pretty successful business on my own. I wanted him to see me. To see my success. I drove down there in my brand-new 328 Ferrari Dino GTS worth six figures. I thought it was appropriate seeing that Enzo Ferrari had designed this car in homage to his son. I had a 4-carat diamond in my right earlobe and enough gold on to show that I wasn't Kevin the short-order cook anymore. I was a player in Lukie's world. I had fucking arrived. What could be clearer? I am your heir, I was saying. I want to be like you.

I roared right up to the entrance and slammed on the brakes. I got out of the car and walked into the restaurant. Lukie had seen me pull up. He was sitting at the bar with Nickie V and one of his captains, Mikey, a musclehead with a crew cut and the IQ of a slug. There was a plate of steamed shrimp in front of him and he had the kind of tan you get from spending most of your time out on the water. The same piped-in Greek songs that I'd listened to as a kid when I swept the floors were still playing. They didn't change that fucking shit for twenty years.

"Lukie," I said.

"What's up, kid?" he said. "Sure you can handle that thing?" Mikey snorted with laughter. I gave him a hard stare and my lip curled into a smile. I turned back to Lukie.

"Funny. Why don't you tell these people my real name?"

His smile died. His face got calm and the wrinkles around his eyes disappeared. He was never calmer than when confronted by an adversary.

"What the fuck are you talking about?" he said quietly.

"My real name. Kevin Pappas."

Mikey started to get up from his chair.

"Sit down, Mikey," I said. Lukie touched the guy's shoulder and he sat down.

Lukie looked at me, calm as a fucking monk "I don't know what you're talking about."

"Lukie, I'm asking you, man to man . . ."

"I said, I don't know what you're talking about."

I dropped my head a minute. The Ferrari, the fact that I'd gone out into the world alone and made it, hadn't dented him at all. The last time he'd offered me money, which had been like ointment on a fresh wound. But this time, he was point-fucking-blank.

"I wanted to give this to you," I said. I took a green Rolex box out of my pocket. "Open it," I said.

Reluctantly, he opened the box. Sitting inside was a Submariner with a diamond-studded bezel. Lukie always loved Rolexes. And this was the newest model, with the custom diamonds gleaming. I wanted to give him something he loved.

I watched his dark brown eyes as he looked at the watch, hoping for some acknowledgment. But there was nothing. He didn't even take it out of the box and try it on.

He closed the box and left it on the counter. Like it was stolen goods or some shit. Like it was nothing.

It was as if he had spit in my face. In Greek culture, refusing a gift is the worst insult imaginable. He hadn't even read the inscription. It read simply, FROM THE SON YOU NEVER HAD TIME FOR.

I turned around and walked down the steps of the restaurant and jumped back in the Ferrari. I buried the rage in my heart and vowed to put it out on the streets.

# CHAPTER 14

Lee, the redneck junkie, started showing up at the Gold Mine at all hours. Tyrone brought him around and I tolerated him. He was snorting up more coke than I thought was humanly possible, but back then I didn't know that many junkies. Lee was a stone addict.

He was also a narc.

His cover was that he was so fucked up. No one thought he was an undercover guy because he was a pill-popping, drug-smoking maniac. Narcs have this thing of saying that they do drugs to protect their cover, but Lee was way beyond that. He was hooked, no question. And we all would see it. And that was a kind of badge of authenticity. If you're that strung out on the stuff, there's no way you're a pig.

Later Lee got busted for being a dirty cop and having a drug problem. But we just thought he was a redneck who liked to party.

So one Christmas Eve, I had an event at the Gold Mine. I had about twenty guys who came in—the champagne was flowing, everyone was dressed to the nines, and at the end of the night, the tradition was that each man would buy his girlfriend or wife a nice piece of jewelry.

By one or two in the morning, there were only a few people left—Tyrone and a few of his guys. And Lee, of course. You couldn't pry him out of my store with a crowbar if there was blow around.

So Lee asked one of the guys, "Hey, let me get a bump."

I was sitting behind the counter, and one of the guys gave me a baggie and I handed it to Lee. He put lines down on the glass counter and snorted it. No big deal. It was just Lee being Lee.

A week later, I was working with my mother behind the counter. All of a sudden, cars squealed up into our little gravel parking lot and guys started pouring out. The Georgia Bureau of Investigation and the Sheriff's Department and a couple of other agencies busted down my door and stormed in with guns drawn, screaming, "Freeze, stand against the wall!" And I was like, "What the fuck?" They told me they were charging me with the intent to distribute cocaine. One gram. Fucking Lee.

The detectives took me in the back room. My jewelry store had a hair salon adjacent to it, and they had a storeroom with a table and chairs. We sat down.

"Listen," this one good ole boy detective told me. "We really don't give a shit about you. We know you got caught up with this thug Tyrone. We've been after him for a long time. He thinks he's slicker than butter. Tell us where the merchandise is coming from and you walk. Or better yet, why don't we work a deal and we'll set him up?"

They actually said that to me. I couldn't believe that. These guys were below amateur.

"Listen," I told him. "It's been an hour since you arrested me and it's already all over the street. Tyrone Meeks knows everything that happens in this little redneck town."

They told me they had a plan to get him. There's only one thing worse than getting busted. It's getting busted by cops who have no idea what you are facing. Tyrone had Douglas, and Douglas would come see my mother with an electric drill if he had to.

"I got my mom and my family, that's all I got. And I know they'll hurt them."

"Son, you can forget about all that. We'll protect you."

That's all I needed to hear. There was no way these guys would put my mother and her family on twenty-four-hour protection. The case just wasn't that big.

I told them to call my lawyer.

There was a prosecutor in Atlanta who was on a witch hunt for Tyrone. I had fallen into the trap; they barely knew who I was. I refused to rat. And the judge and the prosecutor were so angry that I wouldn't flip they ended up giving me ten fucking years. For one gram.

When I heard "ten years" in the courtroom, I wanted to throw up.

I turned around and looked at my mom, but before I could say any-thing they handcuffed me and they took me out of there. They took me to GDCC, Georgia Diagnostic Classification Center, where the state's death row is housed. That's the highest-level penitentiary in the state of Georgia and that's where they put me because I had so much time.

I was nineteen years old.

I didn't have the ability to feel remorse; I was too busy being eaten up with aggravation. I was already aggravated that my mom moved my ass from Florida to Georgia. I was already dealing with this whole idea of "Am I a Pappas or am I a Cunningham?" I wasn't getting any-body's acceptance. And now I was sitting there thinking ten years of my life was gone. Ten years in an eight-by-ten cell, twenty-three hours a day.

And all I could think about was my brother Louie, free and safe. I couldn't get the idea out of my head that he was much better off with me out of the picture. That he'd be thrilled my sorry ass had ended up in jail. The desire for revenge was all I could feel.

In the prison system in Georgia, you're not allowed to have any outside contact for the first eight weeks. You're allowed no visitation, no letters, no communication of any sort for eight fucking weeks. It fucked up my world.

I was scared and confused. I spent four months at GDCC, work-ing as an orderly and making friends with the guards. It was all I could do to keep sane. I'm naturally hyperactive and there's nothing worse for that than being locked in a cell. I was climbing the walls inside of a week.

To pass the time, I would write to my mother, still my first and only real friend. I would dash off whatever was in my head, sometimes sending three or four short letters a day. I would take no shit from the other prisoners, but in the letters I poured my heart out.

*September 12, 1983*

Dear Mom,

Today I'm hurting. I look outside and see freedom and God how I wish I had it. My buddy Yal got out today. Why is it every time I get close to anybody they wind up going away? I hope that one day all this emptiness within me will be filled.

Mom, your friendship has saved me so many times. I love you and always want you to know that. I feel like half my heart is gone. This prison will do nothing but make me harder.

Thanks for the shoulder to cry on. I love you.

Kevin

*October 22, 1983*

Mom,

I love you!

Today was store day. I had $5.80 to spend so I bought you this card, along with some ice cream, a writing tablet, pencil and stamps. The card made me feel young again. Remember when I was a kid and I would go out and spend my last dollar on a flower or a card for you?

Mom, the Bible study was great. Jehovah has been so good to me. I feel so much better after sitting there for an hour and hearing the Word.

I'm hoping Jehovah allows me back in his home. I know it takes time but when I get out, I could help so many people.

Please keep in touch.

Love,
Kevin

My life had been reduced to my cell: a shit jack, a bunk, and a state-issued Bible. My mind was flip-flopping from high to low and from anger to repentance. I had to find a balance in my life or I was going to go insane.

In prison you don't have a mirror, only the polished aluminum over the shit-hole to see yourself. Consequently, the only way to get a reflection of yourself was to look deep inside. Everything in jail is cold, metal, and concrete. That's how the place hardens you more than when you entered. These letters I would write were my only way to open my heart and find reason and solace in my new life.

After four months, they transferred me to a chain-gang work camp in the north Georgia mountains. I was cleaning the side of the road, swinging what we called a yo-yo, otherwise referred to as a bush axe, with a corrections officer behind me with a pump shotgun.

I wrote to Lukie asking him to use his connections. He sent me money to help hire a lawyer, but that was it. Money always seemed to be Lukie's way of showing me where I stood: *You're worth a few grand, but not my name or my acceptance.* It was always a bittersweet thing for me: I would have much rather had a note where he said that he cared about what happened to me. But it was always cash and no message.

Thank God for Alexis. She was my girlfriend at the time, the *Penthouse* centerfold model. Alexis was 5′3″, 101 pounds, blond hair, and emerald green eyes, with an ass that would stop a clock. She was a good ole country girl from Conyers, Georgia. And she loved me to death.

In jail, you are judged by the quality of the women who show up to see you. You don't want some broken-down old lady coming in and embarrassing you. Alexis would show up and everyone would know that she was a centerfold, and they would crowd in to see her and be like, "Oh my God." She'd walk in wearing this cute little skirt and the officers would do anything she asked them. And when Alexis came in, she came with cash because she was a stripper. So she'd put a couple hundred bucks on the books for me every week so I could get extra food from the commissary.

The *Penthouse* model with a heart of gold. God bless her. What folks don't realize is that when you are put in the slammer they seize all your money, close all your accounts, they take all your clothing, jewelry, cars, and any other assets. And the streets close their doors on you. Any money that's owed to you is simply written off. Alexis helped me save my image when I was really down and out.

On one of those visits, she said to me, "Kev, I can't go through this anymore. When you get out, let's get our shit together."

"I will," I told her. And I had every intention of doing that.

The Colombians stepped into the picture when I went to jail. They knew of me through my Lebanese suppliers, half the Colombians are of Lebanese descent and they all knew one another in Atlanta. When they saw that I wouldn't roll over on Tyrone, they made some payoffs and greased some palms to rush my case through the Pardons and Parole Board.

I had no idea what was happening. But after the Colombians worked their magic, all I knew was that I would be on parole for eight more years, but fuck it, I was free.

# CHAPTER 15

When I got out of prison, I had nothing. When you go to jail, it seems like everything you had in your life, you lose, because everybody rummages through your shit like a fucking raccoon. I didn't even have a place to live. Alexis had a little apartment, so I ended up staying with her. The clothes that I had didn't fit because I gained a little bit of size in the joint. I was a scrawny little bastard when I went in and I came out like a fast linebacker.

I had a beat-up old Isuzu, light blue. I had been driving the latest Porsches when I went in, but now I was left with this wreck. It was depressing. All my cars were gone, repossessed or just jacked by associates of mine.

And I'd heard some news that made me extra depressed. Alexis had been seeing some hotshot drug dealer when I was in the pen, a guy named Todd who was one of the top Ecstasy guys in Atlanta. I'd nearly ripped her head off when I heard about it. And deep down, it only confirmed how I felt about women, starting with my mom: They were vipers.

One night about a week after I got out, I got hungry and there was nothing in the apartment. Alexis was out stripping to pay the bills. I drove up to McDonald's, which was the only place I could afford, and I ordered a Quarter Pounder with cheese, an orange drink, french fries, and a cherry pie.

The guy said, "That'll be three twenty-five. Please pull up to the first window." And I reached into my pocket and I only had a dollar and eighty cents.

I was sitting there in the drive-thru lane unable to do anything. Big tears were rolling down my face. I felt lower than a rat. I was a washed-up ex-con, broke as fuck at twenty years old.

I took the fucking dollar eighty, threw it out the window, and gunned the engine. I went to the shopping center and pulled into the parking lot at this nightclub called the Limelight. I was leaning on my broken-down Isuzu, hungry as shit with high-water jeans on, looking like a dumb dog that's just been released from prison.

I was lost. After getting used to having thousands of dollars a week to blow on anything I liked, I didn't know where my next nickel was coming from.

This Lebanese guy I knew came up to me. Hasid Kidad was married to a Colombian girl named Zamida, and her family was hooked into the cartels. I later found out Hasid was my guardian angel. He was the bagman who delivered the cash to the right hands to get me sprung.

He said, "Hey, Kevin."

"Yeah, Hasid." I couldn't even look him in the eye.

"How you been, man? How long you been out?"

"Coupla days, why?"

"What'cha doin'?"

"I'm just doing, what's it to you?"

He put his hand on my shoulder.

"Boy, you look like shit."

"I appreciate that."

"You're pretty fucked up, aren't you? Hey, Willie wants to see you."

I just looked at him. Willie Moises was introduced to me as a very close member of the Ochoa clan from the Medellín Cartel. He was in the United States on a student visa, attending Georgia State University on a soccer scholarship. At the time, Colombians were looked on as terrorists, much like the government views Middle Easterners now. Every headline was Colombian cartels this and Colombian massacre that. Back in the eighties, the DEA was out to eliminate the dope trade by targeting certain ethnic groups, principally South Americans, and specifically the Colombians.

But Willie was legit. That was unquestionable.

"I can't see Willie looking like this," I said.

Hasid said, "No, no, no, come on in." We went inside the Limelight, cut through the line, and went down the steps into this ornate office. Willie was sitting at the desk counting some money, stacks of it.

The surprising thing about the Colombian cartel guys is that they're almost all of Lebanese descent. They don't even look South American. Light-skinned, Arab features. Willie was like that. He looked like he should be selling rugs in some bazaar in Morocco. He was an ugly dude with a big nose, but dapper. Dressed in a suit with these handmade $400 shoes and an Ebel watch on his wrist, the only kind he wore.

Meanwhile, I'm looking like a dodo fuck.

Willie said, "How you doing?"

I thought to myself, "I've seen this movie before."

I said, "Fine."

"Congratulations on getting out. How was it?"

What could I say? "It was prison," I said, meaning I didn't rat out any of my sources. Then I admitted I didn't think he knew who I was.

"Oh yeah, I've kept my eye on you. I was hoping everything would work out for you. I made a few phone calls to see what I could do to help to get you out."

I said, "Thanks." I didn't know what part of that was true or not, but I was going with it. And honestly, he had a very thick Colombian accent, so I was just trying to keep up with him.

He said, "Yeah, we've got some people in high places. I'll make a deal with you. You want a job? You sure look like you could use one."

"I'm not going back to prison for nothing."

"No, no," he said. "I'm not interested in you selling drugs. Those days are gone. I know you did a lot of work for the guys in Griffin. All the black guys."

I said, "Yeah."

"They're good people but now let them start working for you. My friend over here, Hasid, speaks good about you. You're strong and you come recommended."

I said, "Thank you."

He said, "You look like shit, babe."

Again, I said, "I appreciate that."

He said, "Here," and threw me an envelope filled with cash. It was a down payment on my services. "Give me a call tomorrow. We'll talk."

I practically ran out of there and jumped in my little beat-up Isuzu. I was so excited and scared that I didn't even look at the envelope. Turns out it had $10,000 in it.

I rushed home. Alexis was in the kitchen chopping some carrots or something and she had a knife in her hand. I burst in there and scared her half to death. I fanned the cash out in my hands and said, "Look, look, look, look, look." I handed it to her, the whole wad.

She said, "My God, Kevin, where did you get it?"

"Willie."

She knew the name. She took the money and threw it back in my face. "I told you, those days are done."

I said, "Listen, he wants me to work with him. He's given me his unconditional word that I don't have to move any merchandise. I don't have to do anything. He just wants me to introduce him to people."

I didn't know anything about conspiracy laws at that time. Nothing at all. So I believed my own bullshit.

Alexis calmed down. She knew we needed the money. I said, "You're done stripping. I don't want you back in the nightclubs anymore. You can stay home and hang out and do your thing and let me do what I'm doing." I said this to her because I was sincere. I wanted to take care of her, pay her back for everything she gave me while I was in jail. But I couldn't look at her anymore the same way because all I could see were her lips locked on someone else's dick while I was in the pen.

Willie told me to make sure to buy a couple of really nice suits, as I'd be going to some locations that would require me to dress up. So I did. And I bought a couple of pairs of shoes and some sneakers. I bought some gifts for Alexis, jewelry and perfume. I paid a few months rent. It felt so good to be able to do that.

That little taste of being broke was enough to send me right back into the game.

So once again, I was dealing with Willie, who's a fucking target because the cops already know he's a multi-kilo dealer. But in his own eyes he was a businessman. He had the supply chain coming into the country, but he needed someone to work the distribution end.

"I don't need you to sell drugs," he told me when I went to see him the next day. "I only want you to speak for me. You see, I got this thick Colombian accent and every time I open my mouth, people think I'm a bad guy, some kind of a drug dealer."

That was funny. He was completely serious.

"But you, Kevin, you're likable. You know people on the scene, and they dig you. Plus you proved you're a stand-up guy. Help me work the streets. Front my business deals. Be my point man. I'll make it worth your while."

I told Willie, "Listen, if I'm representing, bro, I cannot be driving this fucking Isuzu."

And he laughed and said, "We'll take care of that. Meet me at this location," and he gave me directions to the Days Inn at Piedmont.

I met him at the spot, all excited. I opened up the door to the room and there's probably 250 kilos in there. It had just come in from Colombia and was waiting for the captains to come in and pick up their parcels.

I shut the fucking door and stepped outside and my heart was beating a thousand miles an hour. Willie came out, laughing at me. He said, "Dude, I just wanted to see your reaction. I told you, you don't have to fuck with this no more."

I wanted to grab him by the throat. "I told you I don't want to be around this shit; I just got out of prison. I don't like this game playing."

"No problem." He threw me his keys and said, "Listen, take my car, take it back to the house, and I got a little surprise for you over there." He had a little black Nissan Maxima. I wanted to get the fuck out of there so I took it and tore down Highway 285. When I was driving, Willie called me on the band radio we always used. I picked up the mike and Willie said, "Hey, by the way, Kev, drive slow because there's five ki's in the trunk."

I said, "Oh fuck!" And he broke off contact.

So I was tripping like a motherfucker. I turned around and raced back to where he was and cussed him out. Willie was laughing at me. He said, "Dude, the car is clean. I just wanted to see how you'd react."

I calmed down. We laughed about it and slapped hands.

Well, come to find out there *were* five ki's in there. Willie used to hide stuff inside spare tires and they would fit the tires back on the rim and you'd never know it. The fucking idiot.

Right then I should have known that only someone who's uncertain about his own position in the game plays those kinds of mind games. That kind of nonsense would cause problems between us later.

I was right back in the coke world. But now I was going to do it right.

had to build a team around me and start making connections almost immediately. First I went to Tyrone and let him know that I was working for Willie. It was a little awkward; I'd jumped up in the food chain so that he was now technically underneath me.

Tyrone knew I easily could have snitched on him in the Gold Mine case, but I'd kept my mouth shut. He accepted the decision. Once you're with the Colombians, the conversation is really over. They set the rules.

I brought a lot of my former Chippendales friends into the business, and I started letting it be known in the clubs and in the business community that I had a pipeline to 98 percent pure product direct from Medellín. That was the best publicity a trafficker could get. Purity sells. Getting orders for ki's turned out to be easier than putting together a team to handle all the aspects of trafficking: security, logistics, accounting, collections.

There were twenty-five or thirty people who I dealt with regularly. Out of those, four guys emerged as my core group. We became the Band of Five. Those were the men that I would die for; the rest were associates, customers, contacts.

But I had to kiss a lot of frogs, as they say, before I found my Band of Five.

Let me give you an example: Jimmy Coulos. Jimmy was one of the first I connected with. He was more fun than a truckload of strippers, and about as much trouble.

Jimmy was, of all things, a hairdresser. He owned a really nice salon in Buckhead and it became a hangout and drop-off point; our female customers especially could come in, get their hair done, and leave with a few ki's in the bottom of shopping bags. It was a great setup, perfect cover because the salon was already established.

Jimmy was a piece of work. Both sides of his family were from the old country and he spoke the language fluently. But he was a typically hotheaded Greek. He could not control his temper. Literally.

Maybe some of it had to do with being a hairdresser. It's not the manliest thing to do for a living, and he was hanging out with a bunch of gangsters. Plus he was a small dude—135 pounds, with shoulder-length hair tied in a ponytail. He got more pussy than you could believe. Jimmy loved women; he had five or six girlfriends stashed around the city at the same time. He was a sadistic freak when it came to sex, but they loved him back. Still, he always had to prove he was the baddest Greek around.

One day Jimmy was driving around Buckhead in his BMW M Series when a guy cut in front of him. I happened to know this guy also: Michael Stein, a little Jewish guy who owned a Ferrari dealership. Jimmy got out, lost his temper, and snapped on him. He came screaming out of his BMW with his Desert Eagle in his hand and shoved it in Stein's mouth. Over a traffic argument. This was typical fucking Jimmy: trigger-happy to the extreme.

Sticking a gun in someone's mouth in the middle of Buckhead does not go unnoticed. The police knew he and I were friends, so when they couldn't find Jimmy anywhere else, they came to my penthouse, knocked the doors in, and did a complete search. All the while Jimmy was across the street at Jose's house, but now I had cops crawling all over my house.

I was in my office when they came in. I had a snake pen at the time, with two big boa constrictors in there behind glass. They looked menacing as hell, and for a good reason. Underneath the floor of the pen I had stored ten kilos.

So the cops were tearing apart my place and finding nothing. Finally, they came to the snake pen. This detective was looking down into it, right at the rubber mat, under which there was enough coke to send me away for the rest of my life.

But he was nervous about the snakes. I could see his eyes get wide as he looked at those two twelve-foot-long monsters curled up at the bottom.

"Those boas are all upset with you guys disturbing their home," I told him. "I wouldn't do that if I were you."

The sweat was popping off his forehead. I could tell he didn't like snakes.

He reached his hand in and one of the boas coiled back.

"Oh, now, you better watch yourself," I said. "He's getting ready to strike."

Of course, boa constrictors don't strike, but the dude didn't know that. He pulled his hand back out of there right quick.

He took another look at the snakes and just walked away. The cops eventually found twenty-two grams of pot and gave me a $500 ticket. They were happy to have found something. I was laughing inside when he handed me the ticket.

But the whole thing had been instigated by Jimmy being Jimmy. When there was something going down, he was always in the middle of it. And usually he had caused it in the first place. My guys would come back to me and they'd say, "You can't believe what he's done now."

Jimmy was going to cost me a lot more than $500 before he was through. I never stopped liking him, but it was one thing after another with that guy. I was always doing damage control with everything he did. He just couldn't get it through his head that he wasn't me, that he was a Greek hairdresser who got lots of pussy but was not, in fact, a gangster.

# CHAPTER 17

Jimmy was good as an outlet, as well as a crazy motherfucker to tell stories on, but I would never have trusted my business to him. He was too erratic. When I put my team together, the guys that were going to take me to the top or die trying, I was looking for loyalty.

Jose Diaz had been with me since the beginning. Our history went back to the Chippendales days. At Packets, the club where Jose and I met, Saturdays were always Ladies' Night, and that meant they shut the club down to men until eleven. Everyone in town knew there were 300 horny bitches out there that we were responsible for rubbing up against and priming for the eleven p.m. cattle call. One evening this beautiful blond-haired, blue-eyed darling who had the hots for me arrived at the club. I started to get a little cozy with her. Unbeknownst to me her boyfriend was one of the bulls outside waiting to get in. I was busy nestling my nose between her breasts, and before I knew it, her boy was coming at me with a longneck Budweiser bottle that had my name on it. Then, in the corner of my eye I catch this Larry Csonka coming out of the backfield to intervene on my behalf. As he body-tackled this guy into the bar, I realized it was Jose.

Everyone was screaming and glasses were breaking. Next thing I knew Blondie was gone and so was her boyfriend. But Jose, he was right there. He didn't owe me anything. Until then, we were just entertainers making a living and enjoying it along the way. That night changed everything, and from then on he protected me. He'd just won his first Mr. Georgia contest, weighing in at a trim 235 pounds with four percent body fat on his 5′11″ body. He was one impressive motherfucker.

And he was as loyal as they came. Whenever there was a meeting that I felt unsure about, or a drop where I didn't want to be, Jose would volunteer. We were as close as brothers. I was his main family and he was mine.

Mark Jordan came into the Band around 1987. He was a former Army Ranger sniper who had seventeen confirmed kills in the Panama invasion. Mark was a bodybuilder and a weapons expert, with a specialty in machine guns, which he loved. Mentally, he'd never really left the Rangers. He could sort of stay in a bush or stay on a stakeout for three days without showering or eating a sandwich. He was just sort of weird like that. He wanted to be put in those extreme situations.

Mark was in charge of all loads and distribution coming back and forth from Miami. When we had a shipment coming up by car, he'd either be in the chase car or he'd be in touch with the drop guy by radio. He was also my personal bodyguard when I needed someone absolutely reliable.

I met Rob Schaeffer before my first bid in prison. Rob was a lost child, a street kid who was so confused in his life. He always looked scruffy, with a three-day beard and clothes that were one size too big for him. Rob was a strange-looking dude: He liked wearing trench coats, which was an uncommon look in Atlanta, with these strange-looking English hats. And he wore a pearl-handled 9mm in his waistband. After I got out and I went to see him, I found him chopping up kilos with his mother in her kitchen. No parental direction at all. His family was demented and so Rob was looking for something better.

He always sensed he didn't belong to this world. When he joined the Band of Five, not two days later he said, "Kevin, I want to let you know how I want to be buried."

"Buried?" I said. We were riding high. What the fuck was he talking about?

"Yeah," he said. "Put me in the coffin with a dozen black roses, my fucking hat, my dancing shoes, and my gun."

I was like, "OK, Rob, whatever you say." To me, Rob seemed invincible. He was too crazy to die. I didn't take him seriously.

We grew very close because he needed me more than the others. He was a split personality, very loving toward his friends but dead cold to everyone else.

Rob was in charge of distribution. He took over the product once Mark had delivered it safely and got it to our retail guys. He also knew our personnel: who had gotten busted, who was getting divorced and might be looking to steal a little extra money, who was starting to look coked-out from sampling our merchandise. You don't get a bunch of straight-arrow accountants when you put together a drug-trafficking gang, and Rob was the guy who found out who was going off the plantation.

Willie was the last member of the Band of Five. The god of the business. Willie knew the industry. He dealt with everything over the water, arranging the deals with the Colombians and smoothing over any controversies. Technically, I worked for him. That would cause tension later on. But in the beginning, we tore up Atlanta and the whole Southeast. Willie's forte was his arrogance and his accent. It being the eighties, everybody who spoke Spanish or had an accent was considered a drug dealer, which gave the Band a certain international panache. It's like Brooklyn. Everybody with an Italian last name and a New York accent must be from the mob.

I was responsible for both the personal and business affairs of the Band. I was like a surrogate big brother/father figure to this group of young misfits. I was spanking these crazy fucks, slapping them over the head at times just to knock some sense into them. They loved it. All that was missing was a little dog with a patch on its eye.

But I was never their boss. They all knew that whatever I told them to do, it was always in their best interest. Willie was the boss.

While each Band member had their own families, they all came from the same kind of background: fucked-up and missing a father figure. Everybody but Willie, whose family was solid and secure. My leadership and loyalty to them set the conditions for a different kind of clan, one whose members could rely on one another. And find refuge in one another and feel free to express their deepest thoughts to one another without fearing they would be played upon. That was new to them. Hell, it was new to me too.

But Willie always had something over all the rest of us that none of us could understand. And that was the unity of family. Everything we had was prefab, made up from a TV series or bad novel. Willie also had an exit strategy and that was because his roots and family did not reside in the United States. The rest of us were too young and zealous at the time to know that we were being masterfully played.

I had a medallion made up for all the boys. On the front, it had a portrait of Alexander the Great, a man who conquered three or four nations by the time he was thirty-three. He was also a bastard child in a bloodline of a powerful king and wound up redeeming himself by his courage and his honor. I could get with that.

Next to Alexander was a dolphin, which represents serenity. This might sound funny coming from a gangster, but I've always loved dolphins. They're so intelligent and powerful, and they're notorious for protecting their own in a family unit from the day they're born. That dolphin symbolized to me that these men were my brothers, and we would live and die together.

On the back is a Spartan warrior going to battle, riding in a chariot pulled by four horses. Then there are the scales of justice, because we believed we would never get a fair shake from the cops and prosecutors, so we had to follow our own idea of what was right and wrong. We created our own justice. And finally, above them all is Michael the Archangel, our protector.

Written on the bottom of the medal is one word: DUDENIM. It's Greek for "Power."


In the mid-eighties, the money started to roll in. While most of my peers were off doing bong hits at Psi Upsilon Delta or manning the register at Kinko's, I was running a major international company and increasing its sales every year. I was the Gordon Gekko of cocaine in the Southeast. Yeah, our product was a Class-A-felony narcotic, but I really felt I could have sold icebergs to Eskimos.

For the first time in my life, I had unlimited cash to play with. I went crazy. I had four or five of the biggest TVs they made at the time sitting in my condos, some of them not even plugged in. I had Porsches, a Rolls-Royce Corniche, Maseratis. I had ropes of gold chains and diamonds in my ears, and I could eat at the most expensive restaurant in Atlanta or New York or Miami seven days a week if I wanted.

I'd take the Band of Five's girlfriends and our female runners out and we'd go on shopping sprees to high-end stores like Lillie Rubin and Saks in Atlanta. Or if we'd already done the city, I'd fly the girls to New York on a private plane and go to Fifth Avenue. I'd tell the girls, "OK, ladies, you've got an hour." They literally ran down the street and into the stores. An hour later they'd come back dragging store assistants helping them with the bags: purses, Louis Vuitton glasses, shoes, diamond bracelets, whatever. We'd be in Manhattan for the afternoon and back in Georgia by midnight.

It was Christmas and I was Santa Claus. And it was strictly on a cash basis.

With the Band, I'd fly down to Florida for the weekend or get a convoy together and go to Helen, Georgia, up in the mountains for Oktoberfest and wear that place out. And we'd go for Mardi Gras down in Louisiana and barely escape without getting thrown in jail. The Bahamas was another favorite spot. It was cocaine, women, Ecstasy, and Crown Royal.

We'd have three or four bodyguards with us wherever we went, and they saved our asses time and time again. They made between $3,000 and $5,000 a week, and they knew that part of their job was to keep us out of jail, so they performed. They had cash ready to slip into the hand of a cop or restaurant manager or random civilian whose car we accidentally plowed into. And we had a fleet of cars at our call. We'd go out in a bunch of Porsches and end up in a limousine coming home.

I also sent money to my mother every week, religiously. I had cut my mother out of my life after finding out that Lukie was my real father, but we had reconciled. The bond was just too strong. She had been my best friend since I was in baby shoes. And as I got deeper into the treacherous drug game, where so many people had nobody they could trust, I wanted her close to me.

I even bought her a brand-new Cadillac Seville, the one with the tire on the back. She nearly jumped out of her skin when she saw it. "Beautiful, beautiful," she kept repeating. She even drove it down to Tarpon Springs and showed it to Lukie.

"See what your son bought me?" she told him. "What do you think of *that*?"

Lukie didn't say a word. But she said he stared at the car and seemed real impressed. I loved that.

A few months later I sent my crew on a search to find a car exactly like my father's new ride. I wanted to emulate everything about him to prove to him once and for all that I was someone to respect. In D.C., the crew found a white, 560 SEC Hammer Mercedes-Benz that was identical to Lukie's. The car was owned by a promoter named Ommie, and he insisted it wasn't for sale. A tricked-out 560 SEC was like a once-in-a-lifetime kind of car, and it went for $300,000 and up. Mark and Rob made this guy an offer he couldn't refuse. While negotiations went on for days, Ommie eventually came around and handed over the Benz. My guys were very persuasive.

A week later I drove down to Tarpon Springs in my new Mercedes in another attempt to reconcile with my father. I thought that enough time had passed that he would acknowledge me for what I'd achieved. Here I was driving into town in a car that was identical to his. I thought he'd be real impressed. I wasn't expecting much, but I was hoping for a small gesture. All I wanted was recognition for what I had achieved from him. Some respect for what I had accomplished. After all, I was imitating him.

But looking back, I must have looked like a rolling ice cube with my ridiculous vanity license plate that read NO CUT. What was I thinking? No wonder Lukie rejected me and distanced himself from me. The Greeks like their flash, but it's a different degree from where I was at the time. All he saw when I came rolling into town was the same immature punk that he drove out years earlier.

I got nothing. I just didn't know how to get into his heart.

I expected the lifestyle would fill the hole my dad's rejection had left. But I wasn't happy. Really, I was lonelier and more miserable than ever.

I wanted so much not to do what I did. I had this façade on me, this veneer that I was tougher than nails. I didn't do drugs, that wasn't a part of me. I wasn't a crackhead. I'd go out with four or five or six beautiful women, pull up in a white Mercedes limousine. I had a slant-nose, wide-body 930 Gemballa Porsche, a Corniche convertible, a couple of 911 C4 Targas and Carreras. I had a penthouse apartment in Pennington Towers on Peachtree Street and a condo in Plantation Heights.

But I couldn't get away from my childhood. I still felt like I was cursed.

# CHAPTER 18

After I joined up with Willie, there were three main groups of traffickers in Atlanta. First of all, there was our clique, the 5100 Group. 5100 is the federal code for drug trafficking. We used that as a kind of fuck-you to law enforcement, but also as a reminder to our guys. You slip up, you're dead.

The Southside guys were our first competitors. They were a bunch of extreme white dudes, better known as the Dixie Mafia, led by a guy named Mike Jauber. He looked like Howdy Doody, 6′1″, red hair, freckles. He was also a big partier. He had the good ole boys, the ones driving the four-wheel drives and the pickups with the Confederate flags. Let's just say, whenever Lynyrd Skynyrd came to town, Mike had the concert locked up as far as drug sales went.

He also supplied the bikers. But coke isn't a biker drug; it's not crazy enough. Bikers want to get fucked up and then go fuck up someone else; they were really into fighting and kicking ass and shooting people every so often. So the bikers got Mike into crystal meth, which was the outlaw biker's drug of choice. The 5100 Group tried dealing a little meth, but we never could make it work for us. It made coke look safe.

So Mike the Redneck and I had an understanding. I would do the powder business and he would do the meth business. He had the blue-collar guys, the hillbillies, and the biker outlaws. I had the business-

men, the lawyers, the club people, and anyone else I could find. I
didn't consider Mike that much of a threat; his gang was violent but
they weren't the most ambitious guys I'd ever met. They were happy
with their choppers and their bike chicks. That I could handle.

Every Saturday night, Mike the Redneck would have a party.
There would be choppers and Harleys and pickups lined all around
his house, and inside the good ole boys would be getting whacked out
of their minds. He'd always have five or six whores on hand and they
would be passed around as party favors, just like the drugs.

I'd learned my lesson with Lee, the narc who'd got me for one
gram back in Griffin. I stayed away from those parties and I told my
men to stay away from there. They could go in, pick up a girl, and
leave, but by no means were they to get sucked into Mike's world. If
they did, they were banned from our circle.

Right from the beginning, I emphasized security. If someone came
to me and wanted to be a distributor, taking ten or fifteen kilos a
week, I'd say, "Let me think about it." Then I'd do a full background
check on them. I'd have my contacts at the DMV run their names, see
if they had a stupid habit of getting nailed for speeding or having their
cars towed. I didn't want anyone getting pulled over with my merchandise in their wheel well. I ran a criminal background check to see if
they had any recent arrests: Most snitches are trying to deal with the
authorities for a reduced sentence on their own crimes, so anything
above jaywalking disqualified you from doing business with the 5100
Group. I asked around among my contacts in the clubs to see what
their rep was: Did they do a lot of coke themselves? Were they in
money trouble?

Getting into the 5100 Group was harder than getting into Studio
54 in 1977. Believe it.

I even followed people. I'd tail them for a few days, see who they
hung out with. I became an expert in following people by car. I'd look
in their garbage to see if they had any correspondence from the feds. I
eliminated a lot of people that way.

I wasn't going back to prison for anyone.

I knew Mike the Redneck didn't have the same kind of checks in
place. These guys weren't major thinkers. They'd kind of stumbled
into the drug business and gotten lucky.

I wanted to be different. I wanted to build an airtight organization that would be the number one conduit for coke along the Eastern Seaboard. Atlanta was just a launching pad.

The other group was the Sanders brothers: Jay, Tommy, and Randy, three black guys from the projects who'd risen up from nothing. Along with Tyrone, they had the black neighborhoods locked up. Jay was the brains of that outfit, but he got into a confrontation with the Mexicans. He actually had a lot of money come up missing, a million-plus in a briefcase was gone, and so Jay had to go on the lam. For five years, he was on the run and the business was run by Randy and Tommy. Bad news.

Randy was the guy in charge. Everyone thought he was gay. He was 6'2", thin as a garden rake, and dressed like some prep school homo: alligator shirts in pink and green, with the collar turned up and a sweater tied around his neck. There was something feminine about him, but he was actually a playboy, and he had half a dozen women with him when he went out.

I didn't like Randy. He was showy and he did stupid shit. When he got drunk, he'd take out his pistol and shoot it into the air, just to get people's eyeballs on him and intimidate them. I wanted to choke the son of a bitch. He became a pimple on my ass, always there, always irritating.

But he carried weight and he was dangerous. I was always paranoid that he'd send his brother Jay to kill me. Because Jay was a fugitive, I had no idea what he looked like. He could have snuck up on me any day of the week and turned the lights out.

For all the time I knew them, the Sanderses had bad luck. People in the gang were always getting indicted, or going on the run, or defecting, or disappearing—they had an older brother who'd been missing for twenty-five years, ever since he was indicted for trafficking. They kept losing their top people. But they had the projects locked down, and they had the street black business and some of the richer black customers, too.

The Sanderses were the flashiest outfit out there. We drove Porsches, but in the drug game, that's fairly unassuming. The Sanderses drove Testarossas, snow-white Rolls-Royces, the latest exotic cars that came off the block. We wore a lot of gold, but they had diamonds in their

My hometown Greek Orthodox church. Hymns would play over the loudspeaker for three to four hours in the mornings. Tarpon Springs, Florida

Statue of Louis Pappas, my grandfather, representing my ancestors who led the sponge industry in Tarpon Springs, Florida.

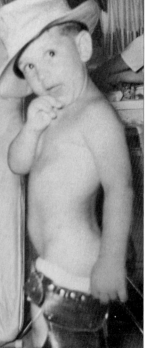

Me at age five. Male stripping and gangster life must have been in my blood from the beginning.

The 800-square-foot house I grew up in with my mother and Jim Cunningham. Tarpon Springs, Florida, 1968

Me, age nine, outside
of the house in
Tarpon Springs with
the dog, Duchess,
and the man whose
attention I was
constantly seeking—
the man who I
thought was
my father.

Here I am at seven years old
on the hood of Jim's
car with Duchess.
I must have been
in deep thought.

Willadean
Cunningham:
my heart,
my soul,
my Mom

My mother was more than a
mom—she was my best
friend.

Me, eighth grade, with my
Mom and Jim Cunningham in
a rare but happy moment.

Me, ninth grade, with my buddy Steve.

Ninth grade yearbook photo:
Always asking the question
"Why me?"

A gangster's briefcase.
You live by the sword.
You die by the sword.
Don't forget the Cuban.

All my men wore this
medallion as a badge of
honor and were buried
with it when they died.
I still wear mine to
this day in honor
of my men.

In loving memory of my #1 bro, Jose. This was the last picture I took of him. He was the first of the band to fall. I miss him still to this day.

A 930 slant nose wide-bodied Gambella, K3 Turbo. This was one of my favorite getaway cars. It goes from 0–60 in seconds.

Jose partying hard with one of the late cartel boys.

With my *Penthouse* girlfriend, Alexis. Ain't she a beauty?

This was one of a few wedding photos we were able to capture before I was called back to prison and put away for four additional years. They got me on an obstruction of justice charge in relation to Rule 35.

Cathie was a professional model before I met her. She snuck this picture in with one of her first letters and I had no idea then how she would change my whole world!

Cathie, Mrs. Hawaii 1992. That's my pageant wife! Not 2nd, not 3rd, but always 1st with me!

A photo from Cathie's early modeling career.

This is the sheet Cathie held up outside the prison on our first anniversary. February 14, 1997

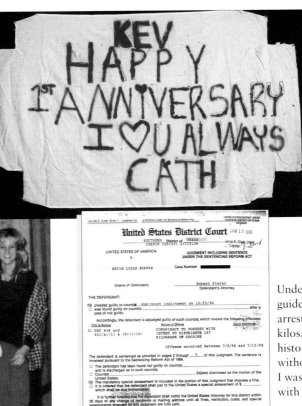
KEV HAPPY 1ST ANNIVERSARY I ♡ U ALWAYS CATH

Under the new guidelines, any arrest over 5 kilos, with history, is life without parole. I was busted with 107.

Me in the visiting room at the Gainesville, Geogia, county jail with my sister, Kathy, and my girlfriend, Alexis.

Atlanta Penitiary—The most violent pen in the nation, with the highest homicide rate.

One of our Saturday visits with our daughter, Jourdie.

This photo was taken of me the day I met Cathie. I weighed 238 pounds with 4 percent body fat. Maxwell Air Force Base, 1994

After 1 year and 14 days of solitary confinement, I weighed 155 pounds. My eyes were jaundice and my skin was green. This was the first time I saw my son, Mikal. He was 4 months old.

The day Mikal met his grandfather, Lukie, for the first time. He was beaming after Lukie bought him a Shirley Temple.

My children: The #1 reason for not going back to the life.

A portrait of my family, taken in 2006. They gave me hope and hope changed my life.

I was invited to lunch with the Sopranos in 2004. Here I am with James Gandolfini.

During lunch with the cast of *The Sopranos*, I found out that Tony Sirico knows my family from the horse track in Tampa, Tampa Bay Downs.

Just another day at the office. Here I am at a NOPI promotional event.

My elite security team, made up of military special forces, ultimate fighters, and former secret service personnel.

A portrait of me with my wife, Cathie, taken in 2008. She stood by me and has more strength than anyone I've ever known. She has my heart and my undying love.

teeth and any other kind of outrageous jewelry. Not subtle. They didn't want to be. They were rich and they wanted to show it.

I was flamboyant myself. I've been known to drive my white Mercedes 560 convertible down Peachtree Street wearing a white silk shirt, white linen pants, and a white mink coat. Hell, it was advertising. A drug dealer should be able to deduct the cost of his wardrobe and his vehicles on his taxes because that's what gets you contacts and soldiers. These working dudes on the street will see you out at a club and say, "Shit, I want to be like Kevin." I can't tell you the number of guys who signed up with the 5100 Group because they saw me out one night with six slamming bitches on my arm, the furs and the jewels, and were like, "Fuck, yeah, that's the lifestyle I'm after."

Even though the Sanderses did 95 percent of the cocaine business in the projects, I still had my connections there. I could go into Techwood Homes—which they called "Little Vietnam" because of all the shooting that went on there at night—and do business without any trouble. I was one of the few white guys who had that kind of access. If you didn't know what you were doing and you went into the Techwood or the Adamsville Projects, you'd have a gun stuck in your mouth before you reached the elevators.

I had a gentleman's agreement with the Sanders brothers and with Mike the Redneck. We didn't go into their clubs and they didn't come into ours. We didn't share the same girls and we didn't steal one another's customers. It was tense as hell. Everyone was watching one another's backs, looking for defectors from one group to the other. If one of the girls we hung out with showed up at one of Mike's parties, I'd know about it within five minutes of her walking in the door.

These weren't the sharpest knives in the drawer. But if you showed weakness, they'd be slicing your territory up before you knew it.

After a few months with Willie and the 5100 Group, we were moving 500 kilos a month. I'd gone from selling grams in the clubs and being a donkey for deliveries to places like D.C. and Miami to being the leader of the best coke outfit in Atlanta.

I had more money than I'd ever imagined I'd have. I had a get-out-of-jail-pass for the small shit. And I had a crew that was as crazy as I was. I felt like the town was mine.

One night, a year after I hooked up with Willie, I was flying down Peachtree Street in my Porsche 930, doing about 120 miles an hour. I loved Porsches. They expressed my personality: fast and uncompromising. I always had at least two in my garage, and I had just gotten this 930 and I was enjoying myself, a little looped on Crown Royal. The gang movie *Colors* had just come out and I was blasting the theme song by Ice-T. I'm usually an old rock-and-roll kind of guy, Bad Company, Led Zeppelin, Eric Clapton, Santana, but that song just captured my life: "I am a nightmare walking, psychopath talking / king of my jungle just a gangster stalking."

I was singing along when I saw the flashing lights in my rearview.

I knew a lot of the local cops by then, but I'd never seen this asshole before. He was clearly the guy who'd grown up watching cop shows. His name tag was polished and his hair was buzzed in that military cut underneath his hat, and he treated me like I'd just run over Mother Teresa. I had hair down to my shoulders, a 9mm in the glove compartment, and I wasn't down for playing.

He asked me for my license and registration. I handed them over.

"Do you realize you were doing one-twenty in a forty?"

"Yes I do, officer."

"What do you have to say about that?"

"Uh, 'Buy Porsche'?"

"That's funny, asshole."

He expected me to be groveling. Little did he know we had a guy who was in charge of prosecuting all kinds of moving violations and DUIs. And he had a real bad dope habit.

You can't operate in the drug-trafficking business without being able to move around, so once I heard what this dude did for a living, I made a deal with him. I'd keep him supplied with Grade-A Colombian cocaine, and he would keep my guys clean at the DMV.

It was a beautiful arrangement. Anything that happened on four wheels, we were untouchable. I could have mowed down the mayor in front of City Hall and they would have ticketed him for jaywalking.

Cops, even the guys who weren't dirty, would walk up to give us a ticket and then laugh. "You again? Slow the fuck down, will ya?" They'd turn and walk back to their cars. They weren't going to go to the mat for a lousy speeding ticket.

This guy wasn't hip. He wrote me up and handed me a ticket. I took it and hit the engine and roared off, spraying gravel in his face. This prick had a lot to learn.

Two nights later, I was driving down the same street in the same car doing the same speed. I see the blue lights in my rearview and I said, "There's no way." Of course, here comes Mr. Clean striding up to my window. I saw him coming up in my side mirror and I couldn't help it. I just started laughing.

"What's so funny, you piece of shit?"

"Officer, how are you? Did I beat the record?"

He just didn't know where I was coming from. He was speechless.

"What did you just say?"

"I was doing at least one twenty-five, don't ya think?"

Before he could get charged up, I decided to give him a chance.

"Listen," I said. "Why don't we forget this ever happened? Because if you write me up again, you're just going to look like a complete idiot."

He leaned over. "I got you now, Pappas. Just wait in the car."

He went back to his car and punched me up on the computer. My previous ticket wasn't there. My DMV guy had got it erased. The cop was back there punching the buttons like a maniac. He must have tried three or four different times, and all the time I was cackling like a motherfucker in my front seat. It was pure comedy.

The cop came walking back.

"Get out of the car. We're going to Piedmont Hospital. Blood test for suspicion of DUI."

"The fuck we are."

He put his hand on his gun. "Are you refusing?"

Poor bastard. I just sighed and walked back to his car. He threw me in jail for the night, but the next day the charges were dismissed.

My DMV connection eventually ended up paying for his drug habit. When I was doing time in the Atlanta federal pen, his name came up in a dirty cop's case that I heard about. What I didn't know was he'd gotten caught up in it, so the feds started looking into all the cases and the tickets he'd fixed for gangsters in Atlanta.

His coke habit was, if anything, worse by then. He knew he was hooked and cooked. He took his briefcase filled with the records of every ticket he'd fixed in the past fifteen years and went up to Amicaola Falls in a little town called Toccoa, Georgia. And he jumped.

But while this guy was on the job, we had the run of the city. Anyone who says they wouldn't want that power is lying. It was addictive.

We also had cops, judges, court clerks, and county commissioners on our payroll one way or the other. There was even a powerful U.S. senator who would take our calls and do us the occasional favor for the right price. I wish I could name names. But one thing I learned in the drug game is that you have more to fear from the guys in the white hats than you do from the thugs you're competing with.

# CHAPTER 19

I was all business and partying in those days. I weighed 240 pounds, with four percent body fat. I had long hair that went down to the middle of my back. I wore a gold Rolex Submariner, just like my dad, thick gold-rope chains, bracelets with four rows of diamonds, and I had a reckless attitude.

I had women falling over themselves to get with me.

Technically, I was back with Alexis, but it wasn't what you would call a traditional relationship. The craziness and the power that was par for the course in my business quickly crossed over to my personal life. I recognized no limits in either. If I wanted something, I took it. If I wanted someone hurt, they just might have a bad day.

And the knowledge that she'd cheated on me with that Todd dude when I was inside the joint still tore me up. Even the name pissed me off. Todd. I couldn't let it go.

Alexis didn't deny it. I felt like she was the latest in a long list of women who'd let me down, betrayed me. But I don't hit women. So I went looking for Todd.

I found out where Todd lived and I actually went to his house at about two in the morning. It was a typical suburban home, brick on three sides, paneling out front, in a nice neighborhood. It was brand-new, paid for by club kids buying Ecstasy, I'm sure. As I pulled up, I saw two Corvettes and two jet skis sitting in his driveway. He must have just gotten back from the lake that day.

I got out of the car, took out my .45, walked up to his side door, and knocked out a pane of glass. Then I reached in, opened the lock, and let myself in. I walked through the dark house. I could have gotten my ass shot dead if anyone had been up; they would have thought it was a push-in robbery. But the house looked deserted. There were some cardboard boxes in the living room, as if Todd hadn't even finished unpacking.

I didn't know the layout, so it took me a minute to feel my way to the stairs. They were carpeted in shag, so I didn't make a noise. I reached the top of the stairs, turned right, and saw a closed door. An empty room with a treadmill and some free weights. I shut the door. I could hear someone breathing now. I turned around and walked back past the head of the stairs. I could see him now through the open bedroom door, lying on the bed in his boxer shorts. He was alone. And snoring.

I walked over and stuck the .45 in his mouth. It stopped his snoring, at least. He made a choking sound and his head snapped up.

I said, "Hey, Todd! Don't move." I reached in my pocket and grabbed the handcuffs I had brought. I snapped them on his left wrist, then pulled his right wrist over and snapped that one in too.

"What the fuck is this, Pappas?" he said. I pulled him up, caught him as he stumbled, and marched him out of the bedroom and down the stairs. I'm sure he thought he was going to be executed that night.

When we got to the door, I nudged it open with my foot and pushed him through the door. He tripped on the stairs and tumbled down into the dirt, landing on his side. I pulled him up halfway until he was sitting. He made a kind of whining noise through his nostrils. I've heard that sound before. It's an involuntary response. It's terror.

I squatted down and looked him in the eye. He had dark black wavy hair and he was puffed out like he was doing steroids. He actually reminded me of a younger version of myself, when I was just coming up. That didn't make me feel any better.

"I want to ask you something," I said. "When I was in prison, why for God's sakes would you be fucking my girl?"

"She wasn't your girl."

I walked back to my car and took out took two big five-gallon tanks filled with gas. I walked over to the two Corvettes. They were brand-new. A yellow one and a red one.

He started yelling, "No, you crazy motherfucker, don't do it."

"You see what pussy rustling will get you?" I yelled back and started pouring gas over the cars. I was enjoying myself.

I took out my Zippo and lit it. I slowly turned the flame up to the maximum as Todd begged me not to light up his cars. He was only about fifteen feet away from them, so I think he was worried that he was going to fry along with his Corvettes.

I took the Zippo and flipped it into the front seat of the yellow Corvette. There was this giant sucking-in sound and then WHOOOOSH. The interior bloomed into an orange flame and the car was engulfed in ten seconds. I used matches for the red one, and soon there was a big-ass Chevrolet bonfire with flames shooting twenty-five feet in the air.

I walked over to Todd. His head was dropped and he was shaking it back and forth. He couldn't watch.

"Now, why did you do it, Todd?"

He didn't say a thing.

"I only used one of these jugs, Todd. And the only things left to burn are you and your house. Now why did you do it?"

That got his attention.

"I swear to God, Kevin, I never fucked her."

I shook my head. I picked up the remaining jug and went over to his little porch. I splashed a little gas on it and turned around.

"You sure about that?"

He was screaming at me. I couldn't catch the words. I finished dumping the gas around the foundation of his house. I threw the jug in the bushes and came back to him.

"Now I've only got a few minutes before the fire department gets here. The good news is that I'm not going to shoot you. But I want you to realize something. Can you hear me, Todd?"

"Yeah, yeah, I can fucking hear you!"

"I'm a lunatic, and Smokey the Bear says don't fuck with lunatics. I don't ever want to see you around Alexis again."

I could hear the fire trucks in the distance. I left him there and jumped in my car.

I guess I have a hard time letting go of the past.

# CHAPTER 20

People think that the drug business is like any other business. You call up the supplier and fix a price for the product. Friends who weren't in the business ask me, "So, the Colombians must have been tough bastards to negotiate with, huh?" They've seen the movies. They think you sit down at a desk and hammer out a price.

But this is one of the first things I learned with Willie: Dealing with the cartels isn't like buying a fucking used car. You don't negotiate. They are the source; they control the supply. You don't walk in to them and say, "I'll give you $3,000 a ki for 100 ki's" or "Fuck you, man, I'm not paying at that price point." They would have looked at you like you just landed from Mars. And then they would have busted your skull for being such an idiot.

So, they set the price, period. There are really only two choices at that level when you're dealing directly with the cartels. There's the drop point price and then there's the U.S. price. The drop point means that the Colombians would package the product, load it onto a plane or a fast boat or whatever, and guarantee delivery at a transshipment hub, like the Bahamas. You get a fifty percent discount on that deal. But then you have to figure out how to get it into the States. And that's really the whole ballgame. Any asshole can stake out some land in the Colombian mountains, grow some coke, pay off the local cops, harvest the shit, process it, and get it to the Bahamas. The hard part is getting the stuff over the American border.

If you want to pay the U.S. price, your kilo goes from, say, $4,400 to $8,500. I almost always opted to let the Colombians take the chance to cross the water. After all, they have a whole network of corrupt officials that they can use to make sure the load doesn't get discovered. If you go solo and take the lowball price, they're not going to offer up their customs guys and Bahamian ministers. You're on your own. And, if you take the U.S. price, you are guaranteed the product will reach you safe and sound. If they lose a load across the water, they have to replace it. I don't care if they lose five loads, you will get your coke. It was like buying an insurance policy from State Farm.

The cartels would usually bring the merchandise in by go-fast boat, which is essentially a custom-made fiberglass shell outfitted with three outboards. Very basic; they don't even bother throwing a tarp over the bundles of coke. If they catch you, they catch you, but when you're doing sixty miles an hour, you have a good shot of making it through. And you can load about three tons of powder on one of those things, with a crew of three. Those boats were the workhorses. They traveled at night, and you might lose one out of five loads, either to law enforcement or to accidents. In the drug business, that's more than an acceptable loss ratio. One out of three is considered good.

They had other ways of getting the shit through. Submarines, Learjet, commercial airliners, even by FedEx before the company started X-raying everything. And then there were the body packers, or mules, which I hated using because the human element is so unpredictable and the loads they could carry were so small.

We would also cut deals to pick up and protect loads that weren't ours. We were considered an office of the cartel in the United States, which meant that if we ordered 250 ki's and the Colombians wanted to drop 750 ki's for their other suppliers in the United States, we'd agree to do the pickup and warehouse the stuff. We'd take our share and hold the remaining 500 ki's for pickup from their sources. So instead of passing this merchandise through fifteen hands once it reached the United States, it would go through only one outfit, us.

Sometimes they would drop, you know, a couple of tons, ton, or ton and a half of reefer. They would come in and drop us 1,500 pounds of pot, and we would be able to find a home for it. But coke was the bread and butter. It wasn't worth your while to mess with anything else.

Just as I wanted to take security to a new level, by checking on all our dealers' backgrounds, I also wanted to step up the warehousing of our shit. So I found five or six stash houses around Atlanta ready for use at all hours: condos, residential homes, and even a lake house. These were mostly unoccupied. We'd occasionally party there, or crash there if we felt the cops were looking for us. But mainly these were temporary homes for the coke.

You couldn't just stack the product in the bedroom, though. If there was a raid, you wanted an extra layer of protection. If we lost the shit, we were liable for it, so I took an interest in seeing that we hid the product very well. At the lake house, we had an equipment shed out in the backyard—the kind you would buy at Home Depot today. We stored lawn mowers and jet skis in there, but underneath the wooden floor I built a secret compartment. We dug down four feet, lined the walls with cement block, and then sealed it.

Cops are lazy, like most people. Every hour of work you added to finding a stash was an extra hour of work for them, and so an extra layer of protection for us. Build enough work into a safe area and you eliminate ninety percent of the authorities. It's really the DEA and the FBI that will rip your house apart. The local dickheads? You can outwork them.

Even if some water got into the lake house stash, we were safe. The Colombians had perfected the waterproofing of the bundles by then. They either dipped them in this red wax, which was incredibly tough, or they actually immersed them in liquid plastic and let them dry. I've seen bundles fall out of airplanes, hit the water at fifty miles an hour, and never crack open.

At the houses, I found a carpenter we could trust and we went to work making secret drawers and fake bottoms. Those places were like mazes: The cupboards had false backs where we could store fifteen or twenty ki's. We did this to walls, to bathroom cabinets, to floors and ceilings.

My favorite piece was this sleeper couch. We bought it and then hollowed out the center, removed the bed, relocated the support slats, and built a wooden cache that could hold twenty-five ki's. It was comfortable as hell and you never knew you were sitting on hundreds of thousands of dollars' worth of cocaine.

When we got up to 500 kilos a month, we needed even more storage space. So we went out and bought a twenty-five-story high-rise condo building in Marietta. The maintenance guy was on our payroll, and we would get the master key, and when the tenants were out working, we'd put our merchandise inside the drop ceilings. When we needed a few ki's, we'd call him up, he'd go into Apartment X, retrieve the merchandise, and meet us at the service entrance with it.

That was my innovation. Who's going to search Joe Blow's apartment when he's got a clean record for the past fifty years and doesn't even know he's storing millions of dollars' worth of cocaine in his apartment? It was beautiful. No one ever suspected a thing.

When we needed to move small amounts around, we'd stuff it in our Honda CBR1000 motorcycles, known as Hurricanes. We had a whole fleet of them. They were as fast as anything and they had little compartments in the center console where you could fit two kilos in perfectly. We'd stuff the coke in there and send one of our runners out to deliver to anyone who needed an emergency supply.

When it came to security, we were Brink's. And when it came to delivery, we were Domino's. Mike the Redneck and the Sanders brothers just couldn't match our service.

We had to find another place for the money. A lot of stuff was placed in sealed private vaults that you could rent in Atlanta. You'd go to this place that looked like a nuclear fallout shelter, all concrete, no windows, with just a keypad by this armored door. You'd punch in your pass code and walk in, and there would be security there that would direct you to your private vault. It almost looked like something out of the future. Millions of dollars moved through those places every month.

When we had too much money even for the vaults, we'd go to Willie's brother. He was high up in the Bank of Bogotá, a vice president. That never ceased to amaze me. Willie's family was like royalty in Colombia, but they all had their hands in the candy jar. They didn't use drug trafficking to gain respect; they were already respected.

When the money came in, we'd pay off our guys and get reimbursed for expenses. No one paid rent, no one paid a car note, no one paid for a meal. Everything was paid for through the 5100 group. Then Willie and I would take our cut and the rest of the money would go back to Colombia to pay for the merchandise. And that was handled through the Bank of Bogotá.

Willie told us that for every $100,000 we made, we should put $10,000 aside and never touch it. That was your "disaster fund." You get killed, your family gets it, you get arrested, your lawyer gets it. I took that to heart and started stashing money all over the place.

I even took bags of cash down to Tarpon Springs and buried them. No one in Atlanta knew my hometown, so I figured it was safe. And I had a special hiding place picked out for my loot.

When I was thirteen, my dog Hambone and I had been out riding one day. I had my bike with the big sissy bar and the steering wheel, and I was working on a big ice cream cone. It was the middle of the summer, hot as anything, without a hint of a fucking breeze coming off the water. And Hambone was jogging behind me, like he always did.

Now, Hambone's big flaw was that he liked to chase cars. He would run them down and bite the side of the tires as they moved. And this one day he went running after a city dump truck, and the damn thing made a turn and ran him over.

It broke me up. I really don't know how I survived that. I took Hambone in my arms, with the blood coming out of his mouth, and I took him to my yard and buried him with my own hands. I even said a few words over his grave.

When I became a bad guy making shitloads of money, I made a special trip down to Tarpon Springs with a headstone I had made. It said IN LOVING MEMORY, HAMBONE. I had gone and gotten some paint and varnish and written the words on there myself, made it look nice.

So when I needed to hide some cash, I went to my mom's old house in the middle of the night, dug a hole next to the gravestone, and buried a bag. We didn't even own the house anymore. I thought Hambone would guard the money, give me good luck.

I had money buried all over town, near the bayou, in the woods. I did it all at night. It was eerie, but I felt good as I was doing it—I'd come back to my hometown a rich gangster. It was $150,000 here, $200,000 there. I just wished I could have woken Lukie up and waved that cash in his face. Showed him he wasn't the only one who could buy the Stamas yachts and the expensive bitches.

In Atlanta, money was there for the taking. People would front you ten ki's on a handshake. When your sales keep going up and up, there's enough cash sloshing around for everyone.

# CHAPTER 21

Growing up I didn't have holidays or special family events I could look forward to and memories to build upon. The Jehovah's Witnesses don't believe in the traditional holidays; they don't recognize Easter or Christmas. But they do have a celebration that is commanded by God based upon their belief that Corinthians 11 states that Jesus Christ gave his soul and his blood to mankind. The ceremony is called "The Memorial" and it falls on Nisan 14 in the Jewish calendar, which is the first full moon of the spring equinox. That's the day the Witnesses commemorate Christ and his death, because scripturally Jesus said that it was not his birth but his death that should be remembered.

I always made every Memorial Service whether I was a gangster or not. I wasn't feeling guilty. I never asked God to get me out of the life. I can't really explain why I went—I was just drawn to it.

I always like to hear the passage about King David, a biblical figure that I really had a passion for. King David was a man who made many mistakes, who slept with the wife of one of his most trusted men and then sent him away to war so that he would be killed. It shows that an imperfect man can be redeemed. I would always turn to that and the Song of Solomon. And Psalms to me is like a melody.

And in those brief moments when I would duck into a Kingdom Hall, I would open the Bible and read things like Isaiah 41. I would remember sitting in the Hall as a kid and reading that same passage. In it, God says, "I am your God of righteousness. I will hold out my right hand of righteousness; please grasp on and hold and I will hold you under my wing and I will never forsake you." That had great power for me. God never forgets, but always forgives. No matter what you do in life, if you understand that God is the spirit of love, not just some entity that you're afraid of, then God will be there to hold and He will be part of your life.

I loved the Memorial. It was the only time I would feel OK being alone. But after it was over, I would always go back to the streets.

I stayed in touch with the Greek side, too. When I was a kid, Black Spot had given me a thirty-minute dissertation on Greek superstitions. And I continued to live by those beliefs.

The Greeks believe that the walls have ears, literally. They believe that your enemies are always near and that anything you let come out of your mouth will eventually come back to haunt you. Greek mobsters are also deeply cynical: They believe that in this business, your only friend is yourself; you can't even trust your own mother.

In Greek life, Tuesdays are bad luck. I tried not to do my business on Tuesdays. And it's bad luck, too, to see a priest walking down the street. All these little things were drummed into my brain and I couldn't let them go.

The last superstition I followed was that if you're going to do a deal, like if you're transporting drugs or putting yourself in harm's way, then the night before needs to be a night of meditation. You don't go into a war zone being still half coked-up after partying until dawn. All my men lived by that. They never rolled in at four and then went out at seven to do a deal.

After all, why tempt fate? The drug game is hard enough.


As the drug game heated up in Atlanta, I tried to outthink my rivals and the feds at the same time. One example is drop points for the ki's that we needed to get into the hands of one of our distributors. The Sanders brothers or Mike the Redneck might call their guys up and say, "Come over and get your shit." That was crazy to me. I needed something more secure.

I developed a sector system. We gave all the neighborhoods that we operated in a number. Buckhead was 21, the airport was 15, and so on. And within those sectors we had pay phones that we had designated with another number from 1 to 10. Those were our safe phones. If I wanted to talk to you about a drop, you'd get a message on your pager and all it would say is "21-8." Completely harmless from law enforcement's point of view. So you'd go to Buckhead and go to the number 8 phone booth and stay there until the phone rang.

We had all kinds of different codes on our pagers. Each product had a number: cocaine was 8, pot was 13. So if you got a message saying 5100-100-13, that meant "I need 100 pounds of pot." If we were talking about kilos, we'd use "1000" because there's 1000 grams per ki. So if you did 5100-8-2000, that meant that the group will bring you two kilos of coke.

If you wanted a specific kind of coke, each one had a number. If people wanted the yellow base, they'd punch in 5100-272-12500 and that would mean 12.5 ki's of coke with a yellow base. And if they didn't know the going rate, they'd add 333 and we'd respond with our price. If someone wanted the price on the ether base, they'd put 5100-2764-333, the middle four digits being my birthday, which signified our premium stuff. We'd confirm with the price and they'd kick back 10-4 2764-5000. That meant send five ki's of the ether immediately.

The same went for security. There were three levels of 911 pages: 3, 2, and 1. A 3 meant lock and load, there was gunplay involved; 2 meaning "situation tense, come silent"; and 1 meant "come when you can, no urgency." If you got 911-666 from one of the Band of Five, that meant "we've been busted, don't come this way."

We could carry on a conversation via pager and no one would ever know what we were doing.

When someone was going to pick up a package, we'd give him or her brand-new codes. We'd say, "Listen, here's the code identifying you for this operation. You're going to go to this location. Here's the code for it. Here's the number to key in once you're done. You'll have an eye on you all the time. If you need anything, call this pager."

The guy would have to alert us at three stages. When he was departing his location. When he was arriving at the meet. And when he was departing with the merchandise and everything was cool. And he would communicate only with his bird dog, the guy who was assigned to oversee the operation. He didn't even know who the assigned guy was; he was assigned only a number. Because if he got busted I didn't want him to be able to tell who the individual was he was talking to.

Once the deal was done, the runner would page the bird dog and the bird dog would page us.

If you had to speak to someone, we also had code words. Kilos were called birds because they'd flown over the water to get here. And if you were discussing prices, you'd say. "How much is your bird?"

"Dollar eighty-five." Meaning $18,500.

On the street level, if a guy came up to you and said, "Want to play a game of pool?" he was looking for coke.

"What do you want to play?"

"Eight ball, best out of three."

That meant they wanted to buy three eight-balls. Sports were the main slang. You'd talk about games and that was the drug, teams were the distributors, and bets were the prices.

Sometimes it got so complicated guys wanted to write it down in little notes stuffed in their pockets. But I told them, "If you can't keep a bunch of numbers in your fucking head, you're too dumb to work here."


My main problem was collections. I was known around Atlanta for being creative in the way I dealt with assholes who didn't pony up the cash, but there's no question that violence was part of our response to anyone who crossed us. We beat people up. We broke baseball bats over people's heads. We burned their cars. I can't say everything I did personally, but if you owed me money and you saw me coming your way, your day was about to get real fucking bad.

And yet, you still had individuals who were late on payments for no good reason. So we would go out on something called "collection days." That's where you went to everyone who owed you money and applied some pressure.

You have to be in a certain frame of mind to press someone. Once you're revved up, I liked to get them all done in one day. One I'll always remember is this guy named Carlos, a fat Honduran dude in his midforties who had the ugliest wife anyone could remember. He was a slob but he moved ten to fifteen kilos a week, so that made him a mid-level guy for us. Unfortunately, he owed Willie about $200,000 on his last shipment and he was two weeks overdue.

Not cool. Ten days was the absolute limit in the 5100 Group.

So I pulled up to his house in my Corniche Rolls-Royce convertible, a beautiful white one with white interior. Willie was in the backseat, behind me. It was about one in the morning.

Carlos climbed in the backseat. I was annoyed with him already because I'd just had the car detailed and Carlos was a sloppy son of a bitch. I didn't want a speck of dirt on my white carpet and seats. He was annoying me already and we hadn't even driven away from the curb.

I turned around to face Carlos and said, "Listen, put your hands on your legs. Willie wants to talk to you. I'm going to drive. I'm going to watch in the rearview mirror, and if I see you make a move, I'm going to have to shoot you."

That's how I talked to people. Very direct.

"*Si, si,*" he said. His eyes got big in the rearview mirror. I started the car and we headed off to drive around Atlanta so Willie could talk to him.

Willie gave him the usual spiel. "Listen, Carlos, what the fuck? You're into us for two hundred thousand dollars and I haven't heard from you in two weeks."

Willie hated when people were late. He was always a little uncertain of himself. Most guys in the business get where they are because they're smart or they busted a lot of heads on the way up. Willie was Willie because of his family. He knew he hadn't earned his position. So any sign of disrespect, he got a bit hyper.

The guy shifted and dropped his hands to the seat. I rolled my eyes. "Excuse me, Willie." I said. "Listen, Carlos, I'm really not interested in fucking up my car. Not interested. So be a good boy. We're not going to hurt you, we just want some answers. Keep your hands on your knees."

We kept driving. Carlos had his hands back on his knees and he was giving Willie a bunch of excuses: sales had been slow on the street, he'd been having trouble collecting from *his* guys, whatever. He was getting nervous. The meeting was a little heavier than he expected, and he knew his answers were bullshit.

All of a sudden he reached down toward his sock. Maybe he had an itch, maybe he had a gun.

We were driving down Cobb Parkway in Marietta. I turned into a Kmart parking lot and pulled into a corner where no cars were parked. I swerved to a stop and stuck the Corniche in park. Then I turned around in the seat.

Carlos was frantic. "*Por la amor de dios!* I was just scratching my leg! Man you got to believe me!"

"Get out."

He opened the door and got out. Willie moved to the front seat. I got out and came around the car to Carlos. He was sweating like a hog in a sauna.

I said, "Now, what did you do wrong?"

"I had an itch, man. *Por favor, por favor.*"

"Uh-huh, what did you do wrong?"

"I guess I moved my hands."

"There you go. Here's the deal, you owe us a couple of hundred thousand bucks. I'm willing to deal with that separately. But you disrespected the order, and that's the problem on the streets these days. No one listens to the fucking guy in charge. I don't want to play God, but at this point I gotta do something. So here's the deal: Get naked."

He protested, but I made him strip and pile his clothes in a nice little heap on the pavement, his sneakers on top. He was huffing and puffing with the effort. When he was butt naked except for his socks, I stopped him.

"Listen," I said. "I'm going to take this little pistol right here, and I'm going to cap you really quick in the legs. Then it's going to hurt real bad. But that's all I've got for you today. I'm going to give you a week to recoup and then things are going to get really serious. Get me my money by the end of the week. If you don't, we're going to Plan B."

*Pow. Pow.* I shot him in the legs. He collapsed onto the tarmac. I jumped back in the car. I saw Willie looking at Carlos as we pulled away, no expression on his face.

I did this for Willie. I did it to show him I would not let someone disrespect him. I also did it because of the need for order. We couldn't just have chaos all over the streets. I worked too hard building a business for it to just fall into turmoil like the family I came from. No way. Not ever.

Carlos paid up a week later.

The 5100 Group became known as the best drug traffickers in the Southeast. We controlled most of the area from Miami to Atlanta. Everyone wanted to do business with us.

We even had a major defection in the winter of 1986. Tommy Sanders came over to our clique from the competition. Tommy was the twin brother of the gang's leader, Randy, so I was stealing away not only one of their best producers, but also his closest kin.

Tommy looked like Reggie Bush: 6′4″, 245, very muscular, hazel-green eyes, chiseled face, high cheekbones. He came to us because he felt his brother was taking him for granted. He wasn't getting the right money or major responsibilities; Randy had him doing collections from the dealers and running ki's up from Miami. He wanted to see what he could do on his own, and I told him I'd make him a superstar.

Which I did. Within two months, Tommy was one of my top dealers. He was moving twenty or so kilos a month, which placed him near the top of our retail guys. And Tommy felt like he was finally being appreciated.

But in the back of my mind, I always wondered if Tommy was a mole, whether that snake Randy had sent him over to infiltrate my gang and then take me out. I watched him closely for those first few months. But then I figured out he was as sick of Randy as I was.

It was a highly unusual thing—most of the time the cliques held their members tight, and any defection was taken very seriously. I knew that Randy would be in touch. A few weeks after Tommy came over, he called me up.

"That's my brother, you know," Randy said in his high-ass voice. "I don't want him to get twisted up in anything over there. I want him back with me."

"Listen," I said. "Tommy's a grown man. I don't make his decisions."

"You ready to deal with the repercussions?"

"Randy," I said. "Do you know who you're taking to?"

He laughed. "Homeboy," Randy said. "Don't get caught out." And, *click,* he hung up.

I couldn't back down. If I shipped Tommy back, it would have been seen as me bowing down to the Sanders group. And, besides,

Tommy had a lot of potential. He was also hooked into some of the projects where we weren't that strong. There was no way I was giving him back to his brother. Fuck it. Let them take him back.

That turned out to be the end of the golden era. Soon Atlanta would become a fucking war zone anyway. I could feel it.

**B**y the summer of 1987, the business was running smoothly. In fact, it was almost eerie. Everything was going right. Our loads were getting through, our associates were keeping out of jail, and our monthly sales were always rising. The only thing that dampened that trend was the explosion of Ecstasy, which really took off in Atlanta around this time. For a while, it was hard to sell an ounce of cocaine to the club crowd. But we balanced that out in other places.

This was the proverbial lull before the storm. I thought we'd perfected the trafficking game. But it's something you can never do. I was about to learn that.

One reason I was feeling good was that I was finally going to Bogotá. I'd gotten a lot of invites to go down there by the captains of the cartel who'd come through Atlanta. I was the social director of the 5100 Group, the public face. If you were coming in from the jungles, I unlocked the city for you: women, fine restaurants, strip clubs, Dom Pérignon, whatever. I delivered. And that generated a lot of gratitude.

So I made friends with the Ochoa clan, the mid-level guys. And every time they were leaving, they'd tell me, "You have to come to Colombia. Let me return the favor to you. I want to show you how we live." And they promised me that Colombian women were the most gorgeous on the planet. Colombian guys are crazy about their women.

Smoking-hot Latinas? Count me in.

The Colombians are big on hospitality. But I knew that in the back of their minds, these guys were doing more than paying me back for a few trips to strip joints. They knew that Willie could go down at any time: His visa could get revoked, he could take a bullet in the back of the head, or he could get nailed on a conspiracy charge and go away for a long time.

I was American. I knew the country. I had the distribution in Atlanta and points south locked the fuck down. And they wanted me to be tight with them in case Willie disappeared.

This was the next level for me: I felt like I could replace Willie if anything went wrong. I wasn't going to move him out of the way, but if he disappeared, I'd be the Ochoas' main guy in the Southeast. That was another reason I wanted to take this trip.

So I went to Colombia with Willie in the fall of '87. We flew commercial down to the Bahamas and then by private jet to Bogotá and stayed for eight days. We didn't want our names appearing on any manifests for the feds to find later. We rarely flew commercial.

I felt naked going in there without the Band. I trusted Willie but I never really trusted anyone one hundred percent. I'm really just a small-town boy at heart and I get a little nervous when I'm in a culture I don't understand. I didn't know who the real powers were, I didn't know what they wore or how they thought. I like to be in control and Bogotá could have been fucking Jupiter as far as I was concerned.

But Willie just wanted to show me his world and to introduce me to his family. As I look back it was his way of drawing me in further and demonstrating to me that he looked at me separately from the rest of the Band.

The first thing I realized when we got off the private plane and loaded into a black Chevy Suburban and went to Willie's condo was that he was richer than I thought. In Atlanta, Willie was conservative with his spending. We bought Porsches for our birthdays, Cartier watches for Christmas, and generally lived like the world was going to end tomorrow, but he had the lifestyle of a bank vice president. Nice, but not over the top. He drove a big-body Benz but his main ride was a black Nissan Maxima with the windows blacked out, which was a car a street-level dealer would drive. We were like, "What are you, a fucking gangbanger or something?" Willie liked to live conservatively, as if he was trying to keep off the fed's radar. I should have picked up on that, but I was too busy blowing my cash on women and cars.

When we got to Bogotá, I saw where Willie put his real money. We pulled up to this modern high-rise, a gleaming steel-and-glass tower. And when Willie walked in, it was like the President of Colombia had arrived. There were five or six guys taking our luggage, pressing the elevator button, shouting into phones. I don't understand Spanish that well but I understand respect. And these guys were knocking themselves out for the head of the 5100 group. Everyone called him "Willie-Willie." Made him sound like some kind of retarded baby, but to them it was a mark of power.

We went up to his apartment and it was something out of an architecture magazine. Unbelievable. It was the penthouse of this circular steel tower and it had floor-to-ceiling windows all around; the sun was just going down and you had the outlines of these huge, black mountains in one direction and the lights of speeding cars on a highway in the other. The whole city was laid out at your feet.

We went out the next morning and toured the city, always with one security van behind us and one ahead. Two things hit me right away. The military was on the streets with machine guns. This was before 9/11, and I had never seen a soldier on a city street corner with a fucking high-caliber weapon in his hands. And they weren't there for a parade. They were alert, talking into their radios, up on their toes. What could warrant an entire army deployed in a major city? Us, that's what. I said to myself, "Kevin, you are in the third world, my friend."

Bogotá was more modern than I expected. "This is the Miami of South America," Willie said as we strolled around. He was strutting like a peacock. I had never seen him like that before. I laughed. He meant that Bogotá was right up with the times—you could buy bootleg copies of the latest movies or get Hugo Boss suits and Lamborghinis. But I knew that it had a second meaning: Miami was built on coke, and so was Bogotá.

The next thing that hit me was the women. Holy shit. They were so beautiful I was walking around with an open mouth. They were these beauties with dark, dark eyes and the brightest red lipstick you could find, and they were poured into these tight jeans that must have required Crisco to get into. I was in awe.

When you go to Colombia, Bogotá and Cartagena are for partying and the jungle is for business. We were waiting for word from the Ochoa group that they were ready to see us. You could be in Cartagena partying for three days or a week, and then one day someone calls your hotel and says, "Be ready in one hour." And you better be fucking ready. You couldn't just jump on a plane if you got tired of waiting. You weren't allowed to leave the country without first getting the Ochoas' clearance. If you disappeared, they'd think you were cooperating with the authorities, and when you got home you'd better disappear for real because they would come looking for you. I don't know if they had people checking us out before they allowed us to do the meet, but it's possible.

That's how it went on this trip. We were on vacation, basically. We traveled everywhere in a caravan of four Suburbans with blacked-out windows; Willie's guys would go to the restaurants first to check them out. Once they secured the place, they'd call us on the phone and we'd head over for dinner. People were getting kidnapped left and right in Colombia, either by rebels or criminals. Willie was taking no chances.

On the fourth day, after lunch, Willie knocked on my door and said, "It's time."

The black Suburban was waiting for us. We got in and headed northwest. Willie took the passenger seat and I was in back with dark-skinned Colombians holding machine guns. The driver had a .45 on his hip. Playtime was over; you could feel the guys were a little quieter, a little more on alert.

"How long is the trip?" I asked Willie.

"Three hours," he said, turning to me. "But it will take us six. We're not taking the direct route."

I was in the backseat. He turned away from me and looked out the front windshield at the road.

I didn't ask why. This was Willie's show. But I got a little chill at the base of my back. That feeling of "What am I doing here?" Were we really going to the Ochoa compound or was I going to get my face blown off on some deserted road? Did Willie suspect me of something? Suddenly I wished I was back on my home turf.

The roads were surprisingly good. I looked out of the windows and saw a lot of steep cliffs on the side of the road. I prayed that our drivers knew what they were doing, because in Colombia they all think they're fucking Formula One drivers on those winding mountain roads. We passed through a lot of farm villages where chickens would scatter out of the road just before you hit them and the people's skin got darker the farther out you got. It's the same in a lot of countries in South America: The closer you are to the centers of power, the whiter the people are.

I dozed off for a few hours. I do that on long drives. And all of a sudden, I felt the Suburban slow down. I shook myself awake and we were on a small, two-lane road and up ahead was a roadblock.

"What the fuck is that?" I asked Willie.

"Don't worry," he said, laughing. "These are our guys."

It was a checkpoint. We were getting close to the Ochoa compound. The driver pulled up and the guard—who was dressed casually in a black short-sleeve shirt, jeans, and aviator glasses—took one look at Willie, said something in rapid-fire Spanish, and raised the striped bar across the road.

We went through two more of these in the next mile. At the last one, Willie opened his door.

"Come on," he said. "You and me, amigo."

I grabbed the handle on the Suburban door. My adrenaline was pumping hard. I was unarmed. I'd never felt so naked and exposed in my life.

I got out. Willie walked ahead and got into a black Mercedes. I looked back at the guys in the Suburban but they didn't budge. Apparently they weren't coming. That didn't make me feel any better.

I got in behind Willie. We drove down a gravel road, gaining a little elevation. Once we cleared it, we saw the compound laid out in front of us.

It wasn't what I expected. It was like being in Disney World, after all that jungle. They had peacocks all over the yard. Peacocks are God's alarm clock. You can't walk within 500 yards of a peacock without them squealing and yelling at you. So the Colombians would have peacocks everywhere, because if anybody tried to get into the compound they'd start whistling and throwing their feathers and people knew that intruders were around.

American drug dealers have pit bulls. I liked the peacocks better.

The main house was very open, a typical South American place with a big wraparound patio. There were armed guards everywhere with military-issued AK-47s and H&Ks, the mini–machine gun that the Navy SEALs use. You could throw that gun from 20,000 feet in the ocean, leave it sitting for three weeks in salt water, and it still would come out shooting. Amazing firearm. They had sidearms, the same military .45s I saw on the soldiers in Bogotá. But the cartels are long-gun guys. They didn't mess with pistols. If someone came to take out the compound, they wanted to shred him or her into little pieces, not give them a flesh wound.

There were stables off to the left because Father Ochoa actually bred these prancing horses that cost a fucking mint. Dressage, it's called. He was crazy for it. I saw a few of the horses as we passed by on the way to the house; they were putting them through their paces, the horses with their knees curling up toward their chests. I'd never seen anything like it.

I even saw kids there, four of them, who looked about ten or twelve years old, goofing around and talking as they walked through. That shocked me, and I didn't ask who they belonged to. But there were no female servants or maids or stray whores or anything like that. It was almost all men.

We walked to a courtyard where they had a few wooden tables and we sat down and had a drink. The Ochoa guys looked typically Lebanese, a bit darker than Mediterranean people but with those unmistakable Arab noses and eyes. They were one level below Father Ochoa and the other leaders of the cartel.

Willie ran the show. I could catch a few words here and there and in the beginning it was all business: ki's and dollars and loads. Willie wanted to bring in a thousand kilos a month. That was his goal. It wasn't just because no other crew in Atlanta was handling that amount. We needed a thousand ki's just to meet demand. As it was, we were piecing together product from different sources to try and keep our retail guys supplied. Multiple suppliers means more work: Sometimes a source falls short one month and your supply chain runs dry. Or they get you the ki's, but they turn out to have been stepped on too many times and the customers complain that you're giving them weak shit. It also increases the number of drops and pickups you have to do, meaning that there are that many more chances for the cops to catch you.

Willie would turn to me and ask, "Can we handle that big a load?" or "Tell them about how we're doing on the south side." Logistics, distribution, personnel: It was pretty intense. I was surprised how much detail they had: They knew the names of our number twos and they wanted information on the competition and how reliable our street guys were.

The guards with the machine guns looked like they had never stepped outside a ten-mile radius from the compound. You tried talking to them, but they weren't very sophisticated. They were usually used for the grunt work or the killing. But the leaders of the Ochoas knew their shit. They knew their distribution chain and where they made the most money. We finished with the business and they brought dinner out. I smiled and used my kitchen Spanish to fuck around with the guys, but I never let my guard down. I was Willie's gringo American and I was happy to play the role.

The sun started going down and you could hear this crescendo of sound from the jungle monkeys calling, shit I couldn't identify. We said our good-byes, loaded up, and headed back through the checkpoints.

In all my trips to Colombia, I was never allowed to stay on the compound. If you had business that couldn't get done in a day, it couldn't get done.

When we got back on the two-lane road, Willie turned to me. "That was good, Kevin," he said. "But I didn't know you knew so much Spanish." He gave me a smirk.

I wanted to smash his face. What was he insinuating? Willie was one suspicious fuck.

"I know enough to get around," I said. "Why, Willie, you think I'd go behind your back? I'm hurt."

"Happens every day," he said. "Every day."

We eyed each other. I felt like telling him that I could run the business without him but chose not to. I knew I could do Willie's job. But he couldn't do mine.

He turned around and didn't say anything for the rest of the ride back.

I was glad to get back to the States. Little did I know that Atlanta was ready to go off like a Roman candle.

# CHAPTER 23

Atlanta and I had come up together. I'd watched it rise from a conservative Southern business town to a hotbed of music, sports, and the cocaine business. It wasn't the same town I originally came to, and I wasn't the same dude, either. Every year, the city got crazier and more hectic. And so did my life.

One thing that may have accelerated the craziness was steroids. They were a part of this era, too. To be in our gang, you had to be big and cut. Personally I started off with Sethenal 250 and Anadrol, and then I moved on to Deca-Durabal and Clenbuterols. Finally, I got into HGH, human growth hormone from the pituitary glands of cadavers. That's right, dead people. I didn't give a shit. Basically any anabolic steroid you gave me, I took.

At first, the roids made me feel great. You feel invincible, like you can just crush any obstacle in your path. The steroids give you extra energy, and you focus like a laser beam. I was an animal. I was ripping 405 pounds in the bench press for six or seven reps. I was squatting 725 pounds. On the leg press, I could do twenty 50-pound plates on either side, so I was doing a half ton to a ton of weights. I felt like a super-hero.

I even gave steroids to my dog, Kia. This is going to piss off a lot of animal lovers, but he was a nine-pound Shih Tzu and we started shooting him up with Deca-Durabolin and put Anadrol-50 in his food and pretty soon he got to be about thirty-five pounds. His neck and shoulder muscles swelled up until he looked like the Tasmanian Devil. He had to walk bowlegged because he had so much muscle on his legs. We considered him a member of the gang, so doing steroids was a rite of passage.

This dog was passionate; he loved me. I didn't really bond with animals after my boyhood dog Hambone got killed, but this dog and I got to be buddies. And he was an extremely smart dog. Every time I had a bunch of strippers or dopers over at my house, Kia'd be walking around and people would pick him up, feed him, and just party with the damn thing.

One night I got a call from a friend of mine who was down in the city at an all-night place called Club Anytime.

"Listen, Kevin," he said. "Is Kia with you?"

"What are you talking about?"

"I'm in Club Anytime, it's four in the morning, and your dog is inside the nightclub."

"What?!"

"You heard me. Your fucking dog is roaming the nightclub."

I guess someone was at my house, got fucked up on Ecstasy or coke, and had the dog in their arms as they left and just forgot about it. Somehow Kia made it to the clubs—not just Club Anytime, but a whole string of them, as I got reports from three different clubs where he was spotted. He got home around eight in the morning. Just another day in the life of a kingpin's pet. I slowed him down on the roids because who knows how far he would have gone next time.

After about six months of regularly injecting the steroids, the Mr. Hyde stuff starts to take over. Your body turns on you. For instance, I'd be in the supermarket checkout line, and if the checkout girl took three extra seconds taking care of the customer in front of me, I'd want to smash her face into the register. I'd actually visualize reducing her face into a piece of pulp on the register again and again.

I was starting to roid out just at the time I should have been on top of my game. I needed to focus and strategize because the game was getting more dangerous month by month.

It started with the Sanders brothers. They were still pissed about me stealing Tommy away from them. There was a series of tit-for-tat incidents: When I was in Colombia, one of our guys got beat up with a Louisville Slugger outside a nightclub. A few days after I got back, I went up and shot up the vintage Camaro of the dude who had done it—a muscle guy named Smoothie. I took a MAC-10 machine gun and wore that car out, popping its tires and leaving it looking like a prop from one of the *Terminator* movies. Poor old Smoothie loved that car to death. Shooting it up was the Greek in me; it was worse than knee-capping the motherfucker himself.

Not long after Willie and I got back from Colombia, I learned that the Sanderses had twenty kilos coming in through Hartsfield Airport. They had guys in security who would let them pass with anything they brought through, for a price. And they had a donkey—a cute Greek-American girl named Missy—who would pick up the loads and take them to one of their stash houses.

There was only one problem. Missy was sleeping with me. And one day she gave me the stub to the suitcase that the twenty kilos would be arriving in. It was perfect.

I decided to add a little kicker to the deal. We bought a suitcase identical to the one that the coke would be arriving in. The Sanderses always used the same kind of case so that there wouldn't be a mix-up. I sprinkled a little coke inside and around the handles, then I had one of my guys walk into Hartsfield carrying the dummy bag. He went to the luggage pickup, waited for the flight to come in and the bags to hit the baggage carrier. He found the twenty-ki piece, pulled the ticket off it, put it on his piece of luggage, and placed the duplicate on the carousel. Then he walked out with the twenty kilos, showed his stub, and got the fuck out of there.

When they didn't hear from Missy, the Sanderses sent over one of their goons to get the luggage. He came back with an empty suitcase.

I told the Sanderses that if they wanted their coke back, they'd have to pay $1,000 per kilo. That was my going rate. If you were operating in Atlanta and you got your supply from elsewhere and weren't affiliated with me or one of the other two powerhouses, I took a $1,000 commission.

I was really lording it over Randy Sanders. It was fun, and in my increasingly chaotic life, I enjoyed it. But things were about to get a lot more serious than a little horseplay and stolen coke.

# CHAPTER 24

What would have helped me out at this time would have been to have a good woman by my side. But I didn't have that luxury. You might have picked up on this, but I didn't trust women. My mother's lying to me really had a lasting effect. But so did my lifestyle. I mean, I really never dated women. I hung out with strippers and *Penthouse* Pets like Alexis, but that whole excitement of having a date with someone and getting dressed and sitting across from her at a restaurant and wondering if she was going to be special in my life—I never had that. I never had a girlfriend who I was faithful to, who when she yelled at me I would feel sad in my heart. I'd just cuss her out and leave her ass.

I had such bad experiences with women that early on I got the idea that all women are manipulators. Every woman has got an angle. I saw this behavior from my father, Lukie, too. There was this time when I was sleeping on the couch outside my mother's office. It was late and Lukie and Mom were behind closed doors. Suddenly from in the back there was a crash that woke me up. A waitress was delivering some champagne for Lukie and slipped, breaking the bottle and making a mess. Lukie came out and I could sense she was extremely scared, but she apologized to Lukie as she wiped up the mess, down on her hands and knees. There she was on the wet, dirty floor in broken glass, terrified. But Lukie ripped into her anyway, telling her she was going to pay for that bottle.

He saw me watching and I think he bullied her even more just for my benefit. I felt sorry for her but his attitude toward women made an impression on me. And it stuck.

I wasn't ready to be with anybody then. I didn't really want to let anybody in.

Being a kingpin in Atlanta warps your sense of everything. I would go into a club and see a girl with her boyfriend—really enjoying being with him and kissing him and everything—and I knew I could go up to the girl and get her away from him and she'd go home with me that night. Because I had money and the cars and the penthouse apartment and the entourage. As much as I liked it, I wished sometimes the girls would tell me to go to hell. Just to prove that there were good women out there. But they rarely did.

I'm sure there's loyalty between men and women, but I never saw it. It was like I never really had a conscience that made me stop and say, "You know, this ain't right." My motto was: "Take what you want and never apologize." It's almost like a disease.

Things with Alexis started going south when I got back from Colombia. We were living at a nice complex called the Plantation at Lenox. It was a high-toned place. I had a chart-topping R&B star as my neighbor, and I'd go to his parties and he came to mine. He didn't ask what I did for a living, but I think he had an idea.

I had promised to straighten up for Alexis, but by then that was a distant memory. I was staying out every night until five or six in the morning and I'd come in loaded and drop on the bed. Comatose. You'd have a better chance at having a conversation with my coffee table.

So finally, Alexis had dealt with that behavior enough. She laid down the law to me. "Listen, Kevin, I expect you home tonight by two. If I mean that much to you, you'll be here, and if you don't make it back, then I'm done." The poor girl. Really, she did her best to save me, but I was flying down the highway at 150 mph. Hard to catch.

I was getting ready for a night at the club, laying out my clothes, the silk shirt and Hugo Boss pants, and I said, "Yeah, sure." I forgot about it as soon as the words were out of my mouth. What a prince.

So I came home at six in the morning blitzed out of my head, and I'd left my house keys somewhere between one of three different clubs. Happened all the time. I knocked on the door. Nothing. I banged on the door. Silence. She was so pissed at me she wasn't going to let me in.

I lost track of time. Somehow I ended up naked in the hallway, curled up in front of the door.

My friend Jessie walked in around nine a.m. and woke me up. People had been stepping over me on their way to work. I guess I wasn't the most traditional neighbor.

He shook me awake. "Kevin, Kevin, you're butt naked out here."

I woke up and I got angry. That bitch had let me sleep naked in front of my own condo. I started slamming my shoulder into the door. Jessie knew better than to intervene.

The door busted off its hinges and crashed into the room. I was still half-drunk and I started knocking vases and shit and smashing anything in my path. I destroyed every piece of glassware within sight. I could hear Alexis shouting from the bedroom; she was too smart to come out. I was screaming back that she had betrayed me like every other woman in my life.

I went to the nearest gun in the place, in an end-table drawer. I pulled out the snub-nose .38 that I kept there for emergencies. Then I went for the closet. Because there was something in there that I needed to settle a score with.

Remember Todd? Alexis's ex whose Corvettes I'd toasted? I knew he'd bought her a dress that she wore when she wanted to get back at me for something, a really expensive green leather dress. Somehow the thought that Todd's gift was still in the condo really aggravated me that morning.

I walked to the bedroom and kicked *that* door in. Alexis was still screaming, calling me a bastard and a dangerous lunatic, but she'd retreated to the bathroom. I went to her closet and snatched the green leather dress.

I took it out to the couch in the living room. I stood back, took one last look at it, and then I shot it. I emptied the gun into that damn thing. It made me feel better.


I'll admit my mother took a lot of my anger about women. One night, she showed up at the Gold Mine, where I crashed at times. She found me back in my arsenal of a quasi-office, which was fully equipped like a slick studio apartment. I had my gun collection on a wall behind me: AKs, M16s, SIG Sauer handguns, Uzis. And all of them were ready to be fired. It looked like an armaments museum, but it was strictly for practical use. I had my pet boa constrictors and seven surveillance cameras that provided parameter visibility. This gave me the kind of security I needed at the time.

She walked in and right off she could see that I was down. "Are you okay?" she asked me.

"Who gives a fuck if I'm okay? You should have thought about that twenty years ago. Look at me," I screamed at her. "I'm sitting in an office with a hundred guns behind my head like a lunatic. Is this what you wanted? This young religious scholar that you trained, is this where you wanted me to end up?"

She said, "I'm sorry."

And I started breaking down crying and I said, "Do you want to bury me? You want to stand over my casket and watch this kid and say, 'He was a good kid, he just didn't understand life'?"

She continued to ramble about how things were the way they were. Telling me to just let go of it. But I couldn't and this just fueled my pain. I had a five-point ninja star on my desk and I chucked it at her in frustration. It was almost as if I was a knife thrower at a carnival. It grazed her hair and then stuck in the wall behind her.

She stared at me in utter shock. My mom is one tough broad, and I knew I had crossed the line, but she knew I had to be messed up to have reacted that way and lost all control. She walked over to me slowly with her hands reaching out.

Tears were rolling down my face. I felt like I was losing my mind.

She came up behind me and rested her cheek on top of my head as she gave me a hug. I closed my eyes. "Baby, listen to me," she said. "I know you feel like you're all alone, but that is just not true. You have to believe me."

"I know, Mama," I said through my tears.

"What's going on with my boy?"

I had to think about that. Where did I begin? It wasn't just the pressure of running a multi-million-dollar business at that age. It wasn't just that I felt like I was speeding down a road to death without having ever really been alive. I had no one to feel proud of me when I succeeded or to encourage me when I failed. I had a hole in my life that made everything empty.

"I don't know, Mama," I said. "It all seems like it doesn't mean a goddamn thing."

"What doesn't, baby?"

"The money, the cars, all of it. Nothing brings me any closer to having a father. Or a family of my own."

The tears started again. I brushed my arm against my cheek and I shook my head. My chest was heaving up and down; my mom pressed the palms of her hands against it.

"I should just get used to being who I am. 'Cuz nothing is ever going to change, is it?"

"Is that what you want, baby? A family?"

"Yeah, Mama. It is."

She turned me around slowly in the chair and brought her eyes level with me. There were tears in her eyes, too.

"Kevin, God will not deny you what you earnestly seek. He won't ignore your suffering. You will find what you're looking for. I can't guarantee you that Lukie will come around, but you're going to have your own family one day."

"You think so?"

She nodded her head. "I do. I really do."

I smiled at her. I didn't believe her, but it felt good to know she thought I might get what I wanted in life. "Mom, I'm sorry. I'm crazy right now, and if I don't find answers to my pain, I'm just gonna self-destruct." I could see my mom had tears in her eyes as well. And she don't cry for nobody.

I took a deep breath. As bad as things had gotten between my mother and me, she was still the constant in my life.

"Well, Willadean," I said. "I hope to fucking God you're right."

She clucked at me for disrespecting the Lord's name.

I winked at her and thanked her for not running away from me. Even after I threw the ninja star at her face. And I meant it. Blood is blood. At least one side of the family called me son.

# CHAPTER 25

Atlanta got hotter and hotter. As obsessed as I was about security, I kept getting intel that I was next on the hit list.

There was a lot of unrest in the Southeast. The Ochoas lost a series of loads on the way from Colombia and each side suspected the other: The Ochoas thought we were pocketing loads and then saying they never reached us. The supply was tight and the streets weren't paying like they were supposed to because there wasn't enough product.

Then in March 1988, a rogue Colombian group decided that Atlanta was ripe for the picking. This was a group from the Cali region led by a renegade named Don Chepe. I kept hearing that name from people all around town: "Don Chepe is looking at Atlanta. Don Chepe wants to meet you. Don Chepe is going to take over the Southeast." I was getting nervous. The locals I could handle. But some of the Colombians were fucking savages.

In four months there were two attempts on my life. I was standing in a nightclub called Confetti's one night checking out the dance floor. There was a blonde in a tank top and what the Jamaicans call poompoom shorts—very small and tight—and we were giving each other the eye. It was a sunken floor and Rob Schaeffer was at the top of the stairs doing security.

I looked up at him and caught his eye and nodded toward the

poom-poom girl. He made a face like "Yeah, she's prime." I laughed and then I saw his expression change. He was looking over my right shoulder. I turned and saw a Colombian guy who was the size of an NFL linebacker, wearing a pressed white dress shirt. Between the open buttons of the shirt you could see the top of a skull. And this scary-looking motherfucker was bringing a gun up to aim right at me.

Rob had seen him first. As I was turning, Rob jumped the stairs, pulling out his gun as he did so. I ducked out of the way and he blasted the guy, hitting him in the shoulder. My bodyguards came running over, and two of them hustled me out of the club as it turned into a scene of utter pandemonium. Everyone was screaming and pushing, but my men were on it. The guy never even got off a shot. The bitch.

And the funny thing was, there was a limousine at the entrance of the club with a wedding party just getting out. They were all dressed in red satin dresses and black tuxes, and the last of the groomsmen was crouched in the door of the limo. My bodyguards yelled, "Get out, get out," and pointed their 9mms at the guy. This dude almost fell back into his car, but one of my guys yanked him out in one move, shoved me into the car while my other man pulled out the driver. I rolled to one of the bench seats and lay there, checking myself for any blood.

I was shaking, I was so angry. The guy escaped in the excitement so we didn't know who had sent him. That was more dangerous than anything. It could have been Don Chepe; it could have been the Sanders brothers or another faction who had their eye on my market.

It was too dangerous for me to stay at my main place at the Plantation at Lenox. We went to the Embassy Suites on Peachtree Industrial and rented a room. No one in the drug game ever used that hotel. I felt I was safe.

But I didn't lower my profile for long. Even the threat of death didn't slow me down.

I did bizarre things under the influence. For example, later that spring, with death threats hanging over my head, I developed this idea that I really needed a companion in my life. So what do I do, I go buy a dingo. That's right, a dingo, an Australian wild dog. Maybe I was feeling lonely and wanted to get that feeling I used to have with Ham-

bone, the feeling of having someone who would love me uncondition-
ally and never leave my side.

Dingoes are fucking expensive. I dropped about three grand on
this dog, and I brought him home thinking we were going to be best
buds for life. But the breed isn't made for captivity. This fucking dog
was wild; he wanted to return to the outback or wherever the fuck
they get dingoes from. I had him at my house, this million-dollar mansion in Brookhaven Country Club. And I'd be throwing these parties
for the Falcons, strippers, *Playboy* models, gangsters. And this dog
would be out in the backyard howling at the moon.

He wouldn't stop. He'd bark and he'd bounce around like he was
doing hopscotch. He chewed through my leather couches and tore
apart my Gucci shoes. We gave him Quaaludes, but he wouldn't calm
down. I gave up.

Finally, I was having a strippers-only party. All the women had to
be professional strippers or had to join the union that night by taking
off their clothes—a typical coked-out theme party. We had secretaries
and insurance saleswomen and whomever else all over the house. At
four in the morning a cop knocked on the door and told us we were
making too much noise. Either we'd have to calm down or he'd shut
the party down.

"And by the way," he said. "Do you have a dog?"

Sure enough, the dingo was calling to his ancestors. I started talking to the cop in my drug haze, and it turned out the guy's dad lived on
a farm up in North Georgia and his dog had just died. The cop just
hung his head; he was a real country boy, and you could tell his heart
was just broken by the idea of his father living alone way up there in
the boondocks.

It touched my heart, that this guy kept that image of his father so
close to his heart. It was really paining him that he couldn't help his
dad. I saw a glimpse of what it would be to have a real strong connection to your dad.

I ran to the refrigerator, where for some reason I kept the dog's
papers—don't ask why—grabbed them, got the dingo, put it in the
back of the guy's cruiser, and said, "You just take this dog and give it
to your dad."

The cop was so moved, he was practically in tears. He said,

"Dude, I work graveyard shift. You guys do whatever you want until eight in the morning."

I watched the dingo disappear down my driveway in the back of the cop's car. I almost felt sorry for the poor bastard's dad, who was about to get a barking machine. But then I went back to the strippers.

Whenever I got *really* juiced I had this bad habit of giving my jewelry away. I would take the chains off my neck and give them to strangers, anyone who looked down on their luck. Jose's brother Jessie would have to go and collect the jewelry throughout the evening. It was an end-of-the-night ritual. Time to go home? OK, then go and get Kevin's bling before people walk off with it.

My background did make me feel for people who had nothing. I went into restaurants, and if I saw a father sitting at a table with his family and they were being real careful about what they ordered, really studying the prices on the menus because they really couldn't afford it, I'd pay their bill. I'd buy groceries for people who were down to their last food stamps at the register. I'd tip the Chinese delivery guy a hundred bucks.

I liked helping people out. Maybe it was the last bit of my religious training coming out. I felt like I was giving back some of the profits I was making.

I wasn't Robin Hood, but I never forgot where I came from and what it was like to be dead broke and hungry.

You might have called me a menace to society, but I was proud of who I was. I'd been tossed away by my family, my real father and my fake one, and I'd made it to the top of my chosen profession on my own. But there was one thing that prevented me from feeling like I'd conquered my past. And that was Lukie. He was such a mystery to me. I just wanted to get to know him. If he had been a fisherman, I would have been casting nets out in the Gulf. But he was a gangster, and so I had picked up a gun and learned the trade. I felt like he'd determined my fate, even though I barely knew him.

I must have been feeling the heat, the closeness of death, because I finally sat down and did what I hadn't done for years. I wrote my father a letter.

Dear Lukie,

I am writing this letter in hopes of once and for all bringing to a conclusion the situation which exists between you, me, and my mother, which we have been dealing with for the past seven years.

I would like to settle this man-to-man and be done with it without the situation becoming a public spectacle. I'd like to spare my mother the embarrassment of having to publicly relive a particularly painful time in her life. I feel that you, as my father, have a moral as well as a legal obligation regarding the liaison between my mom and yourself many years ago, and the result of that liaison, a son, me. I want to thank you for the assistance that you have provided me during my legal troubles, and for the money which has been both loaned and given to Mom and myself over the past seven years.

These gestures have at least shown me that you're not without a conscience. But being born out of wedlock as a result of yours and Mom's relationship has evidently placed me, in your eyes, as someone to be dealt with only if absolutely necessary. I see the manner in which your "legitimate" children are being prepared for and compare their future prospects with mine. I feel that the time has arrived for you and I to decide how we want to put this situation out of both of our lives.

I understand that you're retired and of an advanced age. I understand that playing this out in public would be embarrassing to you—in fact, I've had a Florida newspaper contact me repeatedly to get my side of the story, something I have no desire to do. I understand a lot more than you think I do, Lukie.

I do not wish to be part of the "legitimate" Pappas family. I have no real desire to become a problem for your heirs and the Pappas estate. I don't want to ruin your relationship with the church. I do not want to screw up your family life, as mine has been screwed up.

I am asking only to be treated as your son.

I am looking to straighten out my life. Part of that process involves putting the fact that you are my father out of my mind, and never having contact with you again. This I am willing to do, but it is going to take a commitment from you to me and my mom.

The time has come for this situation to be put to rest.

Yours,
Kevin Pappas

He never responded to that letter. I just couldn't understand it. Blow up at me, scream, send someone to kick my ass, but at least react. But all I got was silence.

The rejection ate away at me. I started doing some truly unhinged shit.

One night, I was out at a club with my crew and it was probably four in the morning. I was sinking lower and lower, thinking about Lukie, and finally I just up and left. I was driving fifty miles an hour on Peachtree Street in my Porsche and I said, "Fuck it, I don't want to do this anymore." I hit the gas and slammed the wheel of my car to the right. The car started fishtailing, spinning into a series of 360s, and I'm jamming down the gas pedal as it turned. All I remember is my head turning and my car going like a million miles an hour in circles, and I was saying to myself, "Fuck it, let's get this thing over with."

All of a sudden my car came to a dead stop within three feet of a pole and just sat there, idling.

My head dropped to the steering wheel. I thought to myself, "I can't even fucking kill myself." And that actually cracked me up. I started laughing at the absurdity of it.

So I went back to the club and got fucked up and took a couple of strippers and brought them home and made them all get naked with one another.

I realize now why the drug game in Atlanta was getting so insane back in the late eighties. The money was too good and too many people wanted a goddamn piece of it. And the craziness started to affect my people. They started doing side deals. That was OK with me so long as they were careful and they didn't mess with our sources in Colombia.

Even within my Band of Five, the Ochoa group could call someone up and ask them to do a little project for them. And it was hard to refuse. Jose got a call near the end of '88 and he went up to Jersey to do a piece of work for the Colombians. I pieced this together afterward because he didn't want to tell me at the time what he was involved with. He knew I wouldn't approve.

Somebody had hijacked one of the cartel's loads, and it was a monster: around 500 kilos. And of course, the Ochoas found out because they always found out. The drug game, for as much money as is involved, is a small community, and hijacking 500 kilos is like coming into an inheritance of a hundred million dollars. It's going to get out on the street who's buying the Maseratis and who's offering a lot more ki's. And who knows, maybe he wanted more respect, more responsibility in the business. Maybe it was something between him and Willie or just his Cuban pride. We were all pretty drugged out at that point.

I'll never know. I just know this deal went down bad and I would have done anything to have prevented it.

So Jose was tapped to deal with this. He had a reputation as a conscientious dude. Never ripped off a load. Never shorted anyone on money.

I've thought a million times: Why did he do it? But in a way it was like getting a call from the president and being asked to carry out this special, secret mission. Jose wanted to be trusted. I'm sure the money was part of it, but he would have been flattered that the Ochoas trusted him for such a major job.

So he got his own little group together without using any of our guys and jumped in some cars and headed north. He had two orders: extract and exterminate. That is, get the shit and kill anyone who's in the house. The Colombians would kill you for stealing a kilo. For 500 kilos? That's so far over the line that death was a goddamn certainty.

Jose thought it was a stash house, meaning a house rented for the sole purpose of storing cocaine. That was the usual procedure. But in the mid-eighties people started noticing stash houses: If someone in your neighborhood moves in, but only comes to the house once a week, and then in the middle of the night with eight or ten guys, you're going to get suspicious.

So the cartels started storing the product with normal families. Colombians, of course. But people who were mechanics or nurses or whatever—give them $10,000 a month to use their attic or their basement. That way, your merchandise has a cover. It's a normal family.

This was the case in Jersey. But no one had told Jose.

He went up there thinking he was going up against a bunch of soldiers, bad guys, thieves who stole the Ochoa goods. He and his boys followed normal procedures. Move in at night, take no prisoners. So they kicked open the door and started blasting away into the dark, and an entire family got killed. I learned that the family knew what they were doing and shot back at Jose and his guys, but they were just women and young people in the house and had no way to protect themselves from this level of invasion.

Tragic, horrible shit. And Jose was devastated. I saw him the day after he got back, and he looked drained, used-up. I didn't know the details then and he didn't want to tell me, but I knew something bad had happened. I knew we were moving into a different era of our lives, our relationships, and our destiny.

That's when I lost Jose. I wasn't even there, and I didn't know it for months, but my best friend really died that day.

# CHAPTER 27

I was getting it from all sides. There were the Sanderses, there was Don Chepe, there were rumors that the Mexicans were eyeing Atlanta. I was holed up at the Peachtree Suites trying to figure out what's what.

Mark Jordan stayed with me and that was it. I didn't want the whole Band of Five coming around; they would have been spotted and my cover would have been blown. I didn't want to go back on the streets until I knew what was happening.

Mark and I lived like hermits for days on end. We ordered room service night and day and kept the curtains drawn at all times. We had clothes brought to the hotel. I worked the phones, calling my contacts and trying to figure out who had tried to blow my head off. Was it the Sanderses? Was it the Ochoas? Was it, who the fuck knew, Willie? So whoever did it, were they just going after me or were they trying to take out the entire leadership of the 5100 group? After the first couple of days, there were no other shootings or attempts on any of my people, so I knew it was just me.

The third day, about three o'clock, I decided to take a nap. I'd watched a repeat of *Welcome Back, Kotter* and I was just tired of daytime TV. I couldn't work out, I couldn't go for a walk, and I was getting sick of the whole thing. I shut off the lights and lay down on one of the queen beds, on my back as always. My right hand was under my head and my left hand was resting on my stomach. There was a 9mm a couple of inches from my right hand. I was listening to the air-conditioning click on. It was real quiet. Mark was in the bathroom.

I started to fall asleep. I was half in a daze when I heard a sharp metallic click by my left ear. I felt someone above me on the left side. I jerked my head right, and just then I felt this searing pain in my ear. I shouted and tumbled to the right side of the bed and down to the carpet. I heard the bathroom door swing open and Mark shout, "What the . . ." There was a barrage of three or four shots, and I jumped up and reached over to grab my pistol on the bed. All I saw was Mark's back as he ran toward the door, which was open.

Someone had gotten into my room and he'd tried to cut my throat. When I turned my head, he'd sliced right through my left ear and nicked the skin behind it. I still have a nasty scar.

I ran to the bathroom, grabbed a bath towel, and stumbled after Mark, swearing my ass off. I tore through the lobby—people gaping at me with that towel dripping blood—and caught up with Mark in the parking lot.

"Did you get that motherfucker?"

"Negative," Mark said. When he's focused, he tends to relapse back into military jargon. "I unloaded a whole clip on him. But no blood trail at all."

"Fuck!" I said. "This has got to stop."

I was breathing hard. I looked around. There were businessmen and secretaries on their way to lunch, and they were looking at me like I was Charlie Manson. I realized both Mark and I were still holding our guns in plain view and that I had blood all over my shirt.

"Come on," I said. We started walking toward our car in the parking lot. It was a white Mercedes, parked around the corner. We jumped in and Mark put the key in the ignition.

"You saved my life, bro," I said, grabbing Mark's forearm.

He looked over at me. "What else is new?"

I had to laugh. It blew off some of the tension. We peeled out and got the fuck out of there.

How they found me in that out-of-the-way hotel I still don't know. But enough was enough.

I went back to my apartment at the Plantation and called in some of my guys to form a security perimeter. And I started making calls. What I heard from my contacts was that this was not the Colombians.

It was either the Sanders brothers or, and this was even crazier, a *Mexican* outfit.

It just showed how insane the cocaine world had become. There were so many outfits trying to get into the game that I couldn't even get the truth on who wanted to kill me. If it was the Mexicans, I didn't even know who to fuck up, let alone where to find them. They were that new to the game.

Randy Sanders, though, was at the top of my list. I wanted to go and blow his head off, but I knew that if I did that, it would be traced back to me immediately. Our feud was all over the streets. And the one thing I feared more than death was going back to prison.

It was clear to me there was more behind these assassination attempts than Tommy Sanders's defection. It had to go deeper. I spoke to some of my contacts in the projects, and they told me that the general consensus on the street was that Willie wasn't strong enough to hold his retail locations. Willie's deepest fear was that someone would challenge him and steal the business away, embarrassing him in front of his family. And this was becoming a real possibility.

It made sense. If Willie was vulnerable, everyone and their brother would try and decapitate the 5100 group. I was the distribution guy, so I was being targeted by possibly two or three groups.

Willie asked me to put together a plan to accelerate collections on the street. I called an emergency 5100 group meeting to discuss these recent issues with an objective of collecting. Period. I saw an opportunity to kill two birds with one stone. Collect our money and stop the violence. It was interrupting the flow of good business, costing us extra money, and eating into our profits. What the fuck were these crazy gun-slinging motherfuckers thinking? Just go home.

The first thing I did was drive over to Techwood Homes housing projects to meet with Diggory Coleman. Diggory was a born killer. He was the leader of the Down By Law gang, which would later become one of the largest Crip outfits in Atlanta. But back then he was a mid-level dealer for me, and he was part-time muscle. Diggory would shoot at anything, anytime. One time he did a drive-by and the target's grandmother was sitting on the porch. She took the bullet. He didn't give a fuck. His explanation was that she was in the way. And he beat that charge. So you know Diggory Coleman was very well connected and extremely dangerous.

We met in Techwood at about one in the morning. I pulled up in my white Mercedes-Benz and got out with my crew and ran into an apartment complex there. If you walked, you were liable to get caught in a cross fire, those houses were so bad. Georgia had a very elite drug task force called the Red Dog led by a guy named Lightning Bolt, which was assigned to stop the cocaine business in the projects. But where do you think the state government pulled their officers from? Techwood and the other projects. So the ones who had not become drug dealers were supposed to police their old friends. It didn't work. Diggory had them all working for him. Lightning Bolt was as dirty as they came.

I met Diggory and I laid out my plan: I told him the Sanderses were getting ambitious and I needed some muscle on the street. Diggory was a major customer of mine, getting twenty ki's a week priced at $18,500. I agreed to cut that down to $14,500. He was cool with that.

I did the same thing with BTK, the Vietnamese gang that was big in Atlanta. It was headed by a guy named Don Lee, a small frail-looking guy who was actually one of the most feared gang leaders in the state.

Before the Gold Mine arrest, when Jose and I would hang out at Packets, we were right in the middle of the BTK territory. Don hung there, too, and Jose introduced me to him. He was just a stick-up kid then, a nobody. We were all small-time, hustling ounces in the clubs, and we got to know one another. When I went away to prison, Don was moving up the ranks in BTK. In the mid-eighties I heard that he'd been given control over the massage parlors, which is a cash cow in Atlanta. Then he was in charge of the bathhouses. Soon after he became the southeast leader of the Luk Lom group, which is a branch of BTK.

I didn't actually take Don or BTK seriously until I was incarcerated. Southerners think in black and white, even when it comes to the cocaine game. But when I was inside on my first bid, I saw how powerful the Asian gangs were inside the prison. You knew BTK when the guys had the muscle-beater shirts on and you saw a casket on their right shoulder—that tells you they are ranking members within the leadership. And if they have burning candles around it, that tells you how many people they've killed.

The BTK were radicals, fearless killers. On the outside, they did old-fashioned stuff like protection dollars and making the store owners pay fees to operate in their area. If you thought those old days of going in and collecting envelopes are gone, it wasn't with BTK. If you opened an ice-cream store or a massage parlor in their territory, they would come and get their share every month. And if they didn't get their way, they would go in and destroy the location—burn it down or blow it the fuck up, they didn't care. Protection money, prostitution, gambling, drugs, human trafficking—BTK was like the last complete gang in Atlanta.

So after I talked with Diggory Coleman I went to see Don. I gave him the same deal, a cut on the price of the Ochoa product for access to his men in the future. He was down with it. His soldiers were all like 5′7″ and 160 pounds, tiny Vietnamese guys with their cheekbones sticking out through the skin so much you felt like buying them a meal. But they were stone assassins.

I put Willie in touch with Diggory and Don. I'd put together a coalition that no one had ever seen before: Vietnamese, white, and black. I just didn't want to know what Willie did with it.

Willie was getting more and more insecure. He was terrified he was losing his power in the city, that his direct link to the Medellín cartel wasn't enough to keep him the number one guy in Atlanta and the conduit to the Eastern Seaboard. More and more it was violence and muscle that ruled the day. There was too much product available from too many suppliers. Willie wasn't unique anymore; everyone had their own Colombian.

For three months, people were getting shot and dropped all over Atlanta. Most of them were affiliated with the Sanderses, but there were Mexicans and Colombians who got their asses shot, too. I assumed Willie had put the Down by Law and the BTK options in play, but I never asked.

I was now giving Diggory and Don more merchandise at a better price so they were moving more product. It was what Wal-Mart does today. More merchandise at smaller margins equals greater profits, so long as you can move enough product. But now I had more guys I could call on in case the Sanderses or some Colombians tried to move in.

My enemies got the message. There were no other attempts on my life. But I knew Randy was still fuming about his brother, and the low-level shit continued: my dealers getting their faces busted up, the occasional rip-off of one of our couriers. One night I was sitting around with Jose and we were deciding how to end this thing.

"What about torching the brewery?" Jose said. The Sanderses owned a brewery on Roswell Road in Buckhead.

"Nah," I said. "I'm sick of this nonsense. It's not bad enough we have to dodge the police and the feds every day, we have to be fucking with the competition, too? Let's go finish this."

So we loaded up our cars with about twenty guys and went to the brewery. This was their stronghold. They wouldn't expect us to arrive there. But enough was enough.

We walked in, slammed the doors shut, and told everyone to stay put. No one in or out. Their security chief came walking up to us, wild-eyed. He either had to kick us out or lose his job.

"Get out of here," I said and handed him a couple of hundred bucks. He and his team headed for the exit.

We walked through the bar to the back room where I knew the Sanderses hung out. I kicked in the door with my boys right behind me. Randy was at a table counting their receipts for the night and I walked up to him and put a 9mm to his head.

"Hi, Randy," I said.

"Fuck you, Pappas."

I really thought I had miscalculated. This was going to be a massacre. You can't put a gun to Randy Sanders's head and keep the beef on a low level.

"Listen, you fuckup," I told him. "Either we can kill each other right here, or we can stop this nonsense. Tommy's with us and that's that."

He thought about it a while. Randy knew that I wasn't afraid. Either we settled the matter or bodies would start dropping.

He didn't like it, but he accepted the truce.

# CHAPTER 28

By the spring of '89, I was putting out fires like Smokey the Bear. It seemed like the whole organization was unraveling. Starting with Jose.

Jose had a condo right across the way from me in Buckhead. We were at each other's houses all the time, but after the New Jersey incident, I started to see less and less of him. Then one morning I got the *Atlanta Journal-Constitution* and my coffee, sat down at my breakfast table, and just glanced out the window.

I couldn't believe what I saw. Jose's apartment had sun glinting off the windows. It took me a minute to figure out the crazy fuck had put tinfoil over them.

I threw on a T-shirt and shorts and went hustling over there. I pounded on the door. I heard rustling on the carpet inside like he was shuffling to the door, and then I had the sense he was looking at me through the peephole.

"Jose, it's me, Kevin. Open the fuck up."

Nothing. I pounded on the door some more.

"Jose, I swear if you don't open this door I'm going to go back and get my gun and blow the lock off."

I heard the dead bolt open slowly. The door opened a crack and I pushed my way in.

My eyes had to adjust to the place. There were pizza boxes on the floor and soda cans on the couch and tables. He hadn't cleaned up in weeks. He had all the windows tinfoiled up, but there were a few little holes poked in them where sunlight was shooting through. And Jose looked like shit. His skin was pale and he had dark rings under his eyes. He smelled like stale bread and I could tell that he had stopped working out.

"Jose, what the fuck is the matter with you? Why do you have that shit on the windows?"

"Kevin," he said. "They're coming after me. They're watching me all the time."

Now, the dope game makes you paranoid anyway. And I didn't know the full extent of how batshit Jose had gone. So the hairs on the back of my neck stood up when he said that.

I dropped my voice. "Seriously, you've seen people out there?"

"Kevin, I swear to you they're watching me—and your place too. You gotta get some foil on your windows. Look."

And he picked up a Bic pen and walked over to the windows. He put his eye to one of the holes and nodded. He poked another hole in the tinfoil and waved me over and said, "Look."

I put my eye to the hole. The window that he was at faced away from my building and toward this open field of undeveloped land. "What the fuck am I looking at? Where are they?"

"In the trees," he said.

"*Up* in the trees?"

"Yeah, bro."

"I don't see anything, Jose."

"Right there, Kevin. Right fucking ahead of you. They hide behind the tree trunks but they've got binoculars and everything."

I was scanning the tree line like a motherfucker, but there was nothing in those trees except squirrels and blue jays. I took my eye away from the hole. I wanted to bust him in the mouth, but then a feeling of total sadness just washed over me.

"Jose, come here."

He backed away from the window. He walked over to me and I opened my arms and gave him a big, hard hug. I had his head in the crook of my elbow and I brushed my cheek against his. I felt I was holding a dead body. That the Jose I knew was in the process of slipping away, little by little. I wanted to grab hold of what was left and just keep him there with me.

"Jose," I said. I felt like my voice was going to break. "Jose, there's nobody out there."

"Kevin, you have no idea. They have night vision . . ."

"Tell me what's going on with you, man. Tell me what's happening."

He didn't say anything for a while. He just stood there in my arms, his body slack. And he just broke down and started crying. He said, "I can't live this way, Kev. I just want my life back."

I told him, "You got to go away for a little bit. Take a few months off. Go. Take a deep breath."

"Fuck it, I can't leave you. I can't leave what we've got going."

I backed up and looked him in the eye. "If you keep this up, son, you won't be around much longer. You'll drive yourself fucking crazy."

He just looked down.

"Here's the deal," I said. "You need to go on a retreat. Check yourself into rehab. Fucking go to the beach, go somewhere, man, and work this thing out. You're no good to no one, especially yourself."

He started talking about a guy named Tony, one of his second-tier guys. "Tony can run the deal. I've gotten soft, after my little situation, I can't deal with it. All I want to do is just hide; I don't want anyone to see me. I want to get out of here, Kev."

I held him in my arms and told him that I loved him and that he was all that I had.

He said, "I love you too but, Kev, I can't do this no more."

"So don't."

We agreed that he'd take a break and get his head straight. He did go away to the Bahamas, but he was back in a few weeks. The thing that he wanted to escape wasn't in Atlanta, it was inside him.

I knew how Jose felt. I just didn't know how to help him.


One of the things that kept me sane during this time, believe it or not, was dancing. Rob Schaeffer and I had certain nights, two or three a month, when we would just drop everything and hit the clubs. There were two rules: no women and no talking about the 5100 Group. We'd put on our Valentino silk shirts, our Guess jeans, and some cowboy boots, and we'd forget we were dopers for a night. It was our chance to be human beings.

Rob was a fabulous dancer. I mean he could have worked backup for someone like Usher today, no joke. They'd throw on the Gap Band or "White Lines" by Melle Mel, and the crowd would literally stop dancing and watch us take over the middle of the floor. I was good but Rob was so inventive and such a natural. And he'd get this goofy grin on his face when he tore it up.

We had dance-offs where we both tried to outdo the other. We didn't give a fuck what the other clubbers thought, we'd do *anything* to make the other guy crack up: spinning on our backs, tango moves, whatever. I held my own, but Rob could take over a club in a minute. He won more than he lost.

I loved it. I loved hanging out with Rob. For most of my life, I had to act like I was a forty-five-year-old executive managing millions of dollars a week and supervising forty guys out on the street. I had to be a hard-ass to survive. I had to make life-and-death decisions at the drop of a hat. But I could go out with Rob and be a human being for three or four hours. And that was special.

It was on one of those nights that Rob told me about his sister, Katie. She was a couple of years younger than him and they'd been close as kids. But when his mother got hooked on coke, the state had taken Rob and his sister and sent them to different foster homes in Atlanta. Her family had moved out to the Midwest and he'd lost touch with her. That had been ten years ago.

I got the idea as soon as he started talking about his sister. I asked him if he knew her birthday, and he gave me a date. I tucked that away in my mind and I got my DMV guy, Dave, to call one of his contacts in the child welfare department. After about two months of digging, Dave called me up with a phone number up in Dawsonville in north Georgia. I called Katie up and she nearly dropped the phone when I told her why I was calling.

She'd been through hell herself; she had one kid from an abusive marriage. She'd been an alcoholic for a while but she'd straightened herself out and was now working as a cashier in a supermarket. And she hadn't forgotten Rob; in fact, just the opposite. She wanted to take the next plane down to Atlanta, but I wanted to set up something special for Rob.

We used to go to an upscale Benihana-type restaurant called Kobe Steaks where we had a favorite chef whose table we'd sit at every time we went. We called him Johnny Lines. He had a minor coke habit, and we'd bring in a few ounces for him and he'd give us three steaks for the price of one. He'd do all the tricks—the shrimp flying up into his chef hat—but he also knew who we were, because every time we sat down our beepers would be going off all night. That was the sure sign of a doper in the late eighties. Businessmen got their pages during the day. We got 'em at night.

So every time we walked in the restaurant, this comedian would throw some salt on the grill in front of him and chop them into lines. Get it? He had balls. And he could cook. So this was one of our favorite places to go.

So we were in there one night, probably ten or twelve of us, getting ripped on sake and shooting the shit with Johnny Lines. Rob was right next to me. Just before the orders were taken, a woman in sunglasses sat down at the corner of the table. I nodded to her. Rob hardly noticed.

After we gave the waitress an order for more sake, I whispered to Rob, "Who the hell is that chick over there?" I pointed to the woman at the corner. "She's been staring at you ever since you sat down."

"Fucked if I know," Rob said.

"You sure? You sure you don't recognize her?"

Rob just wanted to get on with his drinking, but he took another look at the woman. She was about 5′5″, blond hair, looked older than her twenty years, and she had Rob's high cheekbones. When she saw Rob looking at her, she reached up and took off the sunglasses. Katie had Rob's eyes, too. They were beginning to fill up with tears.

Rob just stared for a minute.

"It's not . . ." he said.

"Yeah, it is," I whispered. "Go give her a hug. She's been dying to see you."

Rob dropped his head and he quickly turned and gave me a crushing bear hug.

"You don't know how much this means to me, Daddy Rabbit," he said.

I got teared up, too. Rob let me go and went running over to his sister. The table started clapping and even Johnny Lines stopped what he was doing and applauded.

I felt good that I could do that. I wanted the Band to know that we were brothers, that it wasn't just about business. Rob went up to see Katie and her little girl a bunch of times. He got to be an uncle and a brother. He got to have a family experience that wasn't a fucking horror show.

# CHAPTER 29

Don Chepe was still trying to move on our territory. The dude had an enforcer named Pepe who came to us with his Uzi-wielding soldiers and told us Don Chepe would like to be our partner. We were like, "We already own the city, why would we need *you?*"

I always tried to be diplomatic, but maybe I was a little rude with them. But the Colombians were always very aggressive, so you had to make your position clear. And my position was: Stay the fuck out of Atlanta.

They took offense. I heard that they were unhappy. And then one day they made their move.

I have to tell this story from the point of view of one of my workers, Keith. Keith was new to the business and this was his baptism by fire. I've heard him tell the story a thousand times, and it gives you a view of the business from a completely different angle.

Keith was really just a gofer for us, a guy looking to make a few bucks. I'd met him while I was dancing with Chippendales and I'd partnered him with Ross Peterson, one of my underguys. He was only eighteen at the time, a wide-eyed kid. I put him into a storefront that I owned. We advertised beepers and pagers for sale, but mostly I used the place to move dope. As Keith said, "I ain't ever sold one pager out of that store." It was a front, both to launder money and to distribute the product.

So Keith and Ross were up in North Carolina running errands, just some bullshit details that needed to get done, when he got a 911 call from us down in Atlanta.

What happened was that the Colombians had come into another storefront we ran, and they started slapping my distributor around. They were like, "We're running this town now." They wanted him to take all of their product from their sources and kick back a percentage of the sales. A classic strong-arm move.

My distributor had stayed loyal. Told me everything. Now the Colombians were coming to let me know they were going to be in charge.

Ross said to Keith, "We're going back to the house to pick up some weapons."

Keith was like, "*What?*" He hadn't signed up for weapons. He thought he was going to be selling wireless plans to yuppies. Now he started to realize that he was in a completely different business.

Ross told him to shut up and follow orders. So he and Ross went to one of our condos and started loading up the car with firepower: handguns, machine guns, shotguns. With each armful they brought out, Keith was getting more and more nervous. He was like, "What do we need all this stuff for?" He kept begging Ross for more information, but Ross was just trying to get the stuff loaded and told him to chill out. But they were loading up for World War III and Keith was like, "Man, *what* is going on?"

I was at a secluded area off the highway called Miami Circle, where we had a bunch of storage units with guns and other shit. Ross and Keith pulled up with the weapons. The street was packed with BMWs and Mercedeses, and it was clear that all my guys had arrived. Everyone was milling around outside wearing long black trench coats to hide the shotguns. Guys would go to Ross's car and choose their weapons; I saw Keith's eyes get bigger and bigger as the guys lined up for their pieces. It was insane that we were doing this on a main commercial strip in Buckhead, but it was going down fast and we didn't have time to be discreet. I came out and said, "All right, everyone meet at the house off North Druid Hills."

Ross and Keith jumped in their car and made it to the house. I saw them walk in. I was giving everyone shots of tequila to steady their nerves. There were about twenty guys and no one was giving back their guns. And Jimmy Coulos. Remember Jimmy, the fucking 135-pound maniac? Jimmy was going crazy. He was just looking for a Colombian to fuck up.

Keith was a wreck. He was trying to get an idea of the situation without looking like a complete jackass, so he would sidle up to someone and ask, "Hey, what the fuck is going on?" The answer was that the Colombians were in town and they were trying to take over Atlanta. He was like, "Uh-huh," and then quietly moved away.

Finally, the Colombians pulled up in a black limo. There were about eight of them, all with ponytails, all wearing light-colored suits, and all with Uzis. They piled out of the car, looking around as they stepped out.

Jimmy was ready to go to war, as usual. He put a .45 automatic down the back of his pants and he walked out of the house with his hands in the air, like he was unarmed. We were expecting this thing to go off any second and everyone was on a hair trigger.

I saw Keith against a wall and his face was just like, "Jesus Christ, what have I gotten myself into?"

Everyone was watching through the windows, locking their guns, when Jimmy grabbed the lead guy by the ponytail, pulled the gun out, and pointed it at his head. "Fuck you, motherfucker, I run Atlanta," he shouted at him.

Now it was on. Guys ran upstairs to get better shooting angles from the windows, and at the same time some of the Colombians ducked and ran behind the condo. I shouted to Keith and Ross to cover the back door. Someone cocked a gun, handed it to Keith, and yelled, "Watch the back door. They're coming in the back door." Keith took the gun, but he was like, "Man, I ain't shooting nobody."

Keith was freaking out. He looked like he was going to pass out. But he went to the back door.

We were all watching Jimmy with the gun at the Colombian's head. All of a sudden there was this *BAAAMMMM* and people ducked, then looked out the windows again. They expected to see the Colombian with his face blown off. But it wasn't Jimmy's gun. It was Keith's. The fucking retard had tried to cock his weapon when it was already cocked, and it had gone off.

Everybody went running toward the back door, thinking the Colombians were breaking in. But it was just Keith, looking down at his big toe. There was a hole in the floor right next to it where the rounds had gone in. He had fired the weapon by mistake and almost set off a fucking war.

"I honestly about shit all over myself," Keith told us later.

Smoke and dust were swirling around and everyone was freaking out. Keith was so out of it that he couldn't tell us what happened—plus the shot had temporarily deafened him. All of a sudden people realized that the cops were probably getting calls right now from the neighbors about shots fired. Everyone went tearing out the back door and the Colombians jumped in their limo.

"I was so scared I can't remember the rest of it" is how Keith ended the story. He nearly got us all shot, but to see the look on his face when we piled into that back hallway was almost worth it.

# CHAPTER 30

Jose came back from his retreat but nothing changed. He was becoming more and more of a cowboy. When we first got together, he'd always been the one who kept me on an even keel. But as I got to be more and more the thinker behind the operations, and the guy who hated risk, Jose seemed to eat it up.

Jose got barred from Miami. Not by me but by the Cubans and Colombians. Every time he went down there, he was getting shot at or he was shooting somebody. He had a cousin in the Miami Police Department, and this guy managed to squash a lot of the charges against him, but it was too hot.

I was getting worried. Jose was my right-hand man. Now he was getting out of control.

And after a period of three or four years when we could do no wrong, it seemed we were getting hit from every angle. I was watching the TV one night, Channel Five, just relaxing and trying not to think about Jose or Willie, who was getting on my nerves. I think *Quincy* was on. Anyway, there was a banner at the bottom of the screen that said something about a drug bust in Buckhead. That got my attention because Tommy Sanders was supposed to drop off ten kilos to our distributor that night. I started watching that little banner real close.

Finally, the shit must have been heating up because they cut away from *Quincy* and went to a live news report. They had sent their traffic helicopter over to report on it and they were hovering over this drug bust in the parking lot of a nightclub next to the Disco Kroger. The suspect was on the run and I could see this black guy zigzagging through the parking lot. And I was sitting there in my recliner saying, "Holy shit, that's Tommy."

The helicopter was zooming in on Tommy with its cameras, and all of a sudden he turned and started shooting at them. The chopper news guy was screaming, "We're taking fire! We're taking fire!" Tommy had ten ki's back in his car and he knew if he was caught he was going away for a nice long term. I was proud of him, in a way. But shooting at the local news team was not going to be good for business.

Tommy ducked in and out of buildings and behind cars, shooting all the time, until the cops finally cornered him. They came at him and forced him to lie on the ground, spread-eagle. The last shot from the copter showed him being put in the backseat of a police car.

Tommy became a legend, but we lost one of our best dealers when he went to prison.

Another time we were bringing a load in by Cessna and the coordinates got screwed up. The guys waiting at the drop site called Willie, and Willie called me, completely freaking out. He was shouting into the radio, "Are the birds in?" He was going crazy. "How come they haven't landed?"

Well, we looked everywhere for the missing kilos and couldn't find them. The pilots swore they'd dropped at the designated point, but our pickup team swore they'd never even seen the plane.

Two days later, I was reading the *Atlanta Journal-Constitution* about the mysterious death of black bears in some forest. The rangers found the bears just konked out, with no visible wounds or anything. But nearby they found bags of cocaine split open. Eight kilos and two dead black bears.

Between copters taking rounds and dead fucking wildlife, it seemed like we couldn't catch a break anymore.

# CHAPTER 31

One thing that Hollywood does get right about the drug game is how everyone thinks they can do it. That becomes a problem for any trafficker. People are paying you these killer prices for the product and they say to themselves, "Why don't I just cut out the middleman?" Or, as happened with Rob Schaeffer, they start thinking they can outsmart you.

Rob started messing with the product. He learned how to take one kilo of cocaine and melt it down into a liquid base. Then he would take the same coke and repuff it and rebrick it. This was a more sophisticated move than just putting in some baby laxative and recutting the stuff. Rob was playing cook, and it's harder to detect when you do it that way. But he was skimming some of the product off and then selling it on the side and melting what he had left to fill his orders for the 5100 Group.

But junkies are the most demanding cocksuckers you've ever met. It seemed like if you watered a brick down by one percent, they would call you up and curse you out. So eventually word got back to me that the street dealers were refusing to pay Rob because the shit was not up to par. And instead of copping to what he was doing, Rob bucked up and denied it. Rob was a true street kid and he had the attitude to prove it. And I heard that things were about to explode. There were people in Atlanta who wanted Rob dead.

I had to go see him. I found him in one of the strip clubs and slid into a booth next to him. He didn't look too happy to see me.

"You got something to tell me, dickhead?"

He admitted what he'd done almost immediately. Rob was such a loyal guy; he didn't really see that what he was doing was hurting everybody.

"Can you fix this, Kev? Come on, Daddy Rabbit, protect me on this one, huh?"

"Can't do it, bro. People need to know that our word is true. You need to pull your merchandise back. Tell everybody that the last twenty ki's was from a bad load."

It was like a product recall on a Cadillac. Sorry, this defect passed our quality control. Full refunds for everyone.

And Rob needed to tell his guys that the problem was with the original shipment. If people knew he was the one melting it down, he was going to get his head blown off.

"Man, that shit's already on the street," he said. "I can't go back and vacuum it back up."

I had to lay down the law. I told him to get whatever hadn't been sold back within seventy-two hours and switch those ki's out for our good 98-percent-pure product. And he took a hell of a financial hit on that. Tens of thousands of dollars.

As close as Rob and I were, he had to respect 5100 or I'd have to deal with him personally. I told him that things were heating up, Jose was going loco, and this was no time to go playing cowboy off on his own. We needed to be together, and that meant that no one could sell subpar shit on the street.

Finally Rob accepted it. He did the right thing and reimbursed his dealers. I thought it had solved the problem. But I later learned it hadn't.

Rob and Mark and I shared more than the drug game. I had long conversations with them about their fathers because they both had dad issues. Mark's father was a strange combination: an alcoholic and a perfectionist. He was a hardworking redneck, nothing wrong with that, but when he drank he'd beat Mark until he was black and blue all over. He was a man's man—never showed emotion in front of the boys.

I could relate. My stepfather, Jim, had been emotionless too, but he seemed to enjoy beating me, like he was hitting something or someone else and I was just the punching bag to take it out on. I could never respect him because he would beat me when I hadn't done anything wrong, so after a while it didn't matter when I *did* do something wrong. What was the difference? I was going to get a beating anyway.

Mark couldn't do anything right either. It was his brother, Rick, who got all the love. That sounded familiar. Rick was a pretty boy, bodybuilder, but he was also an instigator. Growing up, it always seemed like the two of them got into trouble and Mark would always take the blame.

Mark would call me up at three in the morning and I knew he was feeling down. So we'd talk on the phone for hours, real philosophical conversations. Mark was an atheist. He said God didn't exist. He said God was a figment of people's imagination and that the purpose of religion was to make you feel good so that everyone could stay calm.

I think Mark was scarred by what he saw in Panama. We knew he'd had seventeen kills down there as a sniper, but he never wanted to talk about it. He loved the military, but I think he hated what it forced him to believe and to do to innocent people. It had made him into a stone-cold atheist. "I went to war," he would say. "I saw people eating out of garbage cans; I saw men's brains sprayed out against walls, and I'm not sure for what. There's no reason to justify the amount of life lost for some greater cause. I can see now how this so-called God lets you live, and I don't want to worship anything like that."

At the end of the conversation, it always came back to our dads. If we were drunk, I'd punch him in the shoulder and say, "At least you've *got* a dad."

"Dude," he'd say. "I'd rather have nothing at all than what I've been handed."

I couldn't accept that. To me, any father was better than none. That's why I couldn't let the thing with Lukie die. I couldn't die a bastard who had never been acknowledged by his own father. That was like being an animal.

I thought I had it bad until I got a call from Mark. A relative of his had died, an uncle, and he'd decided to go back for the funeral because this guy was one of the few who'd been decent to him when he was a boy.

"I wouldn't go back for my dad but I will for Uncle Willie," he said. I was surprised as hell—usually Mark talked about his family like they were a nest of vipers.

He asked me to go with him. He asked so quietly, in fact, that I had to ask him to repeat it. "Of course I'll go, ya fuckup!" I told him. Mark and Rob both were like fragile children under those bodybuilder exteriors. They never trusted that you truly loved them; they always thought you were going to fuck them like their relatives did.

So we went out to his family's house out in the outskirts of Georgia. I drove, and as we got closer and closer, Mark got quieter and quieter. It was like he was slowly withdrawing into a shell. "For fuck's sake," I thought to his family, "just be kind to this poor motherfucking boy for once in his life."

We pulled up. There were a bunch of cars already parked on the lawn of a green-and-white wooden frame house, which was a little run-down but nothing out of the ordinary for this part of Georgia. We got out, shrugged on our suit jackets, and started walking up the lawn. "They'll be around back," Mark said, and I followed him around the corner of the house to the backyard. They had tables set up in back with coffee and danishes, people were sitting there gossiping, and kids were running around trying to escape the adults. There were a few dudes in military uniform, as you'd see in any gathering of people in rural Georgia.

A few people looked up, but no one said anything. Then I saw this woman making a beeline for us. She was rail-thin with sunken cheeks and a sixties-style bouffant hairdo, and she was dressed in a black two-piece suit. She looked like Mrs. Cleaver if the Cleavers lived in Georgia and didn't have a whole lot of money.

"Fuck," Mark said under his breath. "My mom."

She didn't say a word to Mark; she didn't even look at him. She came right up to me and planted her feet around five feet away.

"I know who you are and I want you out of here," she said.

"Me?" I was speechless. I looked at Mark. His eyes were pointed down at the lawn, like he knew this was going to happen.

"That's right, you," she said.

"Mom, Kevin's my friend," Mark said quietly.

She turned on him right fast. "You want to bring a drug dealer into my family gathering?" she hissed. She had a smoker's voice—like she was gasping for breath. "That's how you pay your respects to my brother?"

"Listen, I don't want to be a disturbance," I said, holding up my hands. "Mark, I can wait in the car." I didn't want to fuck up this one day that Mark would have with his family.

"No!" Mark said, and his eyes were angry. Scary angry. "Mom, he's my friend and he's not going anywhere."

People at the tables were watching now. It was getting a little loud. I felt terrible for Mark.

"Then you can both leave," his mother said.

"Mark," I said.

"Let's get the fuck out of here," he said, and he walked past me.

Mrs. Jordan crossed her arms and watched him go. I could have taken a step and snapped her neck in half a second, and I was just so tempted to do it. "Aren't you going to call him back?" I said.

"He knows my rules," the stupid bitch said.

I couldn't believe what I was hearing. "Go fuck yourself," I said, and followed Mark to the car.

What a fucking piece of work. I took Mark back to an Atlanta strip club and we got hollering drunk. I knew he couldn't be alone that night. The one relative who'd been good to him was dead, and his mother was . . . well, his mother. I got him good and drunk and let him call her every name in the book. I told him to forget about those assholes, that we were brothers and closer than any family any of us would ever have. And I meant every word of it.

had to confront Jose about his behavior. I was getting complaints from all over. I knew what was eating him—that recovery job up in New Jersey—but he still wouldn't talk about it six months after it happened.

One day we were backstage at the Mr. Georgia competition. Jose was competing for the second time; he'd been in serious training for six months and he was down to two percent body fat. I was slapping some baby oil on his chest, getting him prepped for the final showing, when he looked at me.

"I can't do this, man," he said.

"What the fuck are you talking about?" I said. "You worked hard for this, bro. You're going to walk away with this thing."

"Nah, man, I can't get the image out of my head."

Right then I knew he was back on the Jersey thing. I couldn't believe what I was hearing. I tried to stay calm.

"Listen, Jose. It wasn't your fault. You didn't know what you were walking into."

Jose looked down. He didn't even want to look me in the eye. "Kevin, I didn't sign up for this. I can't believe it happened. I don't play God."

He obsessed about what he'd done. His conscience ate him up.

He won the title that day. But he couldn't even enjoy it. The competition had given him an excuse to channel all his guilt into training for a short period of time, but once it was done, he started to lose it again.

Jose started doing a little too much dope. A line here or there doesn't matter; it goes with the business. But he was coming home fucked-up every night. And at the same time he was loading up on steroids as well.

He was a loose cannon. All through that summer he was acting out. One night we were in Tattletales, this strip bar we hung out at, and we were partying and throwing cash at the girls. Just a normal night out. But Jose was acting crazy, smashing cocktail glasses against his forehead to show how tough he was.

It reminded me of when I cut my wrists with the broken wineglass, trying to get the truth about Lukie from my mother. I knew the pain Jose was going through. I knew why he was doing it: The physical pain drowned out the mental pain.

Finally, one of the bouncers came up to me and said, "Listen, you've got to get rid of this man. No disrespect, but he's scaring people."

I knew that Jose wouldn't listen to me at that point. Every time I approached him he would hold up another glass and crack it on his skull. Plus he was armed and liable to pull out the gun and shoot the place up if confronted. The only one he would listen to in that state was Alexis, my *Penthouse* Pet girlfriend. I called her up and asked her to do me a favor. Even though we were no longer together, she still had a thing for me and she cared about Jose too.

I said, "Alexis, just take his ass home, he's acting like a fool." I stayed until she got there and then I went home.

A couple of hours later, around six a.m., Alexis came to my house. She woke me up.

"Kevin, I do not like the way he's acting."

"Christ, what's he doing now?"

"You need to go check on him."

"Fuck that, he'll be all right." I knew Alexis had dropped Jose safely at his house. Tomorrow, he'd be sobered up and full of remorse. Then maybe I could talk to him.

I got up at around 8:30 the next morning and I had this nagging sense that I needed to go check on Jose. I threw on some clothes and walked over to his place. It was early, there was still dew on the grass, and it was real quiet. I went up to his condo and knocked on the door. No answer. I tried it again, but there wasn't a sound from inside the place. Either Jose was passed out or he'd woken up and gone out for breakfast.

I came back down the stairs and I found the maintenance guy who was doing some work on the first floor. "Hey, have you seen Jose?"

He said, yeah, he was in the laundry room.

So I walked into the laundry room and I saw Jose hanging from a rope. His back was toward me. I froze for just an instant and then screamed his name and ran toward him.

He'd taken the dividing rope from the swimming pool, thrown it over a rafter, and jumped off a washing machine. I jumped on the washing machine and tried to save him, but he was already getting cold. I couldn't believe this sensitive man, this warrior, had done this to himself.

The maintenance guy came and we cut Jose down. I unwrapped the rope from around his neck and held him in my arms. I was rocking him back and forth in my arms, crying, and I said, "Oh what have you done?"

I kept asking him that single question, "What have you done?" as I wiped the dried blood on his forehead, still there from busting the glasses.

"God Almighty, why did you do this? Why didn't you talk to me?"

And right then the air in his body just went, "Uhhhhhhh." It scared the shit out of me, but I knew that the dead often give out that last one breath after they've passed. And I sat there and I sobbed.


It was a terrible time. Jose was the first of the Band to die. I felt like this second family that I had built around me to replace my real kin, the Pappases, was now starting to crumble. Why was Jose dead when I was the one who'd led us into the drug game? Why did he have to die when I looked for death sometimes but never found it? Why could I find no peace in the world? I had no answers, just like I had no answers for why Lukie had cursed me.

I seriously considered getting out of the drug business. It wasn't the danger; it was the fact that I couldn't face losing any more people who were close to me. I meditated on it and I spoke to Jose in my heart, asking him what he wanted me to do.

After a week, I knew I was in until the death. How could I leave when my best friend had passed in the game? I felt somehow it would be dishonoring him, walking away from everything we had built together.

But I expected to be released from the game, and from my life, very soon.

I went to the wake to give my respects along with the rest of the Band. It was at this high-end funeral home on Peachtree Street where it looked like a senator or the mayor would come for his last viewing. I almost laughed. *Now* the family had money and time to spend on Jose. They sure as fuck didn't have either before.

And can you believe it? The family kicked us out.

I walked into the wake. It was full of people, maybe thirty or forty, mostly his Cuban relatives. We stood out. We came to represent in black suits with our medallions showing. And I wasn't there two minutes when one of his fat Cuban aunts came up to me. "You killed him," she screamed. And soon there were three or four more cousins and uncles ganging up behind her, saying, "You did this to him. It's because of you he's in that coffin."

I was dumbfounded. After all the stories Jose told me about his family rejecting him and keeping him at a distance, now I was the monster? I felt like capping a few of them right there, honestly.

"You got it all wrong," I said to the aunt.

But they all kept yelling. "If he wasn't with you, he'd be alive."

That was it. I blew up.

"Where were you when he needed family? Now you come to pay your respects and to show your love? Fuck you!"

I brushed past them and headed up the aisle to the coffin. I looked down in the casket. Jose still had the scratches on his face from the glasses he was busting against his head the night before he died. They were so deep the mortician couldn't quite disguise them. But otherwise he looked peaceful. They'd dressed him in a nice Hugo Boss suit and gelled his waves of black hair. This was the Jose I knew before he'd lost it.

I leaned over the coffin and gave Jose a kiss. I could see that the family had taken his medallion and, who knows, maybe thrown it in the trash. I took the medallion from my neck and I put it between his hands. It was to show that we knew the real Jose; we knew his heart. He was with us until the end. It was our way of sending him off.

CHAPTER 33

**W**illie and I were having problems, too. We were always on edge with each other. I admit that the first part of the problem was my fault—I stole his girlfriend. Shoot me. She was drop-dead gorgeous.

Beth Singer was her name. She was half-Italian, half-Brazilian, with hazel-green eyes. She was a gold digger but not a whore—she was always dressed in silks and furs, and she was so ladylike she would wake up smelling like the best perfume.

I decided I had to have that woman in my life, and it soon became clear she was just as passionate about me. The power of feeling untouchable, of going out every day and mastering the streets, had given me the sense that I could have anything I wanted. *Anything.* Even Willie's girl. What's power if you don't test it to the limit every once in a while? That's how you find out how much you've got.

But it was more than an attraction. I knew even at the time I was looking for a way to get back at Willie. I was out there, just twenty-four years old, getting shot at, getting stabbed, hustling to outdo the competition, and what was he doing? Sitting back and counting the money. I felt like I was the blue-collar guy putting in all the hours and he was this spoiled rich kid just reaping the profits.

Maybe it goes back to my father, Lukie. I always wanted to be appreciated by the guy above me. I'd work my ass off, but the minute you took me for granted, you lost my loyalty.

I knew Willie didn't appreciate the complexity of my job. He would drop hints that anyone could do it, which was total and utter bullshit, because guys died every year trying to do what I did. I established the logistics, ran background on customers and employees, made sure the shit was secure once it arrived, mapped out the strategic plans for growing our business, and prepared the code language for the run. I arranged for the chase cars and the decoys; I identified the drop points and organized every other part of the transactions, including knowing which police officers were on which shift, who their commanders were, and who was on our payroll. I thought out everything to the split second.

But to Willie I was just a glorified social directory. A fix-it guy. He had no idea how intricate my job was. And, like I said, he was insecure. I was the one who was making friends with all the Colombians, I was the one who had the loyalty of the lieutenants and the captains. Looking back now, I can see how threatened he would be by that.

A few months after Jose passed, I got a call. This time it was about Rob Schaeffer. My world went dark for a minute. He'd been found executed with two bullets in the back of his head. Someone had made him kneel against his bed in a praying stance and then pumped two rounds into his brain.

No one knew who did it. It could have been the outside deals he was making. Or it could have been one of my competitors in Atlanta, but if that had been the case, I would have gotten a message making it clear. I wish I'd known who did it because they'd have been on a cold slab twenty-four hours after I got the news.

Rob had always told us that we had to come to his funeral. He was so insecure, like a lost child. How fucked-up do you have to be to think your best friends wouldn't come to send you off? It breaks my heart just to think about that.

We had a procession of four black stretch Mercedes limos with all his friends. The family had made it clear that we weren't welcome at the funeral home so we'd slipped a couple of bills to the guys who dug the grave and asked to spend a little time with the coffin before they buried it.

It was a rainy day and nobody felt like talking on the ride to the graveyard. We passed around a bottle of Crown Royal. I looked at Willie and Mark and thought, *Two down, three to go. Who's next?* Willie looked preoccupied with something and Mark just looked blank, like he was afraid to think or feel anything.

*Who was going to be next?* Sometimes I wished it would be me.

I thought back to Jose and his paranoia about being watched, about people coming to get him. Maybe he was right.

I walked to the grave, the mud splashing up on my $400 Ferragamo shoes. I carried a dozen black roses, Rob's special request for his funeral. The coffin was placed on a piece of green nylon carpet beside the freshly dug hole, and the rain was beading up on the shiny top. I went up to the coffin and knelt right beside it. I put my arm across the top and gripped it. I wanted to give Rob one last hug. I remembered his premonition. I thought he was crazy back then talking about his funeral and all to me. "Is this all there is?" I asked myself. My head sank onto the wood and my tears mixed with the rain.

"Your work here is done, baby," I whispered. "God bless you for your loyalty." I wanted to tell him he was a soldier, a warrior, and that he'd died a warrior's death. I wanted to tell him how much we cared for him and that his death left a gaping hole in all our lives. But I was done. No words would come, so I stood up and walked back to the group. Willie went and stood next to the coffin and put his hand on top. "You showed yourself to be strong," he said. "You showed yourself to be tough. More important you made a mark in all of our hearts. We love you."

The world was closing in on me. Fast. Something had to give. I told myself that I'd either be dead in six months or in prison.

# CHAPTER 34

Willie was right beside me at Rob's funeral. But little did I know that at that very moment he was busy arranging a load all on his own. Just to prove he could.

In the first week of July 1988, Willie came to me and said, "Why don't you go down to Daytona? You've been working your ass off." I was like, "Really?" Willie never told anyone to take a break. In fact, I never needed his permission to hit Florida or the Bahamas. But it was cool that he was saying this. It made me feel he realized all I was putting into 5100. So I went.

What Willie had done was go to my contacts and say that he had spoken to me. "Kevin just gave these directions and we are to go ahead and give you guys a hundred grand a load, a hundred grand a person, for this short trip to Texas."

He went to Jimmy first. If Jimmy was in, all my guys would assume that I'd authorized the operation because Jimmy and I were tight. And of course Jimmy took the bait because he always wanted to head up any kind of dangerous mission. Dumbass.

So I went down to Daytona, checked into a four-star hotel by the beach, and started to enjoy myself. Four days into my little jaunt, I got a call from Mark Jordan on the satellite phone.

"What's up, Mark?"

"Hey, buddy, we're down here in Texas and something don't seem right."

I said. "*Where* are you?"

"Texas. In Houston. We're on that job."

I felt a little flutter of nerves in my stomach.

"What fucking job would that be, Mark?"

He told me the whole thing. They'd been cooped up in a hotel for three or four days waiting for their connection to bring the shit across the Mexican border. Even back then, Texas was a good place to get arrested. We didn't have the connections with the Mexican traffickers. And Willie didn't know the local cops; who were straight and who were crooked.

I'm standing there in my swim trunks ready to hit the beach and I am about to go ballistic.

"Fucking Willie, that piece of shit!" I yelled at Mark. "Why did you believe that stupid prick!"

This went on for about thirty seconds. Then I thought of something.

"Mark, what are you guys driving?"

"The van."

Of course. The van. My conversion van. I'd gotten my sister Kathy to sign the registration for it, but it was a fucking jail term waiting to happen. Later I found out that the salesman at the dealership in McDonough, Georgia, had gotten suspicious when we went to buy the thing. Willie and I had crawled underneath to check for space for secret compartments, and the bastard had sidled over and heard me underneath the thing asking Willie how much coke would fit where the gas tank was.

We gutted that thing and ripped out the interior panels and created a dozen hidey-holes for merchandise. Now the van was in Texas waiting for a huge load to come across the border. Not only that, these idiots had taken my 930 slant-nose, which in the back roads of Texas might as well have been a traveling billboard that said "Hi! I'm a Drug Dealer." The operation was fucked up from beginning to end.

I told Mark to get Willie on the phone.

Willie got on the phone.

"Willie, goddamnit, get out of there right now," I said.

"It's too late. They're off-loading right now."

I said, "Oh shit."

"Don't worry, Kevin. It's done now. We'll be in Atlanta tomorrow."

I calmed down. The transfer is usually where the bust goes down. Unless the guys got unlucky at a checkpoint on the roads, they should be good. They off-loaded the merchandise and stuffed it into lettuce crates and covered it over with some fresh produce. Then they put the rest in panels that they'd had built into the interior of the van. And they jumped on the interstate. Every mile away from the transfer was golden.

Halfway back to Atlanta, Willie later told me he got an itchy feeling. He told the others he had to take a piss. They pulled into a truck stop and Willie went to the bathroom. And when he was inside, he heard the bust going down. The arrest was supposed to happen at the drop point, but they hadn't seen me there, and I was one of the main targets of the investigation. So they decided to nab them before they went out of state.

Willie must be the luckiest goddamn drug dealer ever born. Because when he saw what was going down, he bought a guy's clothes in that truck-stop bathroom and they switched outfits. Paid him four or five grand, I'm told. He walked out of there, found a ride, and called me later from forty miles down the road. I helped him get to Mexico and from there he made it to Colombia.

They got the rest of the crew holding 107 kilos of cocaine and nabbed the Mexicans with 3.8 million dollars in cash. That was always suspicious to me. Drug dealers don't order 107 kilos. You go to Colombia and you order 100 ki's, 250, 200, or 500. That load was shorted or someone took 93 ki's or 393 ki's and disappeared. Maybe it was Willie. I've wondered more than once if Willie set it all up to go down like it did. Premonition is one thing, but how he got out of that bust just defies belief.

I was oblivious to all of it. I was chilling in Daytona enjoying my Tanqueray and tonic, just like my dad, on the beach. The only thing that bothered me was that I was alone.

# CHAPTER 35

At age twenty-four, I was facing charges on the intent to distribute 107 kilos. And Texas wanted to get a hold of my ass for other charges associated with Willie's bust. The joyride was over. I knew the federal codes for trafficking and I saw a lot of hard time ahead of me.

In these kinds of cases, your sentence guidelines are decided on a point system that factors in different questions: Were weapons used during the offense? Did you attempt to obstruct justice? What is your criminal history? The higher the point total, the more time you got. I had a "total offense level" of 34 and a "criminal history category" of III. My guideline was 262 to 327 months. Unless I did something, I was conceivably facing life behind bars.

I entered the Atlanta federal pen in October. At that time, USP Atlanta was the most violent prison in the United States, bar none. In my first year, there were dozens of homicides reported on the inside. It is documented to be the most violent and dangerous prison in the entire world. If you were a federal inmate, USP Atlanta was one place you didn't want to land. It made my little stint at the Georgia state prison for the Gold Mine bust look like a trip to Chuck E. Cheese.

The Atlanta Federal Pen is a nasty piece of work. The Hartsfield Company, which owns Hartsfield International Airport, donated a 150-year lease on that land, and that penitentiary was one of the first federal pens ever built. It's six stories high and it was built starting in 1909. Believe me, it hasn't changed much since then.

You walk in through these beautiful columns made with white Georgia marble, down a main corridor into your unit, A, B, C, or D, Alpha, Bravo, Charlie, Dog. They stuck me in Charlie House when I first got there and—just my luck—it was the only cellblock that hadn't been refurbished. There was paint peeling off the walls, and it had about a hundred years of disinfectant smell that you could probably cut a couple ki's with, it was so strong.

My cell was an old-fashioned Al Capone cell, a true eight-by-ten box with two bunks and a shit jack in it. The walls were metal. Air-conditioning? In your fucking dreams. I saw as I walked in that the inmates put pieces of cardboard on the outside of the cell because they put one fan in the end of the unit and it blows down the catwalk. The guys were trying to capture the wind and bring it into their cell. Imagine that on a day when the temperature was 110 degrees in there. Fucking medieval.

It was like a 1930s movie where the guy is going to be executed and he's sweating it out in this old jail. I felt like I was transported back in time and Jimmy Cagney was going to come walking around the corner any minute. I was so pissed off I probably would have knocked him out. I would have laid out my own mother I was so angry.


Thirty-six hours after I was processed in, I was having a conversation with a member of the Lucchese crime family, who was doing a life term for murder. He was educating me as to the ins and outs of prison life. And he told me that one of two things was going to be in your mouth as an inmate: a man's cock or a cigar. And with that, he handed me a Cuban.

I lit up. I would learn to love cigars, and it started right then. The gesture made me feel a bit better about a grim situation because the Luccheses had basically granted me their respect and protection. They knew who I was and who my father was. At USP Atlanta, that was a very good thing to have.

And then I started looking around me. I saw forty-foot walls topped with razor wire. I saw helicopter wire on the yard to prevent escape by choppers and gun towers with machine guns manned twenty-four hours a day. I looked around the yard and I saw Crips and Mexican Mafia and the Aryan Brotherhood, bald-headed maniacs with swastikas tattooed on their foreheads.

And I thought to myself, "I am going to die in here."

You almost had to laugh. It was the classic good news/bad news routine. "Kevin, you have absolutely nothing to worry about. *Except that you're going to rot away in the worst federal prison in the country.*" Hey, thanks.

Right then I knew I had to get out.

After a few days I was switched to B Unit. I was not sure why, but anything at that point was an upgrade. The first floor was a series of cells on either side, and then you walked up this zigzagged stairway up to your floor. I was put on the fifth floor. The noise was just incredible and it got louder the higher you went. But at least it had been updated since 1909 and had central air and all that. But in Atlanta, if they have a disturbance—a riot or whatever—they can lock you down in your cells and they can pump knockout gas through the A/C pipes that will put you to sleep in like twenty seconds. So they can gas the entire unit and it will be as quiet as a nursery within a minute. Insane.

The feds are all about control. At every one of their penitentiaries, 4 p.m. is national lockdown. That means that every day at 4 p.m., they call "Count time" and every federal inmate in the United States of America is counted. When they have the total, they call it in to Washington and the feds there do a master count. And if one inmate within the institution is missing, then the whole country stays in lockdown. It's an unbelievable system and it gets into your head.

Cells opened at 5 a.m. and you were called to chow at 5:30. You go to the cafeteria, you eat, you go back, and then you get ready for work. They have work call at 6 or 6:15. In the Atlanta penitentiary, they make all the fatigues and mattresses for the entire U.S. military throughout the world, and there is a waiting list as long as you can see of inmates who want to work. They pay you ten cents an hour to begin and overtime goes up to $1.30 an hour. If you're a poor bastard with no family and you have no money coming in from the outside, a prison job is the only way to buy your toiletries and all the shit you need.

At 4 p.m. everyone had to be back in their cells for the national lockdown. Then we'd have chow at 5 p.m. and mail call after that, and then everyone would socialize and hear what had happened during the day. That's when all the stabbing and shit would take place, so I usually stayed in my cell. The final lockdown was at 11 p.m. on the weekend and 10 p.m. during the week. That was going to be my schedule for the rest of my life.

I was issued my prison khakis, three pair of underwear, three T-shirts, my so-called "visitation clothes," and my work clothes. I also had a copy of my paperwork, which you get when you're processed. I looked down at it and it said *Kevin Pappas vs. The United States of America.* For some reason, the full extent of my situation didn't hit me until right then. When it's you vs. the State of Georgia, that seems doable. But vs. the entire U. S. of A.? I was like, "Oh my fucking God, what have I done?" I felt a chill run up from my feet, like I was walking in ice water.

On my fifth day of being inside, there was a lot of tension in the pen. Guys were talking about an internal problem within the Nation of Islam. Outside, the Nation is a religious sect, but inside it's a prison gang. They're very easy to identify. They wear their clothes very starched, with black brogans that are polished to a high shine. They always button their top collar and they always carry their Koran with them.

I'd arrived just as a power struggle was coming to a head. One of the main Nation guys from the pen in Terre Haute was coming in and he had more seniority than the ranking guy in Atlanta. So the current leader was going to have to step down, and people were nervous because that's always a bad thing in prison. It's like a coup in a violent, unstable country. Guys do *not* want to give up their power.

I learned all of this later on. I knew nothing of this at the time. You don't ask questions in prison; it makes you look like a punk.

I was sitting at chow hall. The transfer bus had come in that morning and all the new guys were getting their first meal. Lucky me, I had sat down at the table with the new Nation guy who had just rolled in. He was happily munching on whatever garbage the prison had served up that day, when all of a sudden a Nation soldier got up from a nearby table, walked to the kitchen, and was handed a commercial can opener, which is a metal contraption in a metal sleeve that you turn by hand. Weighs about ten pounds. He pulled the sleeve out so that it almost looked like a jack for a car, and he came walking over to my table.

The chow hall was dead quiet. Guys were eating with their eyes up, not even looking at the food. The stress was so thick you could smell it. I'd never felt anything like that before.

Then there was a flash in the corner of my right eye, and the soldier came up behind the new guy and WHAAMMMM, he brought that metal sleeve down and cracked his skull wide open. I had blood and brain matter sprayed over my face and the front of my shirt. I was freaking out.

Right then an Aryan Brotherhood dude named Rico grabbed me and slammed me to the ground. "Do not look back," he whispered in my ear. "Put your head to the ground, put your arms out, and keep them there." I was a new white boy and he was protecting me as a possible recruit.

The Prison Tactical Squad (or PTS) came in and threw a series of percussion bombs, which stun you and leave you disoriented for a few minutes. The inmates were screaming, the bombs were going off, the PTS was shouting, "Get the fuck down!" and the blood was dripping down my face onto the floor. If you looked back at an officer, they'd crack your skull open with their night clubs.

So that was my introduction to the federal prison system. It was absolutely, hands down, the most insane thing I've ever experienced in my life.

It took about forty-five minutes to clear the chow hall. I went back to the unit, got my composure. One of my roommates was named Huckabee, a redneck from Knoxville, Tennessee, with a big beer belly and more schemes than you can count. He was in for embezzlement or some white-collar shit. If you wanted a dozen bananas at midnight on Saturday or a loaf of Wonder Bread, he'd find it for you—for a price. He laid out for me what had just happened. "Thanks, retard," I thought, "I could have used that information a few hours ago."

A couple of weeks later they had a movie call on Fridays for our unit. I saw everybody getting ready to go, shoving *Playboys* and newspapers in their jackets—not in the pockets, but inside. Then they zipped them up to the chin, which is something you never saw. I had no idea what they were doing. So I didn't do it. Huckabee just looked at me and lay down on his bunk—he was going to skip the movie alto-gether. But I figured, free movie? I'm there.

So they opened my cell and I walked to the auditorium. The lights were dimming as I got there, and the inmates were rushing to get in-side, being funneled from a wide hallway into a small aisle. The guy in front of me was a Puerto Rican who I later found out—story of my life—owed $2,000 to the loan sharks because he was a degenerate gambler. All of a sudden a guy appeared out of the corner of my right eye and I saw a shiv in his hand, coming down at me. I ducked left and tucked into a curled position. But he caught me in the right arm, two deep gashes as he punched forward with the shiv. *Wham, Wham.* I thought he'd gotten my kidney.

He wasn't going for me—if he had been, I'd have been dead. It was the poor Puerto Rican bastard in front of me he was after. His side was in ribbons. He bled out and died the next day. So much for enter-tainment after that.

The one thing I did know is that you never go to medical unless absolutely necessary. If you see a doctor with a knife injury, they put you on the next bus out of there. I could have gone to Leavenworth or to some hellhole in Texas. I wanted to take my chances in Atlanta. I became a self-made doctor in the pen. I wrapped up the wound with a towel and then pulled the skin together and taped the sides. The scar was ugly, but if you get out of the Atlanta pen with just a couple gashes, you're doing pretty well.

But at this rate, I figured I was going to need a fucking mortician instead of a doctor. I'd been in for only a few weeks and I was already getting cut up. Not good. I had to focus on an exit strategy.

# CHAPTER 36

Gradually, I learned the system. First I had to find out who had the power and how to stay alive. Then I put my mind to getting out.

One thing I did right off was apply to become an orderly. The orderly cleans up the unit while everyone else is at class or in the yard or whatever. Once you get that area clean, you have a few hours to yourself. I knew I'd need that time in the law library.

We had an orderly closet filled with mops and buckets and whatnot. Every day I'd go in there and get my stuff and race through the halls, mopping. I'd put a glow on those floors.

But one day, I opened the closet and saw a dead guy lying in there. I recognized him right away. He was Pops Washington, an older guy in his late fifties or early sixties. In prison, older dudes get a free pass. Once you pass your fighting prime, no one messes with you unless you do something dirty. He was sitting up, his left arm was over his stomach, his head was thrown back, and his mouth was wide open. He looked like he'd just stopped rocking while trying to cure a stomachache, but underneath the sleeve of his arm I could see blood.

Pops was a lifer. He'd been inside for thirty years on a murder bid. He had an appeal in for clemency and sentence reduction. That much time gets you respect inside, and with his age, Pops should have just been cruising.

But I found out later he got into a regular game of Georgia Scam, which is also called Tonk. It's a dice game, like craps in the casinos. You play for cigarettes or money or whatever you got. And another inmate thought Pops was cheating him. He didn't say a thing. The killer didn't want to get time added on to his sentence, so he waited. And he caught Pops out, stuck him, and then threw him in the mop room. They have a drain in there and the blood was seeping into it. And no one goes into the mop room but the orderlies.

Now, I was green but I knew you don't go tell the officer, "Excuse me, sir, there's a dead body in my closet. What should I do?" You just shut your mouth and go back to your unit. You decide not to use the mop that afternoon, let someone else from another unit find that motherfucker. Because if you report it, you're suspect number one. The best thing to do is walk away. They tell you never to volunteer for anything in the army; well, in prison, that goes double. You get investigated by the hacks and you get looked at sideways by the guy's friends. You'll get it from both ends.

That incident stayed with me. It helped keep me focused on one objective: to get the fuck out. I mean, really. Dead over a lousy pack of cigarettes? These guys were animals and I was not going to be a part of this world, ever. So I had to learn the system that put me here. Gathering information, watching every move, putting a plan in place with a real exit strategy this time. That was my objective, and everything I did from that point forward was related to that mission, and only that mission.

I began to watch and learn in order to survive. There are a million things to learn in the federal joint. You don't roll up one pant leg, or even allow one to creep up your leg, because that's how the Crips and Bloods identify themselves inside. Left pant leg is Crips, right is Bloods. Bloods wear their hair in pigtails, Crips in cornrows. The Puerto Rican gangs wear the front of their shirts hanging out with the back tucked in. The tattoos could take you months to learn: If you had 13 on your left wrist bone, you were a marijuana smuggler, as "M" is the thirteenth letter of the alphabet. If you had three "prison dots" there, you'd served thirty years, one dot for every decade. A spiderweb on the elbow was Aryan Brotherhood. It went on and on.

Another thing you don't do in the pen is talk to anyone on staff. Every chow hall, the whole prison administration would line up along a wall: case managers, unit managers, psychiatrists, wardens, assistant wardens, so that you can go and either make an appointment with them or ask them a question. But it was useless. Anyone who stepped out of line would automatically be considered a snitch, even if you're asking about a death in the family or requesting that the TV be tuned to *The Simpsons*. Doesn't matter.

Instead, what you do is you send a kite to your management office and then the management office within your unit sends it to the warden. But those kites are very rarely answered. So the prison has it set up so that prisoners are cut off from any form of help. And if someone from the outside protests, they can say, "But we line up every day ready for questions." As if they don't know that's a death sentence for any inmate who's dumb enough to take advantage of it.

The only time I ever saw someone use the chow hall system is when one guy shanked another. He stabbed the shit out of the guy, dropped the shank, walked over to the warden, put his hands behind his back, and said, "Take me away."

They took him away. That time the system worked perfectly.

The one thing I will say for the federal system is that you get a better class of inmate there. I met a lot of interesting people, the cream of the crop as far as crime goes. One of my favorites was Louis F. He was a famous race car driver who got into the drug trade and became a real innovator. He basically invented the use of seamless-hull cigarette boats for bringing the dope across the water. He became one of the largest smugglers in south Florida, and the warden had decided that he was a Hannibal Lecter kind of mastermind criminal. So they had him chained in his own cell. He was a real nutcase, dangerous as hell. He had a list of everyone indicted with him that he had torn out from the *Miami Herald* and he just hung it in the front of his cell. He was saying, "I'm watching you. You flip on me and I will reach you." No one flipped on him.

Another guy I got to know real well was Wayne Williams, the so-called Atlanta child killer. He was in my unit. I could recite his case for you from memory. I had a tendency to sort of get into people's cases and look at them analytically. So I ended up talking to Wayne at length.

Wayne was the law librarian in the prison, and a very smart man. Very, very soft-spoken and extremely well educated. A very compassionate guy. He was so skinny he looked like he'd been eaten up with AIDS, but that was just his build. We got to chatting and sharing the details of our lives and our cases. Wayne was very open with me about the injustices he'd seen within the system and how he had used this opportunity as the law librarian to study his case and possibly affect his outcome through appeals.

After going over his case with him detail by detail, I came to believe he was wrongly charged. The evidence that he was convicted on was based on a single dog hair that they found on the floorboard of his car and under the fingernail of one of the children. The problem that I had with the evidence is that the dog hair didn't match the dog that Wayne owned. The government also claimed that he threw the body of this young child named Lubie Jeter over the front of his car into the Chattahoochee River. Well, if you know Wayne Williams, he's 125 pounds soaking fucking wet. And if you've ever felt a dead body, it's deadweight. There ain't no damn way that boy could have done the things they said he did. No way. Not the size of Lubie Jeter when he died.

Was Wayne Williams railroaded? If you want my opinon, hell yes, he was. Why do I feel this? Because I looked him straight in the eyes and I said to him, "Son, is there anything you want to say to me?" He told me he had shared everything he knew. I believed him because I saw into his heart. And it only deepened my hatred for the system that put him in prison.

Wayne's case went to appeal, but some of the evidence that they claim would have exonerated him had inci-fucking-dentally come up missing in the Georgia Bureau of Investigation evidence room. The theory behind his innocence is that these murders occurred during a time of high racial tension in Georgia, and in fact, in the rest of the country. And if the world had found out that it might have been a white supremacy group or maybe some white sicko killing all these children, there would have been a race war.

If I had to take a guess, I think Wayne was probably gay and he may have even messed around with some of the dead kids. But if you would have watched the situation and looked at the evidence and listened to this man talk, you would then know that there is a hell of a lot more to the story than what meets the eye. Wayne's case was an education for me. I saw how some circumstantial evidence could get you life in a hellhole like Atlanta.

I know what you're thinking: "Every convict says he's innocent." Yeah, a lot of them do. But there are real tragic cases inside the bars that get ignored because of the liars and the connivers.

And I met enough of them to know that justice in America is a roll of the dice, and I wasn't going to be a part of that crap game. I wanted to know where everything that related to my case was located in the library, and it was my goal to dissect his head to get to the legal shit I needed to get me the fuck out of there.

# CHAPTER 37

In those first few months in the pen, I was consumed by anger. When you deal with death—and that's exactly what you're living with in the pen when you're doing a long bid—you go through these phases of loss just like anyone else. First you experience shock, and in your mind you try to turn the clock back to prevent this shit from happening. Like with Jose or Robbie. Then you move on to remorse and mourning, where you talk to God and ask for strength. But when God doesn't hear you or do anything for your pain, then you move on to anger. I was in phase three of this fucking death sentence. I had been here before but was able to get loaded or something to work it out. Not this time. I was one rage-filled dude.

Where was the fucking loyalty, the friendships I'd built over ten years and more? Dead and fucking gone, that's where they were. No one stepped up to the plate for me. Willie had set up the deal for the 107 ki's, but here I was doing the jail time, while he'd skipped out and was probably holed up in Colombia with a fine-ass bitch and enough money to get him through the rest of his life. The Colombians had disappeared when I was indicted. Mark Jordan was a no-show. All those friendships that I'd built up over the years as the go-to guy in Atlanta had evaporated. And my father? Please. Not even a word from *him*.

I felt that loyalty didn't exist. The whole idea had been poisoned for me by my father, my own blood. I knew there was something, someone he could have bribed. I mean we're talking business here. It's not like I squealed on anyone. I was simply managing business and this is what I get? When he left me to rot in Atlanta, I was hurt, sure, but I wasn't surprised.

So you better believe that when a little light was shined into my darkness, I was more than ready to take advantage of it.


One day in my third month in the pen, I was called to one of the conference rooms where inmates meet their lawyers. I had no attorney meetings on the docket so I had no idea what was going on. I sat there in handcuffs and leg chains. There was a knock on the door and two FBI agents in suits walked in, showed me their IDs, and said they wanted to show me something.

"Bring it on," I said.

One of them took out a briefcase and took a stack of about five or six Polaroid pictures out. They placed them on the table. It was an object that was charred, with pieces of red material and white here and there. It took me a few seconds to realize I was looking at a human body. The red was bloody flesh and the white was bone or teeth. Someone had obviously poured a few gallons of gasoline on the sucker and lit him up.

"Jesus Christ, what happened to *that* bastard?"

They didn't answer me. "Can you identify this body?"

I looked at them as if they'd just asked me if I was Jimmy Hoffa.

"Are you kidding me? His own mother couldn't do that. It's burned up."

"We understand that."

"You're the cops. Do a set of prints on him, check his fucking teeth, put some barbecue sauce on him and see how he tastes. Because I don't know."

"Can't," the lead guy said. "Most of the teeth have been extracted and the fingers are too badly burned."

"OK. So what do you want me to do?"

The guy took a small bag out of the briefcase, pulled out some gold jewelry, and placed it on the table. There was a Bell & Ross watch and a bracelet and a couple of chains.

I knew right away it was my stuff. I stamped all my pieces with the Gold Mine logo, and besides, these were custom. I sucked in a breath.

I'd made these pieces for Willie.

"Whose jewelry is this?"

I looked at the guy. A million scenarios were running through my mind. I knew the feds probably had surveillance photos of Willie from the Texas deal at the very least, which meant they had photos of him wearing the stuff. This could be a setup, but there was no point in lying.

"Where'd you get this?"

"Don't get cute, Pappas. You made this jewelry, right?"

"Yeah."

"So who'd you make it for?"

"You know as well as I do. Willie Moises."

The lead guy smiled for the first time.

"You're stating for the record that this jewelry was made expressly for the use of Willie Moises and that you saw it in his possession before his disappearance?"

I told them, yeah, that's what I was saying.

"So where'd you find it?" I asked.

"The jewelry was found on and about the person of this John Doe, on Alligator Alley in the Everglades. We believe it is the body of Willie Moises."

I nodded. And I started to laugh.

"What's so funny?"

"Funny?" I said. "Not a damn thing, special agent."

Fucking Willie. He'd outsmarted us all. I wondered who the body belonged to. Because I will give you ten to one odds Willie Moises is within a ten-mile radius of Bogotá, Colombia, right now, and he's living very, very well.

Months later I was in general population when they brought this runner in who'd gotten popped coming in from Cartagena with a load of dope sewn into his luggage. He was a short, dark-skinned Colombian guy and we were just shooting the shit, talking about Bogotá, about the cartels and the whole game.

"You were a partner of a friend of mine," he said.

"Oh, yeah, who?" I said. I'd had lots of "partners."

He smiled. "Let's just say that Willie-Willie says hello."

Man, what did he just say? No one called Willie by that name except the Colombians who knew him real well. This had to be legit. I just let out a long, low whistle.

The bitterness came later. Right then, I had to give it to the bastard. Wille'd arranged his exit like he was directing a gangster movie. And I was the fall guy.

No hard feelings, Willie. But if I see you on Peachtree Street one of these days, motherfucker, you *better* be running.

A few days later, I was sitting there in B Unit listening to the howling and the banging that makes prisons sound like a cross between a zoo and an auto mechanic's shop. I was wondering what my exit strategy was. I had nothing left to trade for my freedom. Except information. The FBI guys had given me an idea: I knew a lot of people, most of them mobsters and dopers. That information had to be valuable. And since no one was stepping up to get me out of this hell, I'd have to do it my own damn self.

I let it be known to the authorities that I had information to offer on a wide range of crimes. But I also made it clear that I wasn't going to rat on anyone. Not my style. Ratting is when you sell out your partners in crime for a lighter sentence. I wouldn't do that. I wasn't going to snitch on the Band of Five or the Ochoas or any of my close partners. They were off-limits. I had a code.

I'd been into the books when I fell on some stuff. Some new rulings in the laws, and I was primed and ready to test the system. I peeled back that stinking onion called a judicial system and I was ready to make the move. I knew everyone worth knowing in the Atlanta underworld and I had connections up and down the East Coast. I could get intel on crimes that hadn't even happened yet or cold cases that the feds were stuck on. That kind of prime shit had to be worth something.

Besides, I was much more comfortable working with the feds. They were at a level I could deal with, do business with, and that's all it was about at that stage.

One of the first deals I made was for a cocaine connection that I knew about involving my Uncle Theo. I knew one of the main crooked officials at Tampa's Port Authority; he was the guy who got the payoff when ships had to come in and unload their cargo without any inspection. He told me that Uncle Theo, the snake wrestler and naturalist who dabbled in big coke deals, was bringing loads in through Tampa. I'd held on to that info; I knew a hole card when I saw one.

I gathered more information on the Tampa drops from guys—both in the legit world and in the drug business—that I had working for me on the outside. It turned out my intel matched up perfectly with what the feds knew, but added a few additional key elements of information that tied things together. They'd been watching my family and Uncle Theo for a while now and my intel added fuel to the fire at just the wrong time for the Pappases. They were bringing a truckload of coke in from Colombia. That's right, a truckload. Three tons of coke. Estimated street value: well over a billion dollars.

The semi with the coke packed into a shipment of wood was driving down U.S. 19 when the feds hit it. There were representatives of six agencies involved—everyone from the FBI, the DEA, even Interpol, who'd helped track the coke from Colombia. Helicopters descended out of nowhere and landed on the highway while agents swarmed all over the truck. The driver and his partner didn't go down easy—they pulled out guns and started blazing away at the agents, who fired right back. Nobody died, but when the agents pulled open those rear doors, dug into the loads of wood, and found all of that coke, a few people probably would have liked to.

The feds never got enough to get an indictment on the Pappases, but I knew losing more than a billion dollars' worth of coke was going to put someone in a world of hurt. They did end up nailing my Uncle Theo to the wall. He's still doing time in federal prison on that deal.

You know what? Fuck them. Fuck Theo and fuck the whole Pappas outfit. That's how I felt. I had bigger problems than worrying about people who wouldn't even shake my hand and call me family. Survival, to name one. So I bounced between the law library and the gym, getting my mind and my body ready for the next opportunity and final test.

The intel had given me an in with the feds. Now I had a buyer and all I had to do was manage the gathering of intel and package it for distribution. Before I'd been just another convict trying to parlay some information into a reduced sentence. But after the Tarpon Springs information, suddenly I was the golden boy. But that would last only as long as my information did.

# CHAPTER 38

There was this green agent who'd been a federal probation officer before joining the FBI and was going through the training at Quantico. Her name was Agent Gardner. She was just out of the academy and looking to make a name for herself. They assigned her to me because my previous agent, Special Agent Stacy Wright, was reassigned to the high-profile John Gotti case. When a criminal is assigned to a federal agent under organized crime status, it is the rule of thumb that the subject is under that agent's supervision until the agent either retires or is reassigned. In my case, Agent Wright was going to be a tough act to follow. She was a highly regarded organized crime and drug task force agent who'd been able to gain the much needed respect to do business on the streets. Agent Gardner definitely had some big shoes to fill, and I was ready to assist her in any way I could.

However, as a newbie, her superiors told her to be very careful with me and her other special subjects. But I knew I would earn her trust and respect, and once I did, it would be smooth sailing from there.

I was in the Atlanta Federal Building at 75 Spring Street on the seventeenth floor, which is where the debriefing rooms were. Gardner walked in and introduced herself. "I'm your new case officer," she said. "And I understand you're a real ladies' man."

I laughed and said, "Who gave you that bogus information?"

"I've got my sources."

"Better check 'em," I said.

She was a hardnose. She may have been new, but I could see that she'd earned every bit of authority she had. And she wasn't about to let some fast-talking Greek doper bamboozle her. She was also a southern girl, 5′6″, 127 pounds, sandy blond hair, very cute, pointed features, very good-looking. I could relate to southern girls. They were my favorite.

Gardner came right up to my face and pointed a finger at me. "You're not going to fool me. I'm not going to play into your bullshit, got it?"

I held up my hands. "Gardner," I said. "You're either going to love me or you're going to hate me by the time we're done working with each other. But honestly, my bet is you're going to wind up loving me."

"I don't think so," she said and she turned and walked out.

*Oh but you're wrong*, I said to myself. I had the street knowledge and now I had an agent eager to use it. I finally saw a way out of USP Atlanta.

Over the next several weeks I began to provide intel to Gardner on cases of interest that other agencies were also working. It dumbfounded them how this new, young agent was able to obtain exact information that other senior agents were unable to come up with. After all, she was yet to be a part of their "boys' club," so how did she manage to crack these cases? Her career accelerated while I earned points toward my freedom. We built an understanding because we knew where each other stood. We also knew the line that divided us and we never crossed it.

You know, the strength of law enforcement is only as good as the trust built between the officers and their confidants on the streets. If they break that confidence, it's a lose-lose situation where the game gets dangerous and nobody wins.

Five weeks after meeting Gardner, I was moved to a holding facility in Conyers, Georgia, without anyone giving me a reason. Two federal marshals picked me up, signed me out of the State of Georgia's custody and into federal custody. I kept asking the transport warden what the deal was, but for once he wouldn't give me a clue. "You'll find out" was all I heard. It was top-secret. I was racking my brain to figure out what I could have done wrong in Conyers during my drug-dealing days. Did I have some outstanding charges that I didn't even know about? My heart sank.

I walked into the holding facility. They held me in a unit separate from all the other inmates. I was there for about twenty-four hours, and they wouldn't even let me get a phone call. Finally, the next morning, I was called out of the cell. They took me to a meeting room, but there was no lawyer or prosecutor there. What the fuck was going on?

Ten minutes later, the door opened and Gardner walked in, followed by two FBI special agents I'd never seen before. I looked at Gardner and raised my eyebrows, like "What's going on here?"

"Kev," she said, "We've got a couple guys here who want to ask you some questions."

"Am I in trouble?" I asked.

"Oh no, you're not in trouble," she said. I trusted Gardner enough by then to believe that. I relaxed. Gardner introduced Special Agent Mollohan. He was this tall, thin dude, around 6'1", fair-skinned with red hair. He had the temperament and the look of an Irishman. I should know; I was raised by one. The number two agent had an Italian name that I forgot. Agent Mollohan was the lead agent and he did all the talking. They were both dressed in Windbreakers and dress slacks, no suits, no ties. They said they were with the Organized Crime Task Force of the Southern District in Tampa Bay. I just nodded.

Mollohan eyed me for a minute. He also eyed Gardner. I think he was checking on any body language between us. "Kevin, you know you've got a lot of problems. It's going to be a long time before you see the light of day."

"I appreciate that." I was keeping my mouth shut until I could find out what his game was all about.

"I want to ask you something," Mollohan said as he leaned toward me, with his hands on the desk. "You know that the state authorities take our recommendations very seriously. If I could recommend, because you know we can never make a promise, Kevin, but if I could recommend that your sentence be reduced to time served for some work that you did for us, would you be interested?"

I paused. The room was so silent it was deafening. I said, "I'd be a fool not to say yes, sir. But can I take a moment to discuss this with Agent Gardner?"

He gestured toward her to say, *go ahead.*

Gardner and I walked over to the corner, and I said, "Listen, is this for real?"

She looked at me straight in the eye. "Kevin, just answer the questions truthfully. I can't discuss the details with you. But you have my word this is on the up-and-up."

That's all I needed to hear. I walked back to the desk, sat down, spread my hands out, and said, "OK, what can I do for you gentlemen and what can you do for me?"

Mollohan smiled. He nodded to the other agent, who started pulling a file out of his briefcase. "Well, first of all, I want you to look at something."

The agent handed him a file stamped "Confidential" in a red stamp, just like the movies, but this one had a government seal on it. Mollohan opened it up and pulled a large piece of paper out of it, and as he turned it to face me, I could see that it was some kind of chart. Then he laid it on the table. It wasn't a chart. It was a family tree. My family tree. And it had photos running across the top. Staring up at me were the faces of Lukie Pappas, Yani Pappas, and George Pappas. Below Lukie's photo was my name and my mug shot and it had "Pappas, Kevin Lucas, a.k.a. Cunningham, Kevin Lee, illegitimate son." There was a line connecting me and Lukie.

I was shocked. "Oh my fucking God, what is this about?"

The Pappases were the farthest things from my mind. I'd done so many deals and broken so many laws that I thought the feds wanted to question me about Willie Moises or the 5100 Group. I never in a million years imagined that they would take me all the way back to my childhood, to where it had all begun.

"I think you know the deal," said Mollohan. I could see they were pleased that I was shocked, that I wasn't denying the relationship with Lukie.

I smiled, thinking to myself: *I can outsmart this guy and eat him up for lunch. I just have to play it cool now and keep my anger in check.* I composed myself and I said, "Shocked? You don't know the half of it, man."

"Kevin, we have a series of questions we'd like to get your answers on. First of all, I'd like you to ID some of these people."

He had a stack of six or seven photos in his hand. They were a mix of what looked like surveillance pictures, mug shots, and faces that had obviously been cut out of other pictures. Some had names beneath them, some didn't.

He laid down a picture of Louis Kon, one of my father's advisers.

"Can you tell me who that is? Real names and street names, if you have it."

I knew I was taking the first step of a long road. That's how they do it—they ask you to do something harmless, like ID a few photos. They probably knew who these people were, anyway. It's just to get you into their club, to make you a part of their conspiracy.

A Greek phrase popped into my head. It's one I heard all the time in Tarpon Springs growing up. The translation goes like this: "*He who reveals his secret makes himself a slave.*"

But I was already a slave to the state of Georgia so I just took a breath.

Count me in, bitches. Anything to see the outside again.

"Yeah, I know him. That's Louis Kon."

They didn't confirm or deny. Their faces were like masks. They laid out some more photos. Dozens and dozens.

"That's Yani Pappas. That's Uncle Theo, and that's Nickie V." And on and on. Hours went by, but it felt like minutes. My mind had not been exercised so much in years and it felt good.

Between the family tree and the photos, they had a lot of the Pappas organization. Not everybody, but the leadership and the lieutenants. I was impressed, actually.

Mollohan turned the photos over. There was a pause. All three of the agents were looking at me.

"Kevin," he said. "Would you be willing to assist us in an investigation of the organization and the activity of the Pappas family and those individuals that surround it?"

I had to let that sink in.

"What's in it for me? I'm not some Boy Scout, Mollohan. I don't do these things for fucking merit badges."

Mollohan smiled. "You can pack your bags. You can go and we'll get with you in a couple of months once this thing gets rigged."

I said, "You're kidding, right?"

"No, you are at this moment in federal custody. And we petitioned the judge, and he agreed that you can be released."

I said, "I'll do it."

There wasn't a shade of gray in my answer. My father had been rejecting me for more than a decade. The line connecting him and me on that family tree was the only thing in the world that said I was his son, the only official recognition. He had so many chances to love me and claim me. Now he had to pay the price.

Revenge is very Greek. Read the fucking plays. Now Lukie was going to feel it like he never felt it before.

I was released from prison that very afternoon. I didn't know their plan, but while they were busy off writing their script, I was out in the fresh, free air, away from the disgusting hole they buried me in. I had some business of my own to take care of.

CHAPTER 39

The deal was for me to go back to Tarpon Springs, hang out with my old friends, gain access and trust, and slowly infiltrate my father's group. In the beginning, Mollohan didn't specify what kind of deal he wanted me to arrange with my dad; that would have handcuffed me and brought me under suspicion. He told me to play it by ear, to see what developed naturally. My code name was Apollo. The feds must have been reading their Greek mythology. If I was Apollo, that made my father Zeus, the king of the gods.

Not for long, motherfucker.

I walked out of prison full of anger and animosity toward my so-called father. Fifteen years of denial and disrespect from Lukie was enough. I could put that bastard away without batting an eyelash. I *wanted* to bring him down.

I was flown down to Tampa on a Marshals' plane and my handlers asked me where I wanted to stay. I told them I liked to stay at the Hilton at Sand Key, so they put me in a corner room on the seventh floor, overlooking the ocean. The hotel had a few rooms set up as efficiencies and this was one. I checked in, hit the beach, and had my first cocktail. I felt like I'd been raised from the dead. Lazarus had nothing on me.

I spent the few first weeks just acclimating and getting used to civilian life again. I tried not to think about my mission. I bought some new clothes and after a couple of months I moved back to Tarpon Springs. I got a three-bedroom apartment by the water, courtesy of the U.S. Government, and a per diem of $500 a day.

I made the rounds. I went to the Costas Restaurant, Paul's Shrimp House, and Barnacles Bar and saw my old friends from Tarpon High. I was interested only in the Greek dudes. Most of them had done well for themselves. They were now in the lower echelons of the power structure: They were lawyers, fishing boat owners, real estate guys. And some of them were moving into the life of the Greek mob as captains.

Tarpon Springs is like the smallest small town in America. Three minutes after someone connected to the Greek power structure walks into one of the harbor-front restaurants or drives down the main strip in his car, the whole town knows. I drove into Tarpon Springs in June of '91, and I'm telling you, I could see the little old Greek ladies who ran the jewelry stores run to their back rooms where the phones were. I could feel the news buzzing in the air. It was exactly like I'd left it. Not a thing had changed. I smelled the Greek food and I heard the hawkers crying out that the last tour boat of the day was leaving and, honestly, I wanted to cry.

No matter how much the people in it have done you wrong, your hometown is your hometown. There were so many memories here, it was like every street corner had its own ghosts. As a kid, I'd dreamt of returning as a big man, a player, what the Greeks call a *padaia*, who had conquered the outside world and earned my father's respect. But that hadn't happened.

When I smelled that salt air, something changed inside of me. I'd come back as an informant to bring down my father and anyone else that the net fell on. I knew that I could end up implicating some of my childhood friends, the Greek boys who eleven years before had charged out of Greektown and come to the Sahara to fight for me when I'd gotten into a hassle with Brian Stewart. My brothers in arms. The guys who had stood up for me.

All those memories came back to me now. All that culture that I wanted to be part of for so many years. Now I was coming back as a destroyer of that culture. How'd I go so far astray from my childhood dreams? If I did what the feds wanted me to, the Pappases and Tarpon Springs would never be the same. Every nasty secret, every bit of corruption, and every connection to the judges and the senators would come out. The "godfathers of night" would be thrown into a harsh, unfriendly light and some of them would probably spend the rest of their lives in jail.

These were the men who had patted my head and praised me when I was Greek-dancing on bright afternoons when I was ten and eleven, never knowing how much those words meant to me. These were the men I wanted to become. And even though they were as crooked as they came, they were also decent men in other parts of their lives. They were fathers who would die for their kids and they were patriots who fought for this country, and they all had the same Greek qualities: passion for life, kindness, absolute loyalty.

And as much as I hated my father and wanted revenge, there was also a part of me that said, "This is your blood. There is nothing lower than a man who betrays his own blood."

The mission changed. Putting my father away wasn't going to be as easy as I thought.

One of the things that makes Tarpon Springs so different from any other place in America is the shrines. People who feel they've been blessed by a saint or by God will build a shrine to them right in the middle of a residential neighborhood. People who have the same affliction—cancer, alcoholism, a missing child—go there and pray.

My favorite was a shrine to St. Michael, who is a very typical Greek saint. Michael was the archangel, the good angel of death, the general of God's army. The Greeks call him *Archistrategos*, Supreme Commander of the Heavenly Armies. The gangsters love him, too. He is God's enforcer.

Sometime in the 1940s, a local eleven-year-old kid named Alex Koolianis was diagnosed with an inoperable brain tumor. He was in a hospital in a coma, twenty-four hours from death, when his family brought the icon of St. Michael the Archangel to his bedside. The next day he woke up. He told his family the Archangel had come to him in a dream, and the sick boy had promised the saint that, if God let him live, he would build a shrine to St. Michael in Tarpon Springs. The doctors checked him over and all signs of the brain tumor had disappeared. He walked out of the hospital and lived for another sixty-eight years. His family built a beautiful shrine on Hope Street in Tarpon Springs.

From the outside, the shrine looks like a small, white house. But as soon as you walk inside, you see these narrow pews and, on the wall facing them, the portraits of Michael the Archangel. Michael with a sword fighting the devil. Michael at the gates of paradise. Michael battling a dragon. The whole wall is covered with these paintings that showed struggle, death. The place is as quiet as a tomb and there's an old Greek lady who takes care of the place, selling tapers to light the candles.

As a kid, I would go to the shrine when I felt like I couldn't handle the stress that was tearing me apart. It was either that or the local crack house. Looking at those paintings of Michael—God's warrior, a man of action like myself—I was at peace for a moment. Most shrines show Christian heroes being stoned or crucified or whatever and turning the other cheek. Not fucking likely, in my case. It wasn't my style. But Michael was different. He shoved his sword through the throat of the Devil, and *that* I could get with. Michael's world was my world.

I sat there for hours sometimes, praying to God to give me strength to do what I had to do. I asked him to open his ears to me, the ones that had been closed by my father's curse.

"Show me the way," I would say. "Show me that you haven't forsaken me." And I would look at St. Michael's face, waiting for an answer.

My reputation had preceded me in Tarpon Springs. The locals knew I was a big-time doper, and they knew that I'd gotten out of the first bid, the Gold Mine arrest, through payoffs and influence. I thought I'd have to create a cover story as to why I was free, but they just assumed the Colombians had gotten me out again, and I went with it.

I started doing small deals. At first, it was diamonds. I still had connections in the jewelry business and I got some hot diamonds—from where, I can't say—and I sold them around town for a big discount. That got me noticed.

All the time, I was talking to Mollohan. He was a straight-arrow annoying motherfucker, but he didn't lie to me. What the feds wanted was to get Lukie on a CCE, or "Continuing Criminal Enterprise" rap, under Title 21, Section 848 (c)(2) of the Federal code. It's similar to RICO: a law aimed at nailing the guys behind the guys, the racketeers who organize the deals to bring coke into the country, or fence stolen diamonds, or sell auto parts from stripped-down cars in the Bronx. The masterminds.

To make a CCE charge stick, you need to have the suspect nailed for two separate criminal acts. That was my assignment: Get Lukie to admit on tape to financing drug deals, or bid-rigging, or fixing a judge, or whatever the fuck he may have been up to that month. I would then have to testify that I witnessed Lukie being involved in other crimes as well.

I started going into my father's restaurant and hanging out at the bar. The first time, I saw him and my heart stopped. I sat down and nodded at him and he just stared at me with those brown eyes, then looked away. He looked older and frailer. He had liver spots on his hands and he'd lost some weight. I hadn't expected that. In my mind, he was always the vital, big-time mobster who just exuded life. But now he almost looked like an old man.

We didn't speak. I'm sure he thought I was back to ask him for his blessing again. But that goddamn era was over. I was here for something else.

Slowly I eased my way into Lukie's circle. I sold him some diamonds for twenty cents on the dollar, including a beautiful five-carat stone that I got from my contact in New York. I dropped it off at the restaurant along with some smaller pieces. Lukie always wanted the best stones. Two days later I saw him on Dodecanese Boulevard near the harbor. It was sunset and he was leaning back on his Thunderbird talking to an old crone in a black dress.

I pulled up in my Porsche.

"Lukie," I called.

He looked up, said something to the woman, then walked over.

"What'd you do, give that five-carat diamond to your wife or what?" I said. "Did she like that shit or did you give it to the whore you're fucking?"

That's how we talked. Not father to son. It was gangster to gangster.

He laughed. "Got any more?"

"Jesus Christ. How many bitches you got, Lukie?"

"More than you, cocksucker."

I laughed. "Lukie, you'd keel over and die if one of my girlfriends even winked at you. Stick to the old broads."

He waved me off and I peeled out.

# CHAPTER 40

Finally, after three months of working the restaurants and streets of Tarpon Springs, the day came, August 12, 1991. Mollohan thought we were ready. I'd spoken to Lukie about financing a mid-level coke deal—twenty ki's—and he was comfortable enough with me that I could ask him about his business. He'd accepted me as a gangster. Now I had to get him on tape.

I'll remember that day until I'm on my deathbed. Almost minute to minute. What really made the hairs on the back of my neck bristle was the fact that later that afternoon I was going to have to choose between spending the rest of my life behind bars or signing my own death warrant. And you thought you had bad days. Fuck you.

There's a saying that in August the devil prefers Hell to Florida because it's cooler. It was barely half past nine in the morning, and I already wanted to climb out of my sweat-soaked skin. But the ninety-seven degrees of mercury and an equal dose of humidity added to my anxiety—I felt I was a hair's breadth away from having a stroke.

I checked my watch again—the diamond-crusted Rolex Masterpiece that had been given to me by Rosario Flores. He was a high-ranking soldier in the Ochoa family. The Rolex had more than eight carats of diamonds in the bezel alone.

"Calm down, buddy," I said to myself. The first sign of a hidden agenda is a guy who keeps checking the time. Bad motherfuckers don't do that. I breathed deeply. At first Mollohan didn't want to give me the watch back, thinking I could hock it and flee the country. Then he'd said they didn't know where my shit was, so I told them. It was sealed in envelope number AG-134-7 in the evidence vault at the FBI's Atlanta Bureau.

"They know me, they know my style. I ain't going in there naked as a two-cent piker," I told Mollohan. They got the watch. And my chains, and my rings. But most important, they gave me back my Band of Five medallion. I'd made a new one for myself after putting my old one in Jose's casket. I picked it up and ran my finger across the portrait of Alexander on the front. Two of the men who'd worn this— Rob and Jose—were dead, and one, slippery Willie, was missing. I wondered if I'd passed on a curse by giving it to the boys and whether that curse was now passing on to me.

I'd gotten the jewelry when they miked me up in the Tampa Hilton. Mollohan and his team had met me there at seven a.m. He brought the coffee and bagels. I brought a nasty attitude. I was still so conflicted in my mind about what was going down that I wanted to fuck with Mollohan. Maybe in the back of my mind I thought he'd call the thing off if I pissed him off bad enough. Not a fucking chance. They treated me with kid gloves. I was the investment that was just about to pay off.

I stripped my shirt off and they placed the wire down the center of my chest, with the wire resting near my collarbone. I was wearing a blue and white Hawaiian shirt and shorts, and they stuck the module just above my tailbone. It felt like I had a thin snake taped to my chest. Sweat was pouring off of me and I felt like my rib cage was shrinking on my lungs.

As the tech guy made the final adjustments, I looked up at Mollohan. He was standing there, with his hand on his chin, looking at me like I was a store mannequin.

"You sure this thing works, pencil pusher?" I said.

"Don't worry about our end," he said. "We've done this a few times before, in case you didn't know."

"Lukie's not some surfer selling grass," I shot back. "He's never been to prison because he's smarter than you cocksuckers. So if you fuck this up, I'm a dead man."

Mollohan just smiled at me. I had no illusions; he didn't care whether I lived or died.

We finished up and I headed down to Tarpon Springs in my slant-nose Porsche. It was five and a half hours until my meeting with Lukie, and I had a stop I needed to make first. I had plenty of time—too much— to think of all the ways this afternoon could get fucked up and how quickly I could be lying facedown in the gutter with my throat cut or a bullet through my forehead. I phoned Lukie that morning and we agreed to meet later. He had invited me down to his restaurant, but I told him I didn't want to talk business in front of his brothers. It was a private matter, so he agreed to meet me at a strip mall in Tarpon Springs at three in the afternoon.

Nice and open and nice and light. Daytime rendezvous in crowded places, that was my style ever since Jose and I got jacked in Miami all those years before. You might get shot, but you have a fighting chance. Maybe the guys aiming for you hesitate that one extra second before pulling out their pieces and unloading a magazine or two in your ass, or, if you were really lucky and the place was crowded, a few innocent bystanders might be kind enough to take a couple of bullets intended for you.

I was on the hunt for something important, and I knew one place that might have it. I drove the convertible down Drew Street in Clear-water; I was doing fifty in a thirty zone. It's hard to drive a Porsche any slower—they idle at twenty-five. I loved the feeling of speed. Some guys took it up the nose, but I loved the feeling under the hood.

Turning right onto Ft. Harrison, I parked in front of Argosy's Rare & Vintage Book Store. Checking my rearview mirror, I watched no fewer than three chase cars pulling over as two passed by me. They didn't bother hiding their surveillance; there was no need to. Besides, depending on how this went down with Lukie, I might even be glad to see these assholes. Without even looking up, I could hear the rotor blades of the Bell-UH chopper hovering above the low-lying commercial buildings of downtown Clearwater.

I went inside Argosy. I'd been in there a bunch of times, and bought and sold dozens of books to or from the owner, an old geezer named Mr. Sweeney. Funny, I never read a damned one of them. Nor did I give a shit about collecting them either. Me and my guys used the place to stash drugs and hot stones. For all I know, we tore out the pages of the Gutenberg Bible.

I guess when you already know you're going to hell, fucking up a few old books doesn't weigh extra heavy on the conscience. But today, I wasn't there to ruin any of old man Sweeney's precious books or retrieve some kilos. I was here to find a book.

"Can I help you, son?" said Sweeney, as he came out from behind a podium on which was spread a rare world atlas. Suddenly I felt really guilty. That is one of the first emotions you lose in my business. Guilt and remorse get you busted or killed. But there was something in his fragile voice, and in the word he used, "son."

"I'm looking for a copy of the *Iliad*."

"Ah yes, I have many," he said. "Do you want the Lattimore or the Pope translation?"

"Um, I was hoping you had one in the original Greek," I said.

Sweeney smiled. "The mother tongue."

Sweeney moved a ladder along its brass rails until it came to rest against a bookcase whose contents had an inch of dust on them. He scurried up a few steps. As I glanced at the various spines, it didn't seem that the books were organized by title *or* by author. This old goat must have known where every single book was by memory.

"Here," he said as he handed me a red leather-bound volume. "It's from 1849—Loeb Classical Library." The old man was almost spitting he was so fucking excited.


I headed north on Ft. Harrison, which was the old Highway 19. As I passed through Dunedin, the road passed near enough to the sea for me to see the turquoise waters of the intracoastal. A scattering of mangrove-covered islets, and the Gulf of Mexico beckoned at the horizon. Having spent twenty-three hours a day for the last three years in an eight-by-ten cell, the expanse at once thrilled and scared me. I grew up on these shores, and as a boy, dove for sponges in these very waters. But in my dealing years, I drove by shit like this so fast, I never had time to see anything beautiful anymore. I knew these back roads—having ridden my bicycle down them from one end of the peninsula to the other. One thing about the feds: They're serious, but so fucking predictable. And one thing that you can count on is that at some point even a DEA helicopter has to refuel. I watched it peel away to the local Coast Guard base at the south tip of Tampa.

I hit the accelerator and cut down an unpaved road that wound right along the edge of the beach. I knew my pursuers would be freaking out, and I soon led them on a hundred-mile-an-hour chase through the side streets of Palm Harbor and Tarpon Springs. Though the thought did cross my mind, I wasn't really trying to escape. Reputations had been put on the line, and if I split, heads would roll. Not only at the FBI, but also at the DEA, and at Justice—that's what the assholes at the DOJ called themselves. Shit, they knew no more about *justice* than my dog knew about physics. I wasn't fleeing—I was just fucking with these guys. An act of definace to remind them that they could cuff and chain me, but I was still a gangster and a man.

As my Carrera flew down Curlew Road, I purposely headed for the causeway that led out past Ward Island. The feds knew that I knew that this was a dead end, so even the stupidest among them would realize I wasn't heading for the border. The speedometer easily passed 110 miles per hour and my hair flew straight back behind me in the wind. I just wanted to create, for a few minutes, the illusion that I was in control of my life—even though I was anything but.

Finally, I slowed down and I saw Mollohan's Crown Victoria pull up to me. He was in the passenger seat. I stopped.

"I'm sorry, Officer, was I speeding?" I said as Mollohan pulled up. His face was noticeably redder than back at the hotel room.

"Very fucking funny, wise guy."

"Don't get all bent out of shape, Mollohan. I stopped to let you grandmothers catch up."

"Maybe you didn't notice, asshole, but not all my guys like you. One of them might think dropping your ass with a 9mm shell would rid the world of one less scumbag."

"Then you won't get Lukie," I said.

"Well, you win some and you lose some," he said. "Quit fucking around."

That terrible feeling in the pit of my stomach, that remorse, was growing more painful again. Even in my craziest nights on the town dealing ki's and riding in limos with strippers and celebrities, I always wanted what people like Mollohan had. A normal life, with love and the chance to make a family. I wanted to be a father, and especially to be the kind of father that I was denied. I was sad and bitter—totally fucked-up inside. I'm not making any excuses for my life, but I know I did fucked-up things because I spent so much time hating myself and the world.

But was that price too high? I couldn't think about it. I headed to Tarpon Springs.

Twenty minutes to three. I was parked two blocks from the rendezvous point. I could have walked from here, but that would have made Lukie suspicious. One mistake, one hair out of place, a breeze that shouldn't blow, any mannerism altered—Lukie would smell the trap and I would be as good as dead. It would almost be merciful to be killed right then and there—it would be over, and with it my twenty-seven years of misery. But the Greek Mafia doesn't want you to die quickly. Sometimes they would spare you and kill everyone you loved. That way you could die a thousand deaths, like Prometheus having his liver plucked out each night by vultures.

I reached over to the book lying in the passenger seat. I flipped through it to find the passage I had been thinking of as I waited for the endgame to begin. The federal penitentiary in Atlanta had a library, but Homer isn't one of the authors they carry. Ten thousand lines of poetry—it's genius, but I didn't care about that right now. I was feeling my life slipping away before my very eyes, and I needed to steady my nerves.

Finally I found the section. Achilles' best friend had been whacked by the Trojans. That really pissed Achilles off, big-time. Even worse, Achilles had lent his buddy his armor, and when he died, the guy who killed him stripped him and took Achilles' stuff. That night, as he slept, Achilles' mom went to Hephaestos—the blacksmith of the Gods—and begged him to forge new armor for her son to go into battle with. Hephaestos was lame from being thrown off Mount Olympus by his own parents. He was an outcast, but he did all right with the ladies—even married Aphrodite. So he stoked the fires, and by dawn he had forged the most magnificent set of armor ever seen for the greatest warrior the world had ever known.

I loved this passage. It was one of my favorites. Black Spot, the old

Greek sponger who was my childhood friend in Tarpon Springs, used
to read this to me on the docks when I was a boy. I always related to
Hephaestos. I too felt shunned by my parents and cast out of my real
family—a wound that had never healed. And like the ancient blacksmith, I fashioned the medallions that my Band of Five wore, like
armor, to protect us when the shit went down.

Agent Mollohan strolled over to my car. The feds' van was parked
a block behind me.

"You ready?" he said.

"Aren't you going to give me a pep talk?"

"Yeah. Fuck up and you're dead."

"If I succeed, I'm dead."

"Let me get my violin."

"Great pep talk, dickhead," I said as I turned the engine on and
pulled away from the curb, nearly running over Agent Mollohan's
foot.

Three o'clock, and Lukie was right on time. I was leaning on the side
of my car, leafing through a local paper. It was just for show for anyone else who might be watching. I got there a few minutes early to
check out the parking lot. I didn't think Lukie had any of his guys
there. I knew how to tail guys, and how to set them up—so I also knew
what to look for. Just ordinary folks coming and going in the shopping
plaza.

I nodded slightly as I walked over to him. It wouldn't have been
polite, in the Greek way of doing things, for me to make him come
to me.

"Lukie," I said.

"What do you want, kid? I got business to attend to."

I had no illusions that this was going to be a warm and fuzzy re-
union.

"I have some friends down south who have some special shipping
needs. They know you control anything that floats in or out of Tampa
Bay."

I didn't speak while Lukie took in this information. He knew exactly who I meant by down south and what they were shipping. He bit
his lower lip. His face was worn by years of salt air and a stressful life

leading the Greek organized crime community. He was as tough as they came, and you didn't live past sixty in our line of work unless you were ruthless *and* wise. But something else had changed. This wasn't the same Lukie I had seen on our previous encounters. Something had aged him and, I prayed, had softened him a bit.

"The margins?" he asked.

"One fifty."

"Tell me more."

Bingo: He had taken the bait, and I knew the guys listening in from the van were starting to salivate.

"First, you and I got a score to settle. And you know what it is." I was committed, and there was no turning back now. I watched as Lukie shifted uncomfortably. His eyes drew closer as he studied my every movement.

"I've written you half a dozen letters. You didn't respond to one of them. You call yourself such a big man, but you can't answer one of my fucking letters!" My voice was starting to crack. "Just tell me the truth, just once and then we never have to mention it again." I was nearly in tears.

I didn't know if Lukie was going to shoot me, tell me to go fuck myself, as he had so many times before, or just turn and walk away. His lips tightened as if he was about to lose his composure, and then he exhaled slowly.

"*Ine cataxe papou* . . ." Lukie said. *Of course I'm your father.* He paused and studied my face. "Look at you, you look just like your grandfather." His gaze lingered on me as a thousand thoughts raced through my mind. I had so much I wanted to say, so many years of suffering and frustration pent up in an angry mess in my soul—but words wouldn't form. He quickly returned to the subject at hand. "Now tell me about these shipments from the Ochoas and—"

Before Lukie could finish his sentence, I lifted my shirt, exposing the small microphones taped to my chest. I pulled them off quickly.

"*Papou, sago pa,*" I whispered, tears streaming down my cheeks. *Papa, just go.*

Lukie instantly knew what was going on. He looked at me with what I realized was respect. Finally, with fucking *respect.*

By the time the feds converged on the parking lot, Lukie had ducked into a bakery, and was gone. They could easily find him tomorrow morning. He'd be at his restaurant. But they had no more on him now than they did yesterday.

I knew my day was going to go from bad to worse. But yet something had happened that even the feds couldn't take from me. A momentary reprieve from the cesspool that had become my life.

Mollohan pulled up in his Crown Victoria. He got out, slammed the door shut, and he looked at me with disgust on his face. "What the fuck was that? We had the bastard dead to rights when you pulled the wires."

It was as if he was talking to me from a hundred yards away. All I could think about was what Lukie had said to me. I didn't say anything.

"Hey, motherfucker, I'm talking to you," Mollohan shouted at me.

"They started speaking in Greek," another agent interrupted.

"What did he say to you?" Mollohan said.

"I can't explain," I said to him.

"Not good enough, Pappas. What did he say to you?"

I looked him in the eye. "Mollohan," I said. "Just take me back to prison."

# CHAPTER 41

After the botched FBI summit with my dad, the feds were ready to string me up. I'm sure if they had their way, I would have disappeared into the Everglades, stuffed in the roots of one of the mangrove trees to become alligator food just like Willie. Instead, they immediately shipped my ass back to the Atlanta federal pen to continue my stretch, along with an obstruction of justice charge thrown in for good measure.

I'd embarrassed them; careers were on the line and I'd screwed them. They had to go back to their wives and tell them they weren't going to get that promotion this year because of a slimeball named Kevin Pappas. There were times that I didn't feel safe in a room with Gardner and some of the other feds.

But because I didn't nail my dad, I reentered the system a "made man." The word got out that I took the hit for the Pappas family and remained loyal to my blood instead of ratting on them. I followed the code of honor. Knowing that was the only peace I had as I faced spending the rest of my natural-born life behind prison walls.

As soon as I arrived, they threw me into solitary confinement, just like I'd been ten years before on my Gold Mine rap. Any chance of getting a reduction in my sentence for the Lukie deal was gone forever.

But now I had those words from Lukie. And he knew I'd saved his life. After so many years, my father had finally claimed me. I was his son. No one could ever take that away from me again. I remember the way he looked at me. I was his. He was my dad. No longer was I a bastard child. So many emotions were running through me, but the strongest one was pride. My father finally accepted me. I was a Pappas.

There is a Greek proverb that goes *"He who honors his parents never dies."* It doesn't say never suffers.

I went through hell with the feds. They told the prison administration to treat me like a snitch. They revoked all my privileges. I lost my job as an orderly. As far as they were concerned, I could rot away without the world ever hearing from me again.

But Agent Gardner stood by me, and after three or four months, after I'd gotten through the deep depression of being back in prison, I started feeding law enforcement straight intel from the streets. I was on a mission not to die inside. Information and power were the only weapons I had to get my freedom back. My passion for power made me like an alcoholic craving a shot.

While I now had a father who accepted me, I was faced with hard-nosed government officials who ran the game and the rules. If only I could figure out how those rules could be circumvented and maneuvered to my advantage. After all, the Greek way is to prevail over adversity by using your mind. I was determined to use mental manipulation over sheer brawn and the drawing of blood. That's all I focused on because I knew I was going to get out somehow, someway.

Eventually, the feds wrote off the Lukie incident to emotion. When I started getting them good information on street crime from Leavenworth to Lompoc and Miami to Atlanta, the chill began to wear off. I was giving them premium intel again, while gaining their respect as well as sentence reductions.

So the feds moved me around a lot on various ops. One move was related to an ex–cell mate of mine from a highly recognized crime family. He was scared about going to the pen and opted to give up information to the feds in order to get hidden away in some witness protection program. He wouldn't give up his info to anyone else but me. I was honored.

I was transferred to Maxwell Air Force Base in Alabama to debrief him. I was taken to a minimum-security lockup and given limited access to civilians. This facility was where the government housed other inmates who had been valuable to them. It was a fucking godsend.

Compared to the jungle of Atlanta, this was like Disney World. When I wasn't debriefing my ex–cell mate, I was given the job of cleaning the gymnasium where the military base commanders and the officers' wives worked out. We weren't supposed to talk to any of them. Just "Good morning" and "Good night" and "Can I help you with that?" and that's about it.

This was during the Somalia conflict, so there were a lot more women and very few men on the base. I was beefed-up; my hair straggled down my back and I was weighing in at about 235 pounds. Big, buff, and in my prime. One day I was in the gym, minding my own business, cleaning the floors.

There was a black dude named Reggie who cleaned the gym with me. We were mopping opposite ends of the room when all of a sudden he ran over to me. "Pappas," he said, half out of breath, "you're not going to believe this, but the baddest bitch you've ever seen just walked into the gym. I don't know where in the hell she came from, but that's one bad bitch."

You didn't have to tell me twice. "Where's she at?" I hadn't had any real contact with a woman for months. I may not have trusted them, but I wasn't against looking at them.

So we ran over there and the section was empty.

I looked at Reggie. "You lying ass son of a bitch."

He was standing there shaking his head. "She was right there," he said. "And she was a goddess."

The next day Reggie came up to me and said, "That bitch is back."

I said, "Reggie."

"Pappas, I am not lying to you. She is unbelievable. Come on."

In prison, guys would chew their fingers off on the one percent chance that they might get a glimpse of a good-looking woman. I didn't run this time, but I went for a look.

And then I saw her. A brunette in a striped leotard with black leggings. Green eyes and bright, bright red lipstick. Her legs went on for miles. She was just stunning. She looked like a Miss America contestant and she carried herself like one. Later, I found out she was Mrs. Hawaii 1992.

She was on the exercise bike, so I started cleaning the one in front of her, shooting quick little glances at her.

Finally, I stood up and walked over to her.

"Hi, how are you? I'm Kevin."

She was startled. "Uh, hi, I'm fine. My name's Cathie. How are you?"

"Great. You have a good day."

That's all I could risk. I went out and I felt like a schoolboy. All I could think about was whether I'd get a chance to see her the next day.

I called my mother that day and told her that the promise she made me all those years ago in my office, after I'd tossed a ninja star at her face, had come true: I'd found the woman I was going to marry.

"Oh, honey, I didn't mean in prison," she said.

"Hush up, Mama," I told her. "This is the one."

"Well I hope you're right," she said to me. "It's about time."

"Just get ready. Because you're about to be caring for some grand-kids."

She laughed and I started chuckling myself. But I meant every word of it.

Sure enough, Cathie showed up the next day. I was in my green custodian's uniform and she came in carrying a paperback book and a towel and signed the sign-in book. But instead of turning toward the exercise machines, she headed straight for me. I felt like my heart was going to break through my rib cage.

"Hi," she said. She put the book down on the desk next to me. "There's a letter in this book and it's for you."

How many times have I been speechless in my life? Maybe four and this was one of them.

I watched her beautiful little ass walk away. I drew the book tightly to my chest and tucked it inside my shirt. I could feel my heart beating fast.

I felt like that book was made of gasoline and my fingers were on fire. If I got caught talking to an officer's wife, I'd be out of this cushy job and back in solitary in a minute. I took the book back to my cell and opened the letter when I had some privacy. It was handwritten in blue ink and it was really an introduction to who she was. She told me all about growing up in Hawaii and how she wanted to become an ac-tress and a contestant in beauty pageants. And how nice it was to meet me. She wanted to know more about me, especially why I was doing time.

My heart sank. What should I tell her? Do I tell her the truth about why I'm in the joint and risk blowing my chances? Or reach back into my line of bullshit and come up with a story about being wrongly accused?

I put the question aside while I finished the letter. She spoke about her unhappy marriage. Her words were like music to my ears. Why was she writing me? I had just met her. We didn't even have a chance to speak and yet she was sharing all this personal stuff with me. I guess I made a good impression on her in my green khaki uniform. And you know the old saying, "You never get a second chance to make a first impression?" I had set the bar, now I had to live up to it.

Cathie also told me in her letter that I didn't seem like I belonged in prison. That I seemed so friendly and open and not like the other inmates she'd seen around the base. She wrote the letter because she wanted to find out who I was and what my story was.

No one in my life had ever written me other than my mom. I was shocked that she had put herself out on the line sending me the letter. It meant a lot to me, but I still felt it was a dream.

Everything started right there. I decided to trust her with the truth. I wrote her back, telling her all about my life, about Lukie, what I wanted, and how I felt my life had gone wrong. Thinking back, it was actually a good thing that we met that way. We had a chance to learn about each other and actually become friends before any kind of physical romance developed. We had to get to know each other first through letters, and I found I could pour my heart out to her from the beginning.

I felt like I was sixteen again. All the stuff I'd missed by being a hard-ass determined to get my dad's respect, the puppy-dog stuff, the letters, what people call courtship, I found with Cathie. I'd never had that before.

She told me that she was in a bad marriage with a military officer who moved them to Maxwell Air Force Base. I had to laugh, falling for an officer's wife? If he only knew. What I knew though was I had to have Cathie. Had to. But it wasn't going to be easy.

She told me she wanted to get out of that marriage. It wasn't because of me; it was because she and her husband weren't really in love anymore. And she told me she had a little daughter that she loved to pieces named Jourdan.

Over the next couple of weeks, a system developed. Cathie would come in to the gym around eight a.m. and I'd be waiting for her. She'd get on the exercise bike or the treadmill, and all of a sudden there'd be a machine right next to hers that urgently needed cleaning. I'd get right on it and work away shining that sucker up while Cathie and I talked. Wherever she was in the gym, I would find something near her that needed to be scrubbed down. From twenty feet away, you wouldn't have realized we were having a conversation. Cathie would be doing ab crunches and we'd be talking about our childhoods or something really deep.

We exchanged letters every day, but it wasn't without risk. One day, I slipped her my letter as she was on the way out of the gym and she was reading it in her car in the parking lot. All of a sudden there was a tap on her window. Cathie looked up and there was a lieutenant standing right there. She told me she felt like she'd been caught in some terrible crime, but she kept her cool and rolled down the window.

"Ma'am," the guy said. "I just wanted to make sure you are aware that you are not allowed to fraternize with the inmates."

Cathie gave the guy a "who, me?" look.

"Of course I understand that," she said. "What gave you the idea I didn't?"

"Uh, nothing special, ma'am. Just trying to keep an eye out for you."

She rolled the window back up. One week with me and she knew what it was like to step outside of the law a little bit. But it was worth it. For both of us, it was like being caught up in this conspiracy to make a life together.

I couldn't take Cathie out to dinner or to a fancy nightclub. I couldn't impress her with what kind of car I drove or where I lived. For the first time in my life, I only had myself to offer her. Who I was, not what I had. Cathie loved that.

Just as I was feeling deeper and deeper about Cathie, a female captain started hitting on me. Years without any female attention and all of a sudden I was getting the wrong kind.

I was in the gym giving some pointers to Cathie as she used the shoulder press. Meanwhile, of course, we're talking about dreams and kids and what we want to do when I get out. Then I heard a voice.

I turned around. It was the female captain, a little brunette shaped like a fireplug. She was on the bench press.

"Hi. I'm on my lunch hour and I'm active duty. Can you spot me?" Active duty troops were supposed to get priority treatment, ahead of a wife like Cathie.

I was like, "Uhhhh, OK, can you hold on a second?" But Cathie wasn't having it.

"Excuse me, he's not done with me yet."

Their eyes were shooting daggers at each other. I tried to finish with Cathie quickly. I turned to the captain and spotted her, and then hustled her out of there.

I had to find a way to get Cathie alone. Not only for the obvious reasons: She was gorgeous and I'd been in jail for five years with a bunch of Aryan Nation skinheads, so you do the math. But people were starting to get suspicious.

There was a racquetball loft above the gym that was empty a lot of the time. It was the perfect spot. One day before I went to my cleaning job I took a look in there and it was deserted. I had my hideaway.

I went into the gym and saw Cathie. Her eyes did something whenever I saw her. It was like a combination of melting and sparkling. Got me every time.

The gym was crowded and I knew I couldn't spend more than a few seconds talking to her, so I kind of edged my way over to where she was exercising and out of the side of my mouth I said, "Meet me in the loft."

I started to walk away and I heard her say, all loud and shit, "What loft?"

I stopped. I pretended that I'd forgotten to check on a machine next to her and walked back.

"The racquetball loft," I whispered.

"I don't know what that is."

Jesus Christ. Cathie was new to this spy shit. She was talking like we were at a ball game or something.

I was about to give her directions when I noticed the lieutenant who had read Cathie the riot act staring at us. Rather than blow the whole thing I just walked away and hoped Cathie would figure it out. I found out later Cathie saw another inmate at the drinking fountain.

This was actually a friend of mine who I'd already recruited to look out for me while we were in the loft.

She walked over to him and while she was waiting to take a drink, she said, "Kevin told me to meet him in the loft. Do you know where that is?"

"Follow me," he said.

Cathie was straight as an arrow. She'd probably never jaywalked more than three times in her life. Now she was having secret meetings with a convicted dope trafficker. When she came up the stairs, I was waiting for her in the bleachers that overlook the racquetball court. She looked so scared, it really made me want to protect and take care of her.

"This is probably the worst thing I've ever done," she whispered, and I could see that she was shaking a little bit. And then we were in each other's arms.

We shared our first kiss. It wasn't sexual. It was intimate, a promise of other things to come. All the drugs, women, and money from my past will never replace that first kiss. We held each other, and it was so gratifying to me.

We spent ten minutes up in that loft, but it seemed like it was so much longer. When your whole existence is just survival and you're faced with the worst parts of humanity every day of your life, you have to act like a savage just to survive. Ten minutes with a beautiful woman you're in love with is like an eternity.

All of a sudden there was a sharp crack from downstairs. I knew what that was. I'd told my lookout that if anyone approached the stairs to the loft, drop a broom. Obviously, someone was on the way.

I didn't have time to say a word to Cathie. I just jumped up and got my ass out of there.

# CHAPTER 42

We had twenty-one days together. You're damn right I counted them.

But my good fortune came to an abrupt halt. Three weeks after we met, I was woken up in the middle of the night by the dreaded sound of keys in the lock. I looked up to see three B.O.P. transfer guards yelling at me to get my ass up. "Pack it out, Pappas, time to go!" I could tell this wasn't just a cell shakedown. I was getting on a bus.

They marched me out between guards holding machine guns. The transport Marshal, who does nothing but ship prisoners in and out all day, was right behind me.

"Why am I leaving?" I yelled to him.

"Why?" he asked laughing. "I hope you got some pussy, Pappas, because that's what bought you a one-way ticket back to the pen. Did you get some pussy? Huh?"

They loaded my ass up. I walked onto the bus and saw that I was the only prisoner. The feds never do that. This wasn't just any bus. Somebody must have snitched.

I got back to the Atlanta pen, depressed as all hell. I kept asking myself, "Why can't one thing go right for me? Why can't I have one person to love?" Everyone had disappointed or betrayed me. And now Cathie had been ripped away.

I swore to myself right then: I would find a way to get back in touch with her.

I'd only been back in the pen for a few days when, again, I was sleeping. There was this office clerk who did shifts as night captain during the week and he was gay as anything. I knew he was sweet on me. I laughed about it; he was a cool dude.

But dead in the middle of the night, I feel this hand on my thigh. In prison, especially, that will wake your ass up. I shot up like fucking Dracula in his coffin, and here was the gay captain sitting on my bunk. And what does he do? Puts his hand over my mouth.

I'm like, "Oh my fucking God. He's going to want to fuck me." Which wasn't going to happen. But that meant I might have to bust him up good, and that meant I was going to do extra years in the pen. No good options.

But instead of making a move on me, this captain put his finger up to his lips and made the "quiet" sign. Then he pointed to the showers. I was in an open unit and you could actually see into the stalls from where I slept. I looked over and there was an inmate there who had a *Playboy* strapped to his back and another guy was fucking him up the ass. Just another day in the Atlanta pen.

I saw these dark figures moving through the cots toward the showers. It was a team of COs going to arrest the rapist—because that's what was going on. It wasn't consensual, what was happening in that shower. They grabbed the guy, handcuffed him, and marched him right past my bed, still with a hard-on.

*Welcome back, Kevin,* I thought. *You can forget about Cathie now.*

I found out later that after they sent me back to the pen, the captain took Cathie out to Arizona for a change of scenery. He got reassigned and she had to go with him. But she couldn't forget about me, just like I couldn't forget about her.

I played over those twenty-one days in my mind. There was one time, just two days after we met, when I walked into the gym and there was Cathie. She had her little girl, Jourdan, with her. And Cathie was distracted with something and I could see that Jourdan wanted a drink from the water fountain. She kept trying to reach the water stream but she was too small.

I walked over and said, "Let me help you, honey." And I picked Jourdan up and held her so she took a good long drink. I put her down, and she wiped her mouth and said, "Thank you, sir." I laughed and said, "You're welcome." It was so strange to have someone thank me for doing something that small. In prison, you don't thank anyone—every gesture is a down payment on a future favor. There is no true gratitude or friendship.

I looked over and Cathie was looking at me like she wanted to cry. I guess she'd never thought a muscle-bound doper could have a way with kids. But I loved them.

Later, Cathie told me that Jourdan wouldn't stop pestering her after that day. "Mom, where's that big guy?" "I wanna talk to that big guy with the muscles who helped me get a drink of water." "Mom, go find that nice man again."

Small things like that kept running through my mind. Stuff you probably wouldn't notice on the outside. But to me they were like scenes from the life I wanted and I was never going to have.

Meeting Cathie only intensified my drive to get out of prison. It gave me that image of what could be waiting out there for me: a family, love, fatherhood.

# CHAPTER 43

When I was back in the pen, I got my job as orderly back. Now, as soon as I had my unit clean, I'd head straight for the law library. I knew that's where the key to my freedom lay.

In the beginning, I had to get permission to go to the law library. Once I had my assigned time, I'd get taken out of my jail cell and walk down a long hallway through two series of metal detectors. Once you get inside the library itself, you see this long Formica table in the center with little cubicles where you could take the books and do your research.

When you open the door of a prison library, you're going from one world to another. You're going from desperation to hope. The only place in a prison where you have a future is that library. Everything else—the gym, the cell, the entertainment room—is about killing time. It's about trying to forget where your actions have landed you.

The library is about the future. This is where you might find a way to get back to your family. Outside that room, what counts is how bad you are, how fearless. But here, the question is: How smart are you? How well do you know how to argue?

About five percent of the prison population in Atlanta was practicing jailhouse law. These were the guys who, for protection or money or tobacco or even a blow job, would take your case and see if they could find a flaw in it. Some of the better ones could make thousands of dollars researching your case and writing up motions for you. They'd quiz you about your case, and then hit the law books and look at whether your defense lawyer did a good enough job or whether the judge asked the right questions. About two percent of them are any good. The rest are in there because they want to have an edge. They can't intimidate anyone, so they want to keep out of the way of the gorillas who roam the hallways.

I stayed away from the lawyers. They want to come over and pick your brain and try out their arguments on you. I knew my case wasn't going to be overturned. What I wanted was to be a specialist. Like a kidney doctor who did only one kind of operation. I wanted to master one piece of the law until I was the expert on it, inside and outside of prison. That would give me power.

I soon found that I was made for the law. Because it's very similar to religion: Both have books that are the foundation of the belief system, and then each allows you to make arguments from those books. There is no better training for arguing from a set of rules and traditions than going door to door as a Jehovah's Witness in a heavily Christian town like Tarpon Springs. You had to be fucking sharp. You had to know your Acts and your Psalms and everything else. It was incredible preparation to go to bat against an even scarier institution: the U.S. Government.

What the Witnesses had taught me was that every powerful institution leaves itself a way out. Let me give you an example.

In Acts 5:30, it says that Jesus Christ was slain and hung upon a tree. Didn't say a cross, it said a tree. Go to the book and you'll see. When I was a kid, the Greeks would have these processions around the town and they would do this reenactment of Jesus Christ and they would have a casket and the Greeks would chant, not in the Greek, but in Phoenician, the old, old Greek. And they say during that procession that Jesus Christ was hung upon a tree. Didn't say a stick, didn't say a stake, didn't say a board. Upon a *tree*.

So I would ask my Greek Orthodox mentor who taught me the language and the culture, Mr. Gondas, why is it that they say tree? And he says, "Kevin, the tradition of the Greek people is tradition." That was a great line. *The tradition of the Greek people is tradition.* Meaning, even if the tradition says that the world is flat and two plus two equals five, that's what you believe.

I said, "But the Bible says . . ."

"I know what it says," Mr. Gondas told me. "As a scriptural rule, you are absolutely right. Jesus Christ did not die in a crucifixion. That method of Roman execution didn't come in until 607 AD. But that is the tradition that has come down to us. And we do not question it." Well, being a Jehovah's Witness in America is all about questioning what the mainstream culture tells you. I was taught to always look deeper.

I started hitting the law books. I never stopped until I got the right answer. If I knew the answer was there, I would have kept reading until my eyes bled. Within three weeks I had found Rule 35.


To explain how I began to plot my escape from USP Atlanta, you need to know about Rule 35, and what it tells you about the mind-set of prosecutors and the Justice Department. Bobby Kennedy wrote the guidelines for Rule 35 in the 1960s and never got them fulfilled—and then, on top of that, he got himself shot. They sat dormant until Ronald Reagan came to power and, as a law-and-order Republican, he decided he wanted more convictions in big cases, especially high-profile cases that drove the media and the public crazy. On November 1, 1987, the law was changed and Rule 35 came into effect.

Rule 35 provided that any inmate who offered up viable information on cases could get a reduction in his sentence. It wasn't snitching, it was information-proffering, as we called it. Snitching in prison means testifying against a fellow inmate for favors. And it will get you one of two things: Either you'll be killed or the warden will put you in high-max lockdown, which means you'll spend the rest of your life in an eight-by-ten room, getting out thirty minutes a day. It's death by a slower method. Your choice.

What I did was act as a conduit between prisoners who had information and prosecutors who were often stuck with cases they couldn't get indictments on. I brokered the deals. And as part of each one, my sentence was reduced: two years, or five or ten, depending on the importance of the case. On how desperate the prosecutors were.

Reagan made a deal with the devil. He was willing to sacrifice due process to get the baddest criminals, the untouchables, off the streets. But it was my ticket out.

What my education with the Witnesses told me is that, if you study the sacred text of your adversaries, you will discover something that they don't want you to know. And for the U.S. Government, it was Rule 35. When they had a case that was too tough, they gave themselves this out, this bonus. It was a rule that said they could use testimony from prisoners to build a case against a suspect, even if that prisoner was never called into court to testify.

And here was the key: The information could be second- or third-hand. It didn't have to come from an informant who had a direct connection to the case. I could get a piece of information from Inmate A or Criminal B on the streets and proffer it to the government for the benefit of Inmate C. He could be an accountant or a ditchdigger, and we'd give the prosecutors information on a drug case that had nothing to do with him. Didn't matter. Nowhere in the law did it say that the information had to originate with that inmate. It just had to be true and deemed substantial by the case agent.

That would change. Now the law is that you have to be the first-hand source of the information, or you have to be a relative of the source. When the feds saw how I was working Rule 35, they changed it. But when I first stumbled on this loophole, they'd left it as open as possible. Because they wanted to make cases and they didn't care how the information got into the pipeline.

Who knows more about crime than criminals? So the government said to itself: Who has the largest collection of criminals under its total control, criminals desperate for freedom or a nicer cell or a sweet job away from the possibility of getting shanked?

We do!

And they said to themselves, "Let's use that resource."

That's what Rule 35 was. It was a gold mine for prosecutors. But they only wanted a certain amount of people to know about it. It was their own personal pot of gold, and they didn't want to share. They wanted to extract as much information from inmates while giving them the least possible benefit.

Informants are the lifeblood of the criminal justice system. Just look at Sammy "The Bull" Gravano, who by his own admission had killed seventeen people. He was as close to a natural-born murderer as you can find. He was the muscle for one of America's largest organized crime families. John Gotti was nothing more than a pivot boy, a negotiator. But because Gotti had accessibility to the media and the media made him into this superstar, that's who the feds went after. They went after the headlines. Because headlines make careers.

Let me be clear. I'm not a saint. I didn't get into Rule 35 to expose how messed up the confidential informant system is. I found Rule 35 and I used it to get out of prison and get back to the life I'd always dreamed of. But I didn't create it. I just took the tools of prosecutors and used it for myself and my clients.

People think Rule 35 is just for people who want to go snitch on somebody. I've heard all the accusations, but it isn't snitching. If I'd been a snitch, I wouldn't have lasted a week in prison. Instead, I had inmates coming to me.

The government can take your information as being pertinent and being useful and it doesn't convict anybody. It just can actually facilitate the government in understanding what's going on in a certain area—a drug conspiracy, a bid-rigging syndicate, whatever. If they can use that information to get a better picture of what is going on in a criminal enterprise, that's enough to give you a reduction. You're providing a missing piece to a puzzle and you're getting rewarded. Simple as that.

# CHAPTER 44

I started small, just like when I got into the drug business. Inmates would come to me with little bits of information and I would charge them for my services. I only charged based on results. If I got you into an education program that had been closed to you before, that was $1,000. Medical transfer to a nicer facility? $10,000. Furloughs to a work program on the outside? $25,000. Halfway house was $30,000. I had to find the value of my information. As I got better at judging how much I could get for, say, tipping the feds to a twenty-ki heroin deal, I could get even more bang for my buck in reductions. You know the old saying, "What would you pay for freedom?" It's priceless.

One of my first clients was Gary Abrams, the founder of a multimillion-dollar company in the optical industry. Except I didn't know who he was at the time. I was standing at the window at the pen when the bus arrived with the new inmates and I saw him walk out: 6′3″, white as paper, and looking like he was going to shit out his lower intestine. *That is one scared motherfucker,* I said to myself.

I went down to the commissary and bought myself an ice cream and surveyed the newbies coming in. It's like watching lions as they stalk the antelope at the African watering hole. Everyone's scheming to figure out who is the weakest and how to cut them out of the herd.

I saw Gary standing alone and so I walked up to him.

"How's it going?" I said.

He looked at me. His eyes were as wide as saucers behind his glasses.

"Uh, OK. I'm OK. So far."

"No offense, but you look like a boy scout. How in the holy fuck did you end up behind the walls?"

He gulped.

"Hummus," he said.

"*Hummus?* What the fuck is that?"

Gary told me his story. Apparently he'd been set up by two informants, who he called Pete and Jerry, Colombians who he had bought some coke from years ago. He didn't mention that he used the money he made dealing that coke to start his new legitimate business, which was by then worth hundreds of millions of dollars. Pete and Jerry had gone their own way, but years later they got caught shipping some ki's and they were nailed for trafficking. The feds, as they always do, asked them if they had information on anyone they could give up.

By then, Gary was famous. They spilled everything they had on the guy. And even though this deal was years in the past, they nailed Gary under what is known as a "historical conspiracy" law. He got six years.

As a first-time offender, he was sent to an air force base, which is where a geek like him belonged. Gary was Jewish and he'd grown up eating hummus, which he told me was ground-up chickpeas. Disgusting, right? Well, Gary loved the stuff so much he paid a guard to bring canisters of it in to him. Another inmate found out and squealed and the poor sap was shipped to the Atlanta pen and housed in B Unit.

All for some damn chickpeas. The system was laughing its ass off.

The feds had really done a number on Gary. When he was arrested, he'd offered up information on the Colombians, classic Rule 35 shit. The law states that if the prosecutors deem the info to be helpful to the government, he gets a reduction. But Gary's judge ruled against him. He said the information was not usable. Complete bullshit. They just wanted to nail this high-profile defendant. Not to mention that word had gotten around that Gary was a high-level informer, a rat, and he was worried. But for good reason. That's a death sentence in the Atlanta pen. And he knew it.

He laid out his whole story, leaving out the fact that he was a millionaire a hundred times over, as we sat in our bunks in B Unit. Gary was freaking out. He couldn't sleep. He was convinced someone was going to slit his throat. And he wasn't fucking far from the truth.

Gary and I became real good friends. When his commissary money ran out, the fucking guy would come over and snag my cans of tuna fish and my ramen noodles. That was like taking my dick and my balls and going off and fucking my bitch with them. I was ready to shank the guy myself, but he was just clueless.

He begged me to help him. Finally, I said, "I'll protect you but it's going to cost you $2,500 a week."

"That's no problem," he said. "Just get me out of this place alive, please."

Now I didn't have an army behind me. I had the Italians watching my back but I couldn't protect Gary twenty-four hours a day, which is what would be required if the guy wasn't going to get gutted like a fish.

So I made the rounds. I went to the Crips and the Bloods and the Mexican Mafia and asked them to watch over the guy instead of sticking a knife into him. I wasn't just buying protection for Gary, I was paying them not to kill the guy themselves. Pretty soon he couldn't take a shit without a gang banger standing next to the toilet. They probably even wiped his ass. He'd become the golden goose. I split the $2,500 with the gangs and walked away with $500 a week for myself.

Now that I had Gary off the death list, I had to get him out. That's when I reviewed his Rule 35 paperwork. The prosecutors had testified that Gary's information had been applicable to cases they were working on. But the judge had ruled against them, which was just bizarre.

Under Rule 35, if the prosecutors have already cut a deal with the defense to cooperate, it was SOP (or "standard operating procedures" for the layman) for the courts to follow the recommendations of the deal. This is referred to as substantial assistance. In those days, the sentencing guidelines were broad and vague because the rules were so new. Everybody was shooting from the hip, which often painted the judges into a corner and prevented them from determining their own verdicts. Today it doesn't work that way. You have to have a direct relationship with the suspect in question.

Anyway, Gary's lawyers petitioned the court to remove the judge and get another assigned, citing the fact that the guy had messed up the Rule 35 decision. After a couple of months, it was done. And the new judge did the right thing and ruled in Gary's favor. Pretty soon he was on the bus back to the air force camp and the good life. A year later, he was out.

Just before he got out, I was called down to the case manager's office for an attorney/client call. I picked up the phone. "You got a check for $50,000 in the mail! What the hell is going on?" It was my mother's voice. She read me the name on the check but I'd never heard of it before. I couldn't believe it. I had no idea who would give me that amount of money.

I told my mother to deposit the check and go out and buy herself something nice. It had been a while since I'd been able to send her any cash. She'd written or called me every day since I'd been thrown in jail. I wanted her to have something special.

I was talking with Gary that night and I mentioned the check.

"That's a pretty big chunk of change, $50,000," I hinted. "Pretty generous, huh?"

Gary bowed his head a little bit. "And may it serve you well."

I looked at him. "Gary! All this time, you've been fucking holding out on me? You fucking scumbag!"

He looked at me. "I had to know I was dealing with someone who had my back and my best interest at heart."

I put my hand on his shoulder as we were walking the yard, and said, "I love you, man." And that was the end of it. It was never mentioned again.

I found out it was his father's name on the check, but it was Gary that was banked. After he got out of jail, he bought his optical company back and then resold it a few years later, for some ungodly amount of money.

With Gary, I'd fought to get a basic injustice overturned. I was Erin Fucking Brockovich with a mullet. Gary had given the government some solid leads, but they'd taken the information and screwed him, even endangered his life by putting him in general population in a fucking killing machine.

But now I was ready to turn my discovery into a mini-empire.

I had definitely stumbled across a lucrative opportunity. I was able to convert information into cash payments in exchange for slashing sentences at will. The only thing I was missing was a law degree.

My photographic memory allowed me to easily retain detailed information. While I'm not good with a computer, I was able to farm out evidence and testimony to more and more clients with access to research and information. Word spread and business boomed. I went from being a drug dealer to an information broker.

My access to street information brought me power, which eventually led to doing business inside the corridors of the federal government. My client base grew and represented everyone from "C" level white-collar criminals to organized crime figures and even high-profile politicians. People who could afford representation. People who could pay my fees. This shit rocked! I was able to use the government's own guidelines to my advantage and leverage the law to master the criminal justice system.

When society thinks of hardened criminals in the traditional sense, they think of rapists, murderers, robbers, and drug dealers like me. Over the last several decades a whole new type of criminal entered the penal system referred to as "white-collar." Yeah, it's been around for centuries but it became prolific after the Reagan era. These were some of my primary clients, corporate CEOs of *Fortune* 1000 companies. Everyone would say to me "Kevin, why would you want to help get the bad guys out?" Well, it's a matter of perspective. Who exactly is the bad guy? And anyway, these were high-paying clients, so who am I to judge?

Within one year, business had gotten so good I needed to enlist an old friend and attorney to help manage this growing enterprise. I formed an LLC with my mentor and lawyer, Robert Fierer, and called it Conviction Consulting Services, Inc. (CCS). I'd gone corporate.

The federal pen was filled with wealthy inmates anxious for someone to help free them, reduce their sentences, or arrange lower-security transfers. It was the breeding ground for millionaires and college for the young and upcoming elite criminals. I was able to broker hundreds of deals because I knew how to manipulate Rule 35 evidence to collect time-off credits even for myself without ever having to testify in court.

Bob Fierer handled the legal side, I handled the information, and together we filled the Rule 35 pipeline. We developed information on cases and we fed it to prosecutors. Attorneys and inmates would pay us to arrange the whole thing.

One of the controversial parts of our business was that we provided inmates with specific information based on Rule 35 guidelines. We never told the feds who did the crime. We simply supplied them with just enough forensic information to help them build their case. Evidence that was undeniably involved in crimes. Bob Fierer was a big part of my life. He was a good-looking Notre Dame graduate who dressed in Armani suits and Ferragamo shoes and knew everybody. He was also a sought-after lawyer who was ranked in the top ten in the nation in those "best attorney" lists. His clients were high-rolling celebrities in politics, sports, and media. They ranged from NFL stars to politicians and even a publishing mogul. Bob was a very connected lawyer. When the feds needed someone to assist them in doing an exchange of spies with the Russian government, he acted as co-counsel on the deal.

Bob was the first man, the first real father figure, who stood up for me. Every time I needed help or got myself into trouble, he would be there for me and help untangle the knot I had gotten myself into. He always told me there was a life outside of crime and a right way of doing things. And he emphasized I should always tell the truth, except when it came to your sexual prowess: *Be Caesar's wife.*

I became like a private investigator. For instance, there was a very powerful group in the northern part of Georgia, multi-kilo traffickers who'd built up a pile of money off the streets. The cops couldn't bring them down because they had no idea about the structure of their organization. They had no good informants and no one willing to come forward. These guys were too feared and too good at what they did to let any bozo CI get anywhere near them.

The feds had been trying for seven years to make a case on these guys. Who knows how many millions of dollars of taxpayers' money had been blown on the case. And they still couldn't lay a finger on the top guys.

I still had contacts on the street from my 5100 Group days. I called one up and I said to him, "Look, I need you to do business with this north Georgia outfit and learn all you can about them." I was creating my own confidential informant because I had the Rolodex and the cops didn't. He went out and did some deals with these boys, got friendly with them, learned who the captains and foot soldiers were, where they got their product, and the supply chain involved in all of it.

Within three months, he was buying multi-kilo loads from them. And then he came back to me and laid it out at my feet, the whole organization. His job was done and he walked away a happy man. He had no further involvement in the case.

Now I had prime, grade-A information and a client who had a lot of money to burn. I had a buyer, the feds, who were going around in circles trying to make a case on these north Georgia maniacs who were about as watertight as an outfit can get. I was the fucking puppet master and people were getting results.

I put all of the elements together. The feds got their information. My client got five years off his sentence. My street guy got $10,000 from me and whatever he made off the north Georgia coke deal. And my fees were waiting for me someplace else.

Was I manipulating the system? I don't know, it's a matter of opinion. I was following the rules and leveraging them for everyone involved. Everybody was happy. They were making cases. They looked like heroes. It was a win-win situation and it was a beautiful thing.

Just like in the drug game, information was everything. If I'd been serving up old information or making the shit up, I would have been exposed in a minute. But I had sources on the streets and intel that no one else had. Said differently, I had third-party cooperation.

This had never been done before. Never ever. Before CCS got on the scene, a special agent would bring a suspect in, sit him down, and say, "OK, we're going to put you down for a twenty-year sentence unless you roll over on your friend Fred."

That would get the guy so terrified that he'd flip over and start gushing: Fred did this and Fred did that and he's got money buried here and there's a dude named Billy Joe buried over there. "OK, that's good. If we deem your information substantial, we will recommend to the AUSA and the judge a downward departure for substantial assistance."

They never said the term "Rule 35." They never even talked about it. What they did was make it seem like this was a special, one-time deal that they'd managed to work out for you and you alone. CCS turned everything around and made it a tool for inmates.

Eventually, we had a team of people up and down the coast who would feed information to a sub base. Then we had another group of individuals who would designate and corroborate that information, and word got out that we paid well for it. We started getting hits on crimes, past, present, and future.

Let's just say that there was six ki's of heroin coming in from Alabama and somebody knew about it. They weren't one of the players, but they were close enough so they knew the structure and timing of the deal. I would take this info to the case agent and say, "Listen, I got something for you. Six ki's of heroin, probably $2 million, being brought in by Mr. X on such and such a date. What's it worth to you?"

"Well, what do you need?"

"I got this guy sitting in a maximum security prison where they're going to feed him to the lions if he stays there another week. I need him sent to a country-club-type work-release program within seventy-two hours."

"Okay, let me run it by my superior."

They'd go to ASAC or the U.S. Attorney's office and we'd get word back if it was a go.

If so, they'd call and say something like, "Mr. X is a high-value target for us. Matter of fact, we've got intel on him, so yeah, let's do it."

We gave them a little information, they'd check it out, and if it came back legitimate, they'd get our client into that country-club prison where they have a fucking petting farm and you get to do arts-and-crafts instead of getting fucked up the ass. When I got word back that he's in his new digs, I would give them the rest of the information.

Then we were on to the next case.

This was a clearinghouse for all kinds of information. CCS got the informants, we did quality control on the leads and made sure our clients got what they were paying for. We had people at our disposal who could get into an individual inmate's files to memorize or copy down information on cases that prosecutors from other districts didn't have access to. Either because they didn't know about it or because the two jurisdictions weren't cooperating with each other.

We were doing what every prosecutor in the country was doing to make his bones and win the cases. We had the trust of the best sources in the world: the federal prison population and the street guys. No one could match our sources.

And I started it all out of a two-bunk cell in a maximum security prison. Hoo-yaa. I get goose bumps thinking about it now.

# CHAPTER 45

Cathie was on my mind constantly. For me, there was no reason to get out of prison if I didn't have a chance at being with her. I didn't want to go back to my old partying, whoring, coke-dealing self. She'd given me the hope for a different life.

What I'd forgotten was that I'd given Cathie my mom's address and told her that if she ever needed anything and couldn't reach me, she should write my mom a letter. I'd forgotten all about it, but Cathie took that lead and ran with it. She told her husband she had a modeling job in Atlanta and had to jump on a plane. She didn't write my mother. She got on a plane, went to Atlanta, and knocked on her door.

One day I got a letter and it was from Cathie. My hands were trembling as I opened it. I thought it would be a kiss-off letter, but instead she told me that she wanted to be with me and was willing to do anything to do that. I almost dropped to the floor.

A few days after I received Cathie's letter, I was able to get a call out to her. She told me the whole story of her and the captain and how she'd left him and was going back to Arizona to get a divorce.

"Your mother told me that I was the one," she said. "According to her son."

"Damn right," I said. "Get that wedding dress ready."

She laughed. It was good to think that the two women in my life were together in the same room, looking over old childhood pictures of me, talking about my good points and bad points over a cup of coffee. I felt like a chain that had been broken years before was mending itself back together.

I went back to my cell that night and I made a vow to Cathie in my heart. I vowed that I would do everything within my power to get out of prison and become the man she thought I was. I would have to be utterly ruthless, but it was with a good aim: to finally find the love that I'd been missing all my life.

In 1991, after I'd been in for two years, one of the largest dirty-cop cases in history came out of Atlanta. There was a young man who was my old bodyguard who was a bouncer at a very well-known strip club in Atlanta. He got himself wrapped up in a little situation and was part of a crew that went out to rob an old-school nightclub owner who took his profits out every night in a paper bag. During the course of the robbery, the owner actually got off a round and shot one of the guys. The perp survived. The owner didn't. Someone put a bullet in him. And this was one in a series of seven or eight similar robberies that had gone down in Atlanta in recent months.

The killing was all over the news in Atlanta. You couldn't get away from it. But the cops and the prosecutors had no idea what had gone down, and the pressure was increasing day by day. Pressure creates opportunity: That's the first thing I learned with Rule 35.

My ex-bodyguard knew who had killed the owner. Along with two other guys who'd been involved, he brought me the whole story. So I contacted the U.S. Attorney's office and spoke to the prosecutor on the case, who I heard was whip-smart and up-and-coming. I said, "Listen. For three weeks you've been trying to find the killer and you can't even locate the weapon. Here's the deal. I know who killed the guy and I can produce a gun for you and testimony of a witness that was there during the time of the killing. But to get you that, here's what I need: I want to reduce my sentence down seven points (about a twenty-year reduction). And the witness is willing to do twenty-four months in a state facility in South Georgia called Waycross. And there are a couple of other things."

The prosecutor said, "You're crazy."

I said, "Well, then go find the fucking killer yourself." And I hung up.

A couple of days later, I was sitting in my cell and I was told I had a visitor. Of course, it was the prosecutor. She said, "Listen, we want to make a deal. What do you need?"

I said, "Well, I've got two guys sitting in the federal pen and I want to move those two men to a camp. I want to reduce their terms and then when you do that I'll give you the murder weapon."

They did it.

I went back to the two individuals and said, "Listen, I'm going to get you out of the pen. I'll get your six years down to six months, and I need a half a million dollars. Put the money in my attorney's account and it's done."

They didn't blink an eye. Freedom is precious; freedom makes half a million dollars look like nothing at all.

My guys were sent to a camp, and they told me where to find the murder weapon. I was halfway there. Now I've got to give them the perp. So my bodyguard gave me the name. It turns out he was a bouncer and night security guy and—most important—an off-duty Atlanta police officer. He was dirty. And he killed the owner and got shot in the face in the process.

Acting on that information, the prosecutors checked and found out that the cop had called in sick for two weeks right after the robbery. They brought him in and could see he'd taken a bullet to the face. And the blood they found at the scene matched his blood type.

They had him red-handed. The shooter knew it and he began telling them stories. Eventually, twenty-six other dirty cops were brought down for a variety of offenses: robberies, payoffs, shootings.

My bodyguard never testified; he didn't have to. That was the beauty of Rule 35. He got his twenty-four months in Waycross and everyone was happy.

We provided the blueprints. And the prosecutors built the cases. This is your justice system at work. And if the feds tell you that things have changed since I was operating out of the Atlanta pen, they're lying through their fucking teeth.

And slowly, my prison sentence was coming down. I wrote Cathie every day and we started planning to have a family and a life together.

Everyone at the U.S. Attorney's office in Atlanta was aware of my contribution. Let's just say that, after the cop case, they became real avid listeners. And at the Atlanta pen, I had a nickname: "Houdini."

My guys had gotten taken care of, gotten the deals they wanted. I had my sentence cut in half, and I had lottery money sitting in a bank account. We did this again and again. I built cases the same way a producer packages movie deals. And the money was about the same.

Soon I had twenty-four-hour access to the law library. I could come and go as I wanted. I could bring books back to my unit. I made and received phone calls in the counselor's office, not at the pay phone where you got stabbed if you went ten seconds over your time limit. I even had computer access, and could get into the FTS, or Federal Tell System, which let me pull up inmates' files.

I was known nationwide. I was getting kites passed to me saying so-and-so at Leavenworth or Attica or wherever wants you to look at his case. There are buses taking thirty or so inmates to and from federal lockups all over the country, and these guys would be like walking advertisements for me. They told everyone what I was doing. Better than billboards on Interstate 95.

Now I had power, which is the hardest commodity for an inmate to acquire. Bureau of Prisons officials knew I had access within the federal government right up to the top of the food chain. So they treaded lightly with me. They must have been asking themselves, "Who *is* this guy?" Because everyone was afraid that the feds were putting a plant in the prison to check up on them.

I capitalized on that. I made it very known to the hacks. "Don't fuck with me," I told them. "Just let me do my thing and I won't fuck with you. I'll watch your back and you watch mine."

The skills I used in building Rule 35 cases were the same I used on the streets or making deals with the Colombians. They were the same ones I had soaked in watching Lukie control his syndicate without ever leaving a table at his restaurant. You have to know what people want. You have to be able to provide it. You have to stand your ground. And you have to earn trust.

You can't do this kind of work and not have your view of things change. Some people are going to think my perspective is twisted, but to me certain departments of government represented the highest forms of organized crime. They are so much more powerful than the Gambinos or the Pappases. As I told my guys in prison, these people are part of the system that invades countries and wins world wars. And you think you're going to beat them in a contest of wills? Put down the crack pipe.

You can outthink them, though. Once you understand what they want, and you understand what the game is, believe me, they'll play.

The best illustration I can give is what we call the "FBI beauty pageant." When models go out for jobs, they bring along an eight-by-ten composite card with small little mini-pictures on it. The feds would do the same thing. They would walk into the penitentiary with about fourteen of these little mini-pictures and they would want to know something on somebody. The federal agent would actually put his finger on the photo, and he would begin to coach the informant on what he wanted him to say and do. Because when you're considered a reliable informant, the prosecutor can use that information to get an indictment. Once they have that piece of paper, they pick the guy up and say, "We have a credible witness who says you're dirty on this and you're going to do forty years." Immediately, he flips on everybody.

This was all done in the shadows. There were no juries, no media, no courtrooms. The feds were farming information and using it to turn people on the outside. Rule 35 was completely out of control.

You just had to pray that your picture didn't end up on one of those eight-by-ten composites. Because if it did, may the good Lord help you.

# CHAPTER 46

Rule 35 set me free. After working with Gardner, I had my term reduced from life to ten. The day I was released, they moved me into a halfway house for the next few months. Cathie was right there waiting for me. I got to see her and Jourdan when I earned passes. I had to wear a beeper and an electronic bracelet at all times. But I didn't care. Freedom was freedom.

Cathie landed herself a desk job after she got her divorce and moved to Atlanta to be by me. She was working long hours and always looked tired. It was taking a real toll on her. I could see it when she came to visit. I swore that she would get a long rest beginning the day I got out. I would be the breadwinner. I wanted to take that burden off of her. She was the first woman I ever really cared for in my life, besides my mother.

We got married a few months later in the house she was renting. I cried throughout the whole ceremony. When I say cried, I mean I bawled like a baby. You try having your life taken away from you and then, in a one-in-a-million shot, find the woman of your dreams. Tell me if you aren't reduced to tears when you finally make her your wife. It was the best day of my life.

On my first daylong furlough from the house, Cathie and I decided to get some pictures taken. It had been several months since we were married. The wedding ceremony had been so rushed that there wasn't enough time to get any nice shots.

"What the . . ." I said and looked down at it. The message said, "Call in."

"What's wrong, honey?" Cathie's eyes were so big and filled with worry. When you're married to an ex-con on parole, you always expect the worst.

"Nothing," I said calmly. "Let me just give them a ring and then we'll start shooting."

I called in and the supervisor told me I needed to come back immediately. There was a problem with my paperwork. I wanted to cross every *t* and dot every *i*, so I didn't raise a ruckus. When I told Cathie what the supervisor said, she looked at me with tears in her eyes and asked, "Will this ever end?"

I grabbed her close to me and whispered, "Everything is going to be OK, babe. I'll be back in one hour."

I drove back to the halfway house with butterflies in my stomach. But everything looked normal: no police cars or unmarkeds out front. I walked in and was heading to the supervisor's office when two federal Marshals stepped into my path.

"Kevin Pappas?" they said.

*No, not again,* I thought.

I was charged, along with my lawyer, Bob Fierer, with tax evasion and obstruction of justice. Essentially, the feds had come to suspect that I'd not only gotten my freedom from Rule 35, but earned a minor fortune as well. They were pissed. I'd followed the law as I understood it, but because I had profited by years of my intel, now they wanted to revoke what I'd earned.

And my lawyer had made it easy for them.

I found out that the idiot had repackaged the information I had provided to our clients and used it three and four different times in different courts, something that was possible only because a lot of the evidence was in sealed documents. Of course, he hadn't bothered to tell me what he was doing.

We were both arrested, and Bob immediately blamed me for everything. According to him, it was *my* idea to sell the information over and over again. I was the mastermind. But how was I supposed to be doing this from behind bars? I procured the information and Bob got the deals done with the prosecutors.

I couldn't believe it when I heard the charges. I thought I was going to lose my wife and my family. And then it only got worse.

Not long after my marriage, a former female federal prosecutor in Miami familiar with my past antics as a dealer became a U.S. Attorney General. This prosecutor was thorough, and in my opinion, an overzealous attorney who wanted to stop what had become a rampant epidemic of "corrected" (meaning reduced) sentences that could taint the White House and her new position. I was the poster child for what she was targeting.

She took a look at my case and decided that my actions were "corrupting and shaking the American justice system to its core." I heard from my attorneys that she was coming after me as a top-level criminal, the mastermind of a highly sensitive plot to stop criminals from doing their sentences. But when my attorneys looked into the charges, they couldn't find a single law I'd broken.

The Attorney General pursued and prosecuted me for my exploitations of Rule 35. Bob Fierer turned against me and agreed to provide the feds assistance for essentially doing the same thing we were put in jail for. I was cooked and booked. I was dumped back into the Atlanta federal pen for a third time, to await my trial on obstruction of justice.

I never made it back to Cathie that day. I can't imagine what she thought. Sitting there in her wedding dress waiting for me to come back as the hours ticked by. I couldn't even call her to explain what was happening. Why would she even believe me anyway? I had failed her so many times before. I was locked up for a third time, to await my trial on obstruction of justice.

About a month later Cathie was finally able to come and visit me. She came in and sat down. There was a three-inch-thick piece of glass and two telephones between us. She looked beautiful as always while I looked pretty rough. She picked up the phone and pressed her hand against the glass. She looked at me and started to cry. *Oh Christ*, I thought, *this is not good.*

I picked up my phone. "Are you OK?" I asked. "Is something wrong? What is it, Cathie? Is it my mom?"

But she kept crying. She couldn't get the words out.

"I'll be home soon. Stay strong for me. For us."

Cathie looked up and through her tears she asked, "Do you think you'll be home in six months?"

For a moment, time stopped.

"Why Cathie, are you planning to leave me?"

She started to laugh and smiled, "No silly, I'm going to have your baby."

Five months later, my mother called to tell me Cathie was on the way to the hospital. I was friendly with one of the shift officers who was on duty when she went into labor. He pulled some strings and got me an open phone line to the delivery room. My mom told the hospital that I was a businessman off in Greece, and because the baby was two weeks early I couldn't get back in time.

I was on the other end, coaching her through the pain as the contractions came faster and faster. I could hear her panting in labor. Suddenly the sound of a new life, my son's cry broke all the other noise. Joy and rage competed in my heart: I was so incredibly happy to have a boy, but to bring him into this world while I listened in chains? That killed me.

This was in 1996. About a month after my son was born, they threw me in solitary confinement on the third floor of the high-max Atlanta City Detention Center (ACDC) jail in Atlanta, Georgia. It was my third term in prison, and I honestly didn't think I was going to make it out alive. Or if I did, I'd be completely whacked in the head.

I'd been a gangster for most of my life. I'd been the king of the Atlanta cocaine trade. I'd made millions of dollars trafficking coke from Miami to Atlanta, and I had scars from bullets and shivs to show for it. There wasn't a mobster or a cartel killer that I feared. *They* feared *me*. I wore my medallion around my neck with Alexander the Great on it. He was my hero, my model for life. A true, fearless conqueror.

But now, here I was holding Bible study with cinder blocks. It was one hell of an experience, let me tell you. I never missed a single day. What would those godless cinder blocks have done without me?

ACDC was different from anything I'd been through before. I'd entered at 252 pounds, a bodybuilding stud who could snap your forearm and would happily do it, too, if you pissed me off. Now I was down to 171 pounds. My right eye twitched constantly. I sat in an eight-by-ten room, cinder blocks on all sides painted gray. There was a stainless steel combined sink and toilet and a bunk with a two-inch cracked mattress on it, no pillow. The door was stainless steel with a slot for your dinner tray. Everything was a different shade of gray. Sometimes I thought I was becoming gray myself.

My skin, which had been tanned from the sun ever since I was a boy growing up in Florida, was now sickly pale and I had rashes all over. I dreamt crazy shit: that I would disappear into the walls one day, that the outside world wasn't there anymore, that the guards had gone home and everyone in the world was dead, that my loved ones were informing on me in another room in the prison.

The thing that convinced me that there was still a world outside my cell was a slit window that was a foot and a half high and six inches across. From it, all I could see was a sliver of Whitehall Street and the leaves of a few dogwood trees. The only way I could tell the season was by whether the dogwoods were in bloom or bare. I would stare out at them for hours. When a breeze would make the branches move, that was a good day for me.

But you can't talk to a dogwood tree.

That would be insane.

Cinder blocks, though . . .

Mine were named Michael, Mark, David, Sarah, and Martha. They were the blocks directly across from my bunk. All good biblical names. Michael was my lead block and I'd start Bible sessions by asking him a question.

"OK, Michael, you look like you ate your goddamn Wheaties this morning. Why don't we start today by talking about Isaiah 47, where God says, 'I am your father, your God, your fortifier, I am reaching out my right hand of righteousness.' What is God telling us here?"

I'd grown up with the Bible. I knew its passages by heart. And I'd teach my five gray, rectangular students the ins and outs of Scripture from Acts to Revelations. But if you think the cinder blocks sat there and just listened, you've never been in solitary confinement.

They talked back. They even argued with me. They called me a fake and a bum. Scriptural controversy raged in that little cell week in and week out like it was some fucking monastery. Did the Bible really say that you can't bring the blood of others into your own body? *Yeah, you think so?* Mark told me I was wrong on that for weeks in the summer of '96. Sarah supported him. Ungrateful bastards. I had to straighten them out fast.

The guards must have thought I was headed straight for the mental hospital. When things got hot, I'd be yelling at the wall, "*You don't know what the fuck you're talking about, Michael.*" For hours.

But fuck the hacks. They went home to their wives and kids at night. I was surviving the only way I knew how.

I got out of solitary after a year and fourteen days and was put back into general population. They had tried to crack me this time, and with one more day they might have. One more day without freedom was one day too many. I was a wreck. But the worst time was over.

Like most of the other inmates, I skipped shower call. I washed out of the toilet, which I kept immaculate. I washed my clothes there, too, because if you sent them out to the prison laundry, they'd come back with lice crawling all over them. The food wasn't fit for stray dogs. I ate hot dogs that were electric blue and rice and beans that had maggots and boll weevils crawling in it. I ate those for protein.

The only time I got a visitor was when the feds came to me with a deal. They wanted me to flip on Agent Gardner. I couldn't believe it. Apparently, she'd risen from a newbie agent to the head of a different task force. They accused me of feeding her information but that was bullshit. She earned her stars and became even more respected than Agent Wright. Rumors started flying within the prison that our relationship had gone way beyond a professional one. All I can say is that she was my best friend for four years and she went to bat for me again and again. Without her, I'd still be chewing on the bars in Atlanta federal pen right now.

The internal investigators at the bureau came to me and told me that Agent Gardner was under investigation. If I told them that she knew about the reselling of information and the fact that I'd packaged intel from different sources to get reductions for inmates who had no prior knowledge of the cases, I could walk out of jail within a month.

It was like Lukie all over again. My freedom for someone else's incarceration. The Devil was whispering in my ear: *Take the deal.*

I agreed to a meeting with the investigators. They brought me out of solitary and walked me to a room in the prison where you went to meet your lawyers. They opened this gray metal door, and who was standing there but Gardner. She looked exhausted. She'd lost ten or fifteen pounds. Her hair was all frizzed out, and the look in her eyes told me that she was being leaned on. Heavy.

Our eyes met. She had these intense blue irises but they were bathed in tears. I smiled at her, winked, and mouthed the words, "Don't worry." She ducked her head and let out a quick gasp, then turned and walked into the corner.

The investigators worked me over for an hour with Gardner watching. I told them the truth: The intel I got was real and I had no idea my lawyer was hustling it all over town. And I said point-blank that Gardner had no involvement with how I got and packaged the info. She was innocent of all their slimy accusations.

After the meeting was over, Gardner was escorted out by one of the investigators. As she walked behind my chair, she patted my shoulder. I smiled to myself.

Lukie, I almost sold him down the river, but for good reason. But Gardner? She was my friend. We had a code of honor to stay true to what was true. I would have never let her hang.

# CHAPTER 47

I had a new lawyer working on my case, and he went to the feds and told them what Bob had been doing behind my back. But when he met me in the little conference room at the ACDC facility in Atlanta, I could tell it hadn't gone well.

"Kevin, they're not negotiating," he said. "You're cooked. You're done. You may as well find a male bride inside that fucking prison because they're putting you away for thirty years."

I'd been expecting that. Like I said in the beginning, I'm always looking around the next corner and getting my exit strategy ready. I knew that when it came down to the word of a lawyer versus the word of a doper ex-con, I was going to get ass-blasted every time. I'm a gangster so why would anyone believe me?

As our case came closer to the end, I maintained my loyalty to Bob. After a year of solitary confinement while he was free on the streets, I still didn't give up any information.

But, within a few days of sentencing, when it looked like my fate had been sealed, I had a visit from one of the prosecuting attorneys, someone I had no relationship with whatsoever. He told me I needed to protect myself and I should know that Bob had sold me out and was going to bury me.

So at eight p.m. that night, I requested an attorney phone call. I pulled my trump card out, which clearly showed that I was not the mastermind behind the obstruction of the courts. It was Bob. I had a fax from Bob's office to a prosecutor offering to proffer some information that we'd already presented on a different case. I'd seen it in a pile of Bob's papers when we were in one of our lawyer-client conferences at the prison and, sensing he was up to something, I snatched it.

I handed my attorney the fax. "Well see what you can do with this."

He read it. "Oh my God, Kevin, this is the smoking gun. Fierer was fucking you all along. How come you didn't share this with me before?"

I said, "Jerry, I have no intention to hurt my friend Bob Fierer. I love him. He's like a father to me. But there comes a time when the guilty must pay."

I was devastated when I eventually reviewed Bob's sentencing transcripts. It proved that what the prosecuting attorney told me was true. I never thought in a million years this man I respected and adored would throw me under the bus.

Jerry called the U.S. Attorney's Office and faxed them the paper. They changed their tune immediately. Now they realized that bringing down a top criminal defense lawyer was even sweeter for them than busting Kevin Pappas. It's very seldom that you see lawyers take down other lawyers.

I wasn't going down for Bob Fierer or anybody else. I'd taken the rap for Lee, the narc, for Willie Moises, for my father, and now for Bob. I'd spent almost half my life behind bars. No more. No fucking way. Not this time. I still got a seven-year sentence. The system that had used me now stuffed me in a hole so deep I thought I'd never see the sun again.

Cathie came to visit me. She would sit across a table from me. My legs were chained, and we had ten minutes together every fourteen days. They give animals more time with people who come to adopt them.

Jourdan didn't understand. She came with her mother sometimes, and she would say to Cathie, "Mommy, why does Kevin have those bracelets around his hands and feet?" And Cathie would have to think fast and say, "Well, his boss wants to know where he is at all times, so they have those monitors on him so they can locate him at any time."

But it just broke her heart. That just hurts you in a way I can't even describe.

I was down. I looked like hell. I didn't even want to see her at times. I was afraid she would be disappointed in what she saw for a husband. Cathie would tell me that my skin was a gray color and I knew it was from my time in solitary and not getting out in the sun. I love to feel the sun on my skin; all Greeks want to feel that and feel the sea breeze, but I was in a dark, stinking hole that might as well have been a hundred feet below ground. I felt like I was buried alive.

One night I was talking with Cathie on the phone and she said, "Tomorrow at noon I want you to look out your window."

"What for?"

"It's our anniversary, darling. And I have something I want to show you."

I had stopped looking out that slit of a hole called a window. I had put a piece of cardboard in front of it because I wanted to forget the real world outside my cell existed.

"Cathie, you know I don't do that anymore," I told her.

"Tomorrow, do it for me. Just once. Twelve o'clock, OK?"

"I can't promise you anything."

The next day came and I looked at that piece of cardboard. Eleven o'clock. Eleven-thirty. I was lying on my bunk with the sweat beading up on my forehead. Finally, I lifted myself off the bunk and walked to the window. I grabbed the cardboard, held on to it for a second, and then brushed it to the side. I put my eye to the slit and looked down.

I looked out on Whitehall Street. I could see buses and cars below that zoomed by and the sidewalk on the other side of the street. There were office workers and college students walking there, unaware of the men looking out at them from the prison. Men who would kill to be one of them for just a few minutes. I didn't see Cathie, though.

Then I saw her small figure walking across the street from below me. She had a large white sheet in her hand. It looked like a bedsheet. She got to the other side, walked past a bus shelter, and then turned and faced the prison. I saw her shield her eyes against the sun and search for my window.

She smiled and she took the sheet and unfolded it. I could see some writing on it, but I had to stand on my tiptoes to read it. Finally,

I could make it out. It said: KEV, HAPPY ANNIVERSARY. I LOVE YOU AL-
WAYS. CATH.

Tears welled up in my eyes and I turned away from the window as
if I'd been blinded. I slumped with my back against the wall and slid
down.

I never looked out that window again. I kept the cardboard over
the slit so that I could hold that image in my head, like she was always
out there, holding that sign up for me to see.

That day was tattooed in my heart. No one could take that away.
Nothing could be sweeter.


The house I'd built in my head went up. Cathie had to explain to our
new neighbors where the man of the house was, though. It became the
longest-running soap opera in Fulton County, Georgia. I would probably have told people the truth and let them deal with it, but Cathie is
a straight arrow and she didn't want everyone to think of her kids as
part of a gangster's family.

When people asked where Mr. Pappas was, she would tell them
that my father was really sick and I'd gone back to Greece to see to all
the arrangements because I was the only one in the family with a pass-
port. So now I was in Greece and she had to keep feeding everyone de-
velopments from there. First, my father was on his deathbed, so I
couldn't leave. Then he staged a miracle comeback, and I was celebrating with the Greek cousins. Oh, actually, Papa just died. Kevin's
tying up the details of the will. And guess what? Now Kevin has to
stay over there to save his father's company.

It was comical. But if Cathie hadn't done that, our kids would
have been bullied and marked as the criminal's spawn. It ate me up not
to be able to protect them from that kind of harassment. But I knew
Cathie was strong enough to handle it. All my energy was going into
getting out of prison and staying out.


When I had gone to jail for the 107 kilos, Mark Jordan had disappeared. I had expected that. Mark was loyal as hell but he needed you
to be there for him to stick around. He had vanished off the face of the
earth, and even my street contacts didn't know where he was. I as-

sumed the worst. I thought he had ended up like Rob Schaeffer, with two bullets in the back of his head.

When I was back in solitary, I got a call to Cathie and she told me that Mark had come to see her. I was relieved and I told her to have him visit me at ACDC.

When he came to see me I told Mark that I needed him to watch out for my family. To make sure no one touched a hair on their fucking heads and that my wife didn't even have to get the tires rotated. He was going to be the caretaker.

But Mark fucked up. I got a call from Cathie one day a couple of months later and she was almost hysterical.

"Kevin, you have to talk to Mark."

"Why, what's up?"

"He's saying all kinds of crazy things. He thinks he's in love with me. He's telling the kids that you're never going to get out of prison and that he'll be their daddy."

I wanted to vomit.

"Is he out of his fucking mind?"

"Just talk to him."

I called Mark up and he admitted to me that he'd fallen in love with Cathie. I smashed my fist on the wall next to the phone. I called him every name in the book and swore I'd slice his eyes out of his head if he even thought of making a move on my wife.

"Mark, what's wrong with you? I told you to protect my wife, not try to fuck her. Is this how you prove your loyalty to me?"

"Kevin, I have been loyal to you, man. But Cathie needs someone now. Think about it, she's not going to make it a second time around with you in jail."

I was dumbstruck. If Cathie had a weak moment and went to a bar one night and found herself drunk on tequila, maybe I could understand that moment. After all, she was young and beautiful. But that didn't happen. Instead a member of my own family who I had entrusted to protect them made moves on Cathie and my children. He even tried to convince them that he was their new daddy because I was going to rot in jail. This betrayal was inconceivable to me and it conjured up images of my past, from birth to my first relationships to now, and it just put me on overdrive. I could have expected this from anybody but Mark. I'm a cynical bastard when it comes to people's motives, but he was my brother, the one who'd have given his life for me in the blink of an eye. And I for him.

"You betrayed me, brother," I said. "You know how much she means to me and you just stuck a knife between my ribs. You're a fucking coward."

I could hear him breathing on the other end of the phone but he said nothing. Then there was a click.

I had no idea what he would do. Mark was a trained killer. Maybe he'd go to the house and slaughter my whole family. Maybe he'd just do Cathie. What can I say? When you have assassins as your best friends, the costs can be very high.

But he didn't do that. Apparently, he hung up the phone, drove out to my house, kissed my kids on the forehead, and said goodbye to Cathie.

I got a phone call through to her and she asked me, "Did you talk with Mark?"

I assured her I did, but I was worried more than ever and I didn't want her to hear it in my voice. I could see something happening that was out of my control, and reports were coming back to me that were very disturbing. I made calls to secure the perimeter of our home and had eight sets of eyes watching over them 24/7. Everyone I loved was in that house. My mother, my children, and my wife. And this crazy motherfucker was out on the streets.

It was a long night. The evening unit manager knew there was a family hardship so he let me call home every hour. The next day we learned that Mark was killed. He was hit by a semi-truck on a highway in Atlanta, a victim of an apparent accidental death.

We later got details that he was hit by a flat-nose Mack truck going some seventy miles an hour. The impact was so strong it threw him out of his shoes, but somehow the medallion remained embedded on his chest. Though he had hurt me personally, I knew in the end that he was faithful to the Band. He had always worn that medallion as a symbol of loyalty and a badge of honor. A sense of being part of something bigger.

But now I was the only one left and I kept asking myself, Why am I still alive?

I'm Greek to the core, and Greeks believe in curses, evil eyes, spirits that can be tricked and deflected. So, yeah, a part of me believed that Mark had died so that I could keep living.

But I couldn't be there to protect Cathie and my family. I was getting nowhere with my appeals on my sentence. I decided to go commando on these bastards.

I wrote a letter to *60 Minutes* telling them I had a once-in-a-lifetime offer: a story on informants and the corruption of the justice system. I mailed it off, along with letters to ABC News, CBS, CNN, and whomever else I could think of. I just sat back and I waited.

I didn't want to be a crusader. But I was starting to see that what had been done to me fit a pattern: The government was playing both sides of the street. They wanted to use the information prisoners like me gave them to advance up the ranks, but they wanted to come out smelling like roses. So, once the convicts were milked dry, they had to be turned back into villains and punished once again. Otherwise, it would make the prosecutors' victories look dirty. And they couldn't have that.

I waited for mail call every day, hoping there was someone out there who wasn't crooked, corrupt, or compromised. Finally, a few weeks later, my attorney got a call. My letter had arrived on the desk of Vicky Mabrey of *60 Minutes II,* and she had been intrigued. She'd made some calls, double-checked my accusations, and saw a whole new world open to her: the ugly reality of how justice was really made.

She wanted to interview me right there in the prison. I told the lawyer to set the date. I was going to spill the beans on all the loopholes, deceit, lying, and manipulation the courts got away with. I just lay in my bunk, grinning. This was going to be larger than me. I was going to actually do something righteous and good—and I was going to make them rue the day they ever fucked with Kevin Pappas.

An hour before I was set to do the interview, my lawyer got a call. The government had agreed to set me free two years early. I never got to tell what I knew about Rule 35—until now.

Power. You have to know how to use it.

I finally walked out of jail in June of 2000. When I walked out the prison gates, one of the guards that I'd gotten to know called out to me.

"Pappas."

"Yeah?"

"You're all right, man. Don't let me see you coming back here."

I laughed. "Ain't no chance in hell you'll see me back here, my friend."

The world had changed. I didn't know how to use the Internet, how to send an email, and I'd never held a cell phone in my hand. I felt like I was being born again.

# CHAPTER 48

I went home to Atlanta and I got to do things I never dreamt I would. Push my son's baby carriage around a neighborhood of manicured lawns. Eat ice cream with Jourdan and talk about boys. Get to know my wife without bulletproof glass between us or an iron chain on my ankle.

Cathie and I were like two people who'd lived through a war. We'd fallen in love while I was in prison, in an atmosphere of secrecy, tears, and anguish. Every turn in our life had been like a spy drama or a prison film. Now we had to learn how to live like two normal people.

I took her out to see movies. I bought her little gifts whenever I went anywhere so that she knew I was thinking about her. And I called her every hour of the day. At first, I thought I was doing it for her, to reassure her that I wasn't being snatched away from our home again. But then it dawned on me that I needed to hear her gentle voice or I would lose it.

Our little corner of Atlanta was so normal and American it almost freaked me out. I'd come home from a day directing my landscaping crews, and Jourdan's school friends would be in the backyard hanging out at our pool. "Hey, Mr. Pappas!" they'd yell. In the beginning I was like, "Hey, guys!" I'd wave back thinking to myself, *If your parents only knew who I was.* But Cathie had gotten to know a lot of our neighbors and they were great. I wasn't treated like a circus freak. They simply accepted me.

Cathie realized that by waiting for me, she'd signed up either for the ultimate disaster or for something really remarkable. Some of her friends warned her she was making a terrible mistake. They said that being with me might jeopardize her custody of her daughter. And what kind of life or future could a convicted gangster offer her? We lost some friends over that shit, too.

I tested Cathie while I was behind bars. In prison they say if you are with a woman and it lasts more than nine months, then you've got a keeper. Otherwise the saying is, she's out fucking Jody, your best friend. I needed to know that Cathie was different, that she really believed in me. So I would test her. There were times I even pushed her away, like when I told her she was going to leave me. And I truly believed it. But she never gave up on me. Ever.

She would look at me and say, "If I waited seven years to get you, why would I leave now?"

That was good enough for me. I knew I'd found my diamond. And I was not going to let her go.

At night, when the kids were in bed, I would hold my wife close to me and feel like I was living inside a Hollywood movie. What we had was so deep and real, tested by shit most couples couldn't even imagine.

But there was one act left to play in the Greek drama of my life. A few weeks after I got out, I got a call from Chris Darrius. Chris was an interesting guy. He was my brother Louie's age and had been a successful businessman before being brought in to handle the family's business, both legal and illegal, after a multibillion-dollar family deal went bad. Chris was also a bone-breaker, the successor to my dad's enforcer Nickie V. He was known to have some of Florida's scariest thugs in his Rolodex.

Chris gave me a call and told me the family was interested in me coming in to run the operation. He explained to me that there had been a series of mishaps where Louie had allegedly dropped the ball. He was acting like he was invincible. Chris said, "The confidence in him just isn't there. But we know what you did for your dad, and that's earned you a lot of fans down here. This could all be yours."

This was what I had dreamed of and waited for my entire life. To be a part of the family. The Pappas family.

I had always pictured Lukie inviting me to join him on his boat, not as some deckhand or busboy, but as a respected member of his family. There would be a large group of men, women, and children who welcomed my family and me in a natural and warm Greek way. The boat would take off and the men would move to the upper deck while the women stayed below with the children. I would join my father and his captains and lieutenants, but this time I would be one of them. Between cigars and cool drinks, we would discuss business without losing a beat.

I took a moment and thought about Chris's offer. Scenes from my past flooded my mind. I knew what I had been and I now knew what my destiny could be.

It was tempting. It was such a mark of respect. I'd felt like I'd come full circle with the family. There was no way this decision had been made without Lukie signing off on it.

"I'm flattered, Chris, but I've got to be honest. I just got out of the fucking joint and I'll burn in hell before I go back."

Chris laughed. "You know the Greeks never go to jail, Kevin. You'd be protected. Did you ever see Lukie marched off to the pen?"

I told Cathie about the offer. She hit the fucking roof. Man, I'd never seen her so mad. She told me point-blank that I had to choose between the Pappases and our family. I could only have one or the other. She didn't wait all those years to be the wife of a gangster.

It was the worst fight we've ever had. I couldn't get her to understand that this was what I'd always wanted, to be recognized by the Pappases and asked to step into Lukie's shoes. To be a *nounos*, a godfather of night, in a tradition that went back hundreds of years. I was the prodigal son who'd returned after years in the wilderness, and my father had opened his arms to me. This was my goddamned destiny! How could I now deny him like he'd denied me for so many years? Why couldn't Cathie see that?

The tension was overpowering at my house. She would not compromise. It was either my old family or my new one. I had to get away and get some time to clear my head. I went down to the farm that we'd bought, right on a lake thirty minutes outside Atlanta. I sat there for a few days.

Finally, a month after Chris's call, I took my family to Florida. I had to see the place before making a decision on whether to take the Pappases up on their offer or to go back to my family. This was the place where I'd grown up, where I'd faced my greatest test in life by letting Lukie see that federal wire. I had to feel the salt breezes on my skin before I decided if my future lay in Tarpon Springs or in Atlanta. One way or the other I owed it to my father to give him my decision in person. I finally convinced Cathie to come with me and bring the kids. My son Mikal, who had been conceived just before I went back to prison, was now four.

We drove down in my new black Hummer and we went right to the Pappas restaurant. My family had heard so much about it in so many stories about my childhood that they were dying to see it. And I had told Mikal stories about his grandfather, who he had never met. How he was an important man, a respected man who I had always wanted to measure up to.

It was a beautiful day, the seagulls were screaming, and you could hear the water slapping gently against the hulls of sponger boats. As we walked into the restaurant, I stopped to chat with a couple of people I recognized at the door, and Mikal tugged on my shirt.

"Daddy, is that him?"

"Is that who?" I said, distracted.

"My grandpa."

I followed Mikal's pointing figure and suddenly I froze. Who was sitting there at the bar but Lukie, dressed in a crisp white shirt and tan pants, his hair still jet-black, drinking his Tanqueray and tonic. He was sitting there with five or six of the old-timers, flipping their worry beads. It was the first time I'd seen him since that day in the parking lot six years ago.

I looked at Cathie. She made a face, like, *Well, what did you expect?*

I bent down to Mikal. "Yeah, buddy," I said. "That's him."

"I want to meet him!" he said. But before I could grab him, Mikal was off like a bullet.

As I watched my son running toward Lukie, I realized I wasn't afraid of what Lukie said to me anymore or how he treated me or anything else. He'd looked me in the eye and said I was his son. And the family had asked me to take over the reins of the family business. I was at peace with all that shit.

But for my son? I felt a wave of anxiety and rage wash over me. *If*

*Lukie turns my boy away,* I said to myself. *I'm going to break a beer bottle and gut him right here in this restaurant.*

I wanted to scream at my father. "The curse ends with me! Do you hear me, Lukie?" I felt my right hand grip into a fist. If Lukie had denied him, I would have exploded.

I watched as Mikal ran the last few steps to where Lukie was standing. Lukie looked down. Mikal must have said, "Grandpa?" because I saw Lukie react with surprise. He looked up and saw me. I couldn't react; I was on a hair trigger.

Lukie smiled, reached down, and lifted Mikal into the air so that they could look at each other eye to eye. He put him on his lap, and I could see him signal the bartender for a Shirley Temple. It was the same drink he would order for me after I'd put in a hard day sweeping floors or busing tables.

I watched, but it was as if I was bolted to the floor. I couldn't move.

My son came running back to me. A photo was taken by a local, just minutes after he met Lukie. In it, his eyes are lit up and his whole face is beaming. He'd finally met his grandpa. He knew who he was and where he came from. I'm in the background of the photo and look like I'd just shed a few tears. Because I had.

Of everything I've given my boy, that feeling of belonging is what matters the most. He'll never have to go through what I did. He is Greek. He is a Pappas. He is a link in a long and proud bloodline.

I canceled the meeting with Chris Darrius. I didn't need to talk to him anymore. I had made up my mind. My destiny was my three kids, a loving wife, and a real blood family who depended on me. My commitment was to Cathie and my children. I'd found what I'd come to Tarpon Springs for: not power, but a hard-fought redemption.

I'm a suburban dad now. I pick up the kids after soccer practice. We have a third child, Paris, my beautiful daughter who is more like me than I care to think about. I help the neighbors set up for graduation parties and I'm a shoulder for my daughter's teenage friends to cry on when their boyfriends break up with them. I take out the garbage and I mow my lawn.

If you drove down my street and saw me, you'd think I'm the American Dream. The diamond-studded watch on my wrist and the scar over my ear might stop you cold for a minute, but for the most part, I fit in. I'm a family man and a taxpayer. Who fucking knew?

But that's not the whole story.

Am I cured of my passion for power? Not a fucking chance. I fight the urge every day. To get up each morning and want to control all the people in my life is a sickness that's in my blood. I try to be normal, but there's something inside of me that wants to own you. Manipulate you. And even destroy you. Every day I live with this inside of me. It's like alcoholism. It's like a drug addiction. To fight the urge to take what you have, to find the angle, the edge, the next big score, the power that will make me famous and feared. Just because I can. It's more than an urge. It's a disease that has no cure.

There's no AA for what I have, or NA, or anything else. There is no way to take the power of organized crime away from you. The saying that once you're in you can never get out is true, but not because the other guys will kill you. It's because that life plants something deep in your soul. You can walk away from the lifestyle but not your psyche, your gut, your memory, your nightmares, your desires. They are all still wrapped up in it.

Sometimes I feel like I'm two people. On the outside, I'm just a guy chewing on a cigar, watering the lawn, with a steak on the grill. That's because the nice guy is in charge. But deep down the gangster is prowling around, always looking for an opening. My love for my kids and my wife is stronger than the temptations to go back to the gangster life. But it's a fucking war that never ends.

As for Lukie, I don't see him much these days. He still lives in Tarpon Springs and he still has his yachts and his mistresses. When I pass through town, I'll sometimes see him and I'll nod to him and he'll nod back. That's all. No family reunions for me. But I have his respect, and that's enough.

Every once in a while, though, I dream about him. In the dreams, we're back in one of those little towns in Sparta I visited as a teenager with my dancing group. We're walking through the tiny winding streets with the Aegean in the distance, so blue it looks like it's been painted there. I realize we're back in the town where Lukie grew up, the Pappas stronghold. He's happy, I'm happy. We don't do anything special, just walk around and talk to people, the real Greeks, the old-timers.

I've had that dream more than once. He takes me by the hand and leads me up to the ladies in black dresses and the gangsters with their worry beads, long past their prime but still worthy of respect. The people who must have known him as a child. And he turns and points at me and he smiles with pride, and says, "This is my firstborn son." And that's it. That's where the dream ends. But when I wasn't dreaming, I waited to hear him say, "I love you, son."

I hope I live out my years as a solid citizen. I earned my happiness, every moment of it. But honestly? There are no guarantees in life. I know I am responsible for all that I've created. But the key in all of this was to have my own family someday. That gave me hope and hope changed my life. It is because my wife waited for me and believed in my redemption that I am alive. I've been given a gift. I want goodness. I want to stand for what is right. Not because I'm looking for recognition or to be "holier than thou." It's because I have a son and a family that is going to follow in my footsteps.

This is the story of a man who genuinely had no intentions of becoming the person he became. This bloodline I was given created a monster within me. I've got the battle wounds, the scars, and the skeletons that not everybody could live with. I didn't become a gangster out of greed, money, or to drive fancy cars. I got into it to make a point: To prove my manhood to a father who denied me. I paid my penance. I made my point. It's time to move on.

# ACKNOWLEDGMENTS

I would like to acknowledge all of those individuals, both past and present, who believed in me, supported me, and helped me to reach my dreams, no matter how big or small. They have made me the man, father, and friend I am today.

My Mother, Willadean.

The Cunningham Family: Charles, David, Kathy, and, now, looking back, I guess Jim, as well.

The Greek community, for accepting me for who I am and what I was. That includes Black Spot, Mr. Gambos, and Leon Mavromatis.

My loyal brothers, the Band of Five: Rob Rhino; Jose Diaz; Mark Jordan; Willy Mosies, R.I.P; and Jesus Diaz

I would also like to thank Chaz Lazarian; Keith Walker; Marcus Bagwell; Bahli Mullins; Kenny Flynn; John and Cindy Haigwood; the Fleming Family; Michael Langel and his family; Judy and Gerry Rogers; "King Fish" Gameros; Mary Gameros; Fred Hill; Mike Nickson; John Gadston; Sky McQueen; Rhaz Zeisler; Fred Joseph; Jodie Upton; Barbara Brown; Izzie; Mike Hill; Craig Guillum; Gerry Froleck; Janice Singer; Ron Owen; Lindsey Crawley; the Durrett Family; Roy Hickman; Richard Seibert; Richard Haly; Mark McCardle, R.I.P.; the Bentley Family; the Gurrieo Family; the Lopez Family; Chris Gambino; the Horde Family; the Hughes Family; Mickey Freiberg, agent and friend; Chris Howard; Ben Tappen; Bill O'Zensky;

Eric Stone; Kathy Sholman; Melissa Parker; Randy Blackwell; Serg Mavalyants; the Panettiere Family; Clifton Collins; the Najjar Family; Haven Houllis; Marc Cote; Vince Phillips; Margaret Ward; Toni and Carrie Braxton; Rodney Sampson; Edward Sylvan; Curt Northrup; the Juers Family; Scott Waxmen; Nicholas and the Buckhead Life Group; Chuck Caulkins, R.I.P.; Doug Lacy; Ray Story; Mark Tavani; the Dirty Rats: John Sack and Andrew Tsangranios; Ali Ayden; Randy Crawford; and the many others who contributed to my well-being.

## ABOUT THE AUTHOR

Kevin Pappas grew up in Tarpon Springs, Florida, in a family of Irish Jehovah's Witnesses. Having served eight months in state prison and fourteen years in a federal penitentiary for racketeering and drug running, Pappas now lives with his family in Atlanta, Georgia. He is no longer involved in the Greek mafia.

## ABOUT THE TYPE

This book was set in Sabon, a typeface designed by the well-known German typographer Jan Tschichold (1902–74). Sabon's design is based upon the original letterforms of Claude Garamond and was created specifically to be used for three sources: foundry type for hand composition, Linotype, and Monotype. Tschichold named his typeface for the famous Frankfurt typefounder Jacques Sabon, who died in 1580.